TODAY AND TOMORROW

By Henry Ford

*The vintage 1926 Henry Ford book
now adapted for today's digital devices*

TODAY AND TOMORROW

*Timeless Wisdom for a Modern Digital Age
(Newly Annotated and Illustrated)*

Contributors
Paul Akers (Introduction)
Samuel Crowther (Original Collaborator)
Greg Otterholt (Modern English - Annotations & Illustrations)

Now available in print / eBook / and audio-book

Go to **generositypress.com**
for more details, resources, and a video introduction.

Copyright © 2018 by Generosity Press
All rights reserved,
including the right of reproduction
in whole or in part in any form.
ISBN 978-0-9906010-9-8

Edited and digitized for print, eBook and audio-book by Greg Otterholt
Assistant Editor - Shannon Waterman
Book Cover - Jayme Newby

Manufactured & Produced in the United States of America.
Check out **paulakers.net** for additional books and business resources.

TODAY AND TOMORROW
By Henry Ford

CONTENTS

INTRODUCTION

1. WE ARE BEING BORN INTO OPPORTUNITY
2. IS THERE A LIMIT TO BIG BUSINESS?
3. BIG BUSINESS AND THE MONEY POWER
4. ARE PROFITS WRONG?
5. IT CAN'T BE DONE
6. LEARNING BY NECESSITY
7. WHAT ARE STANDARDS?
8. LEARNING FROM WASTE
9. REACHING BACK TO THE SOURCES
10. THE MEANING OF TIME
11. SAVING THE TIMBER
12. TURNING BACK TO VILLAGE INDUSTRY
13. WAGES, HOURS, AND THE WAGE MOTIVE
14. THE MEANING OF POWER
15. EDUCATING FOR LIFE
16. CURING OR PREVENTING
17. MAKING A RAILROAD PAY
18. THE AIR
19. FARM PROBLEMS ARE FARM PROBLEMS
20. FINDING THE BALANCE IN LIFE
21. WHAT IS MONEY FOR?
22. APPLYING THE PRINCIPLES TO ANY BUSINESS
23. THE WEALTH OF NATIONS
24. WHY NOT

INTRODUCTION:

(Introduction adapted from live video interview by Generosity Press Founder, Paul Akers.)

Well hello everyone, Paul Akers here, and welcome to one the most exciting projects I've ever done. It's called Generosity Press and we're launching it by republishing one of the most important books in business history, Today and Tomorrow, by Henry Ford.

I'm sitting here today with Phil Morgan. He's 88 years old and one of the few people still alive who actually knew Henry Ford. Phil was an orphan in 1944 and was chosen to attend the renowned Henry Ford's School for Boys in Massachusetts. It was a school that Ford himself funded and created to educate, reinvigorate, and completely transform the lives of what we now call, "at risk youth." The automotive genius, business innovator, and icon of the industrial age proved to also be an incredibly generous person as well. One of his greatest successes was how he invested in people. Ford provided the tools to improve their lives by giving them the skills, knowledge, and opportunity to build their own future and live beyond their perceived potential.

Generosity Press is actually inspired by people like Henry Ford for his ingenuity as well as his generosity. Ford's classic book, Today and Tomorrow, was originally published in 1926, obviously long before this digital age of eBooks, digital audio-books, and hi-def video, all now available in the palm of our hand. So, we wanted to make this book available and tell his story in all of these formats for the very first time. If you're like me and lack the time, or maybe the attention span and patience needed to flip through the paper pages, now you have other options. Or, if you just love the convenience and the thought of listening to the book as if Ford is sitting right there telling you the story himself, we made that dream a virtual reality for you too with an absolutely stunning audio-book of this as well.

So I thought to myself, wouldn't it be cool if we started reproducing and recording all kinds of historic and classic business books with today's technology, and made a way for everyone to have access. That concept became the catalyst behind Generosity Press. You might say, why Generosity Press? Well really, it's our opportunity to sit on the shoulders of men like Henry Ford, a very generous man. He had a profound and positive effect, not just on technology and industry, but also on all society by empowering people, just like the guest we're about to hear from, allowing them to set a new course and trajectory for their whole life. That of course, had a domino effect that grew through their families, then flowed through their communities, then grew momentum through the local, regional and eventually the world economy. That's the kind of impact we too dream of making! So with that, welcome to the first book reproduced by Generosity Press.

Now this particular book, <u>Today and Tomorrow</u>, by Henry Ford, is very fascinating because this is a book that influenced lean manufacturing genius and Toyota Production System inventor, Taiichi Ohno. Ohno talks about this book as having a profound impact on how he developed the Toyota production system. So being that I'm a big lean maniac, it absolutely makes sense that I too would want to read this groundbreaking book by Ford. And the backdrop where I'm sitting right now is also absolutely amazing!

Look how beautiful this is – the book was originally published in 1926, and right behind me is a beautiful hunter green 1926 Model T Ford. Right next to that, we have an all original classic black 1924 Model T with its original paint job untouched. You can still see the brush strokes in the few places on this vehicle where they actually hand painted this classic in the Ford factory nearly a century ago.

Now if you're reading this and dying to see the video of this for yourself, just go to my website, <u>paulakers.net</u> and look under the "Books" tab. From there you can find all kinds of additional resources for this book and all the others that we will continue to produce and make available.

This particular interview is also on YouTube. You can simply scan the QR code below that will take you directly to it at https://youtu.be/mFM_Hp-vt5Q

I'd also like to thank my friend, Mike Yeakel, who is also in business here in Bellingham, Washington. He has this wonderful car collection and he also owns an injection molding company, Myco Molding. He actually did a lot of molding for my company, FastCap. Mike made his amazing car collection generously available to us as a backdrop to shoot this interview today to help kick off Generosity Press.

And that's what generosity is all about. You know, as a business owner working with people all over the world, all the successful business owners that I know and work with are also incredibly generous in the same spirit of Henry Ford. It's wonderful to give back, and I want to thank all the business owners that I've been associated with around the world who are constantly giving back to society to make their communities better. That's why we named it Generosity Press – going along and supporting that idea of how important it is for all of us to be generous and give back to our communities and our society to make the world a better place as Henry Ford gave a great example of.

Now to hear more about Henry Ford, and this amazing story from someone who actually had the opportunity to attend Ford's own school, got to meet Ford in person, and the impact that Ford's generosity had on his life... welcome Phil Morgan.

Phil: Well thank you Paul.

Paul: Thank you for doing this! Tell us how it all started.

Phil: I was an orphan as a kid and taken from a home that was very squalid. I was taken by child welfare of Massachusetts and was placed in many foster homes where it would be very much like Oliver Twist taking a walk in the park. I mean it was pretty interesting but there was not really much of a future for me. I was going to public school and then the child welfare department heard of Henry Ford's Boys School. Henry was actually looking for boys to work with supervisors in his automotive plant. The school was called Wayside Inn Boys School (alternatively, Henry Ford's Boys School) in Massachusetts.

Phil holds up the book that catalogues the daily experiences at the boarding school while he attended.

Phil: And here's a book, **Henry Ford's Boys: The Story of the Wayside Inn Boys School** though it's not in audio form. *(Phil says satirically as he laughs.)*

Paul: Oh. It will be soon! *(Paul says with a sly smile and chuckle.)*

Phil: This is a book that tells about Wayside – Henry Ford's best kept secret. There were all sorts of boys from various parts of society. Most of them from troubled backgrounds – orphans or foster kids.

Paul: How fantastic. I love to hear that story that it wasn't a government program but it was Ford, a businessman, who actually responded.

Phil: A very generous person.

Paul: Yes, a very generous person. You know what else, Phil, I thought about when you were telling this story earlier, wow, Henry Ford got waste. He saw your life and the path that it was on as an orphan and ward of the state, how it was basically in jeopardy of being wasted yet he took your circumstances and turned it into something great because you became a top electrical engineer for the Mobil Oil Company. Wow, what an impact Ford had on your life.

Phil: I'm not the only one. Many other boys have had very successful careers and lives.

Paul: Yes, you were telling me earlier how most of the boys who went through this program became very, very successful. All different kinds of trades. Name some of the kinds professions that they had.

Phil: For instance, like the military – colonels in the Army and he took some of the boys into his Ford plants.

Paul: It's kind of nice. So, he both educated them and then brought them into the plant to give them great jobs at the Ford Motor Company as well.

Phil: Yeah.

Paul: So when you met Ford, he actually came to one of the schools that you were in to kind of look it over, go the shop floor if you will, make sure everything was copacetic, and what was he like when you met?

Phil: He was a rather stern person and demanding. He was very keen on work ethic and he wanted to know what was going on and he didn't just take somebody else's word for it. We had academic courses in the morning and in the afternoons physical labor.

Paul: So he was a very practical guy. It was not just about academia, it was also about getting your hands dirty. He believed in getting your hands dirty and getting callouses on your hands.

Phil: Yes, but a melding of both of those things: academics and work ethic.

Paul: Both important.

Phil: He wanted to see for himself what was going on, so he climbed on to the truck which delivered the boys to their various work stations.

Paul: How many boys were on this truck?

Phil: They had several trucks but maybe eight.

Paul: So not a lot. You were right there with Henry Ford and just eight or nine other people.

Phil: Yeah, as a kid I thought he was a strange old character at the time.

Paul: Did you know it was him at first?

Phil: I actually didn't know at first.

Paul: And this was shortly before he died, right?

Phil: Right, he actually died in 1947. I first met him a year earlier in 1946.

Paul: Wow. So, did he seem like he was in good health then?

Phil: Oh yeah. I had no idea what caused his death.

Paul: But he was getting around and still going and checking things out at that point in the game.

Phil: He wanted to know first-hand what was going on.

Paul: So clearly, without a doubt, you would say that Henry Ford's generosity had a profound impact on your life?

Phil: Oh yeah.

Paul: It changed your life. Completely.

Phil: As a matter of fact, the boys had training in their own health care and neatness and learned how to iron their own clothes and sew.

Paul: Doesn't sound like much of a chauvinist to me at all. Wow.

Phil: Yeah, as a matter of fact he had dancing classes one day a week where we also learned etiquette.

Paul: So you started learning how to (respectfully) treat women.

Phil: Yes we did.

Paul: This guy was incredible and that's what I like about it. You know, a lot of people approach life in a very happenstance way. But Ford was not happenstance. He was very deliberate about everything and he thought that everything in many respects should go through a nice process or a formal process even to the point where he thought it was important that you should learn how to dance. You were potentially going to be a supervisor or a leader in his factory, but he thought that those kinds of social skills were relevant.

Phil: Right. In order to be a leader, you had to know how to follow.

Paul: Ah. That's profound! **In order to be a leader, you needed to know how to follow.** What does that mean, Phil?

Phil: Well, you have to know how to take orders in order to know how to give orders. You have to have discipline and to be able to do it properly and to use your human faculties as you would use tools probably, but compassionately.

Paul: This is incredible. You know Bob Taylor is my mentor as Edison was the mentor for Henry Ford. I asked Bob Taylor one time and it's one of my favorite quotes that Bob said. I asked, "Bob, who was your mentor? Who was it that was influential on you?" He said, "You know Paul, today everyone's always saying you need a great leader; we need better leaders." Bob retorted back and said, "No, no, no, Paul. We need better followers". This is exactly what you're saying and what Ford had taught you. You need to first learn how to follow before you can learn how to lead.

Phil: Exactly.

Paul: Wow. How interesting.

Phil: He was also great on work ethic but in order to pass on a bit of that work ethic you had to experience it. You had to be able to be practical.

Paul: I personally, I love Henry Ford. I look at icons like Henry Ford, Tachii Ohno, Sakichi Toyoda, Thomas Edison, Benjamin Franklin, Jefferson, Adams – these people are my heroes. I make no apology about that at all. But a lot of people have spoken disparagingly about Ford, about some of his tendencies one way or another. But really, he was an incredibly generous man, a very thoughtful man, he elevated people in all spectrums across the world. What would you say to that? Are my feelings about him accurate? Or misled a little? What do you think?

Phil: From my perspective, he took care of the boys.

Paul: He took care of people.

Phil: For instance, while I was at the boys' school, I had to have my appendix taken out. Henry Ford paid for that. He paid for the hospital. All the things we learned at the school, we were able to apply later on in life, too.

It wasn't learning from a handbook and getting a degree in History or a degree in English. It was all hands-on plus that. He was even interested in our knowing where our language came from, for instance.

Paul: Isn't that incredible.

Phil: Yep, they even taught Latin at Wayside Inn Boys School.

Paul: Fantastic. So what was the number one thing – I always like to ask people – what was the number one thing... how did Ford's life make an impression on you, or what was the number one principle you learned from Henry Ford?

Phil: I think it was discipline and work ethic and how to get along with my fellow man.

Paul: Wow.

Phil's Junior Class at the Henry Ford Boys School - circa 1947 - Phil second in on the bottom row.

Phil: Now at the boys' school, we would get disciplined; and sometimes we would go through the paddle line.

Paul: Did that scar you and destroy your life? *(Paul asks with a hint of satire.)*

Phil: It certainly did not. *(Phil laughs)*

Paul: You say, "It certainly did not." Wow, okay - opinionated Paul here. *(laughing satirically)* That's incredible.

Phil: I think in the book (Today and Tomorrow) it talks a little bit about Henry Ford's opinion about education. *(Phil picks up the book to look at the Table of Contents.)* Here it is, "Educating for Life". It's chapter 15. It tells about his philosophy of life and philosophy of education, that not only did you have to have the academics, but you had to have hands-on practical experience.

Paul: Which I absolutely love. You know, that's me. I have callouses on my hands, I love the idea of getting my hands dirty. I'm an executive, and yet people walk in and I'm always on the shop floor, I'm always working, I'm always doing, because that's really who I am. So I identify deeply with Henry Ford and I'll say publicly - Henry Ford, I'm so grateful for everything you did for this country and for the world, and especially this book that will now be available in audio (and digital) format to so many people. Phil, thank you so much for everything you've done and the contribution you've made to society being a great engineer for the Exxon Mobil Company. I'm so happy that we got to meet and that you got to kick off the start of Generosity Press. It makes perfect sense. Here we're going to have Henry Ford's book, Today and Tomorrow, as the first book for Generosity Press, and that we would get to meet you and talk with someone who actually knew Henry Ford and was around him, which is just incredible, with the backdrop of these beautiful cars. We are so fortunate!

You know, in the first chapter of Henry Ford's book, Today and Tomorrow, it is so interesting what the first chapter is called. *(Paul picks up the book and opens to the first page.)* I'm going to read it right here: We Are Being Born Into Opportunity. I cannot agree with that more. Everywhere we look, for every human being, opportunity is swirling around them. The question is, are we awake to reach up and grab it and take advantage of it.

Phil: Absolutely.

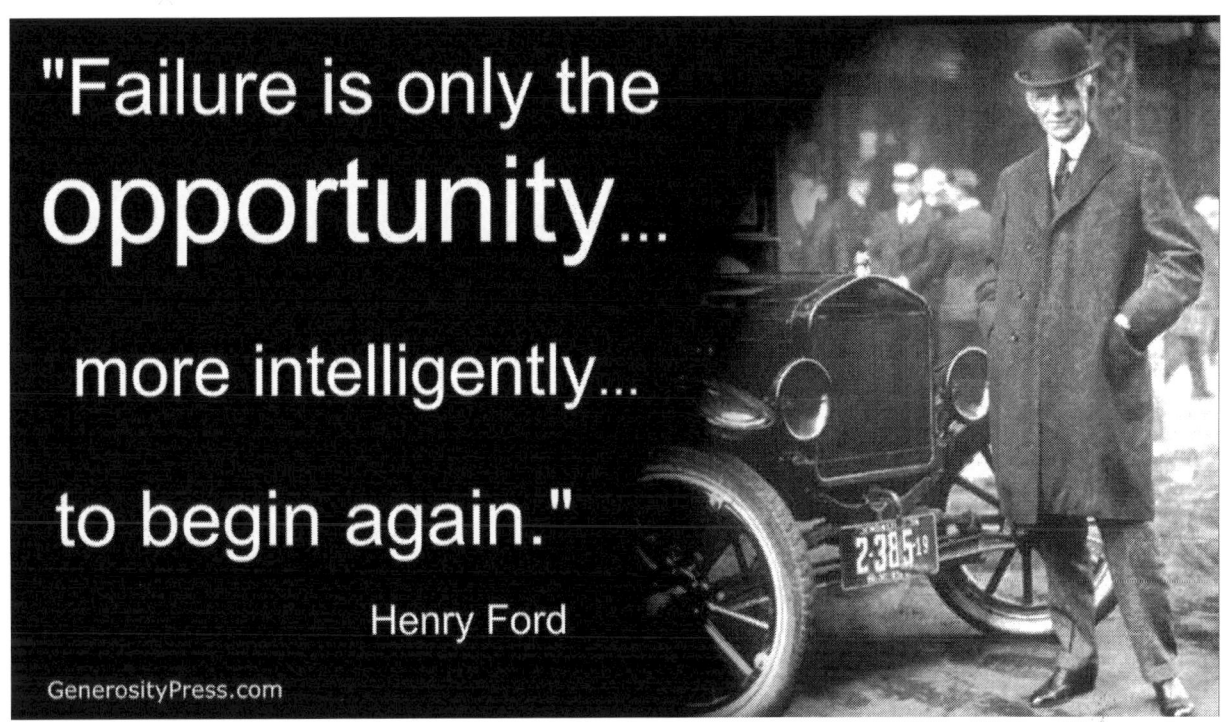

CHAPTER 1
WE ARE BEING BORN INTO OPPORTUNITY

For hundreds of years men have been talking about the lack of opportunity and the pressing need of dividing up things already in existence. Yet each year has seen some new idea brought forth and developed, and with it a whole new series of opportunities, until today we already have enough tested ideas which, put into practice, would take the world out of its sloughs and banish poverty by providing livings for all who will work. Only the old, outworn notions stand in the way of these new ideas. The world shackles itself, blinds its eyes, and then wonders why it cannot run.

Take just one idea – a little idea in itself – an idea that any one might have had, but which fell to me to develop – that of making a small, strong, simple automobile, to make it cheaply, and pay high wages in its making. On October 1, 1908, we made the first of our present type of small cars. On June 4, 1924, we made the ten millionth. Now, in 1926, we are in our thirteenth million.

Henry Ford and his 1924 ten-millionth automobile next to his very first model from 1896.

That is interesting but perhaps not important. What is important is that, from a mere handful of men employed in a shop, we have grown into a large industry directly employing more than two hundred thousand men, not one of whom receives less than six dollars a day. Our dealers and service stations employ another two hundred thousand men. But by no means do we manufacture all that we use. Roughly, we buy twice as much as we manufacture, and it is safe to say that two hundred thousand men are employed on our work in outside factories. This gives a rough total of six hundred thousand employees, direct and indirect, which means that about three million men, women, and children get their livings out of a single idea put into effect only eighteen years ago. And this does not take into account the great number of people who in some way or other assist in the distribution or the maintenance of these cars. And this one idea is only in its infancy.

These figures are given not with any thought of boastfulness. I am not talking about a specific person or business. I am talking about ideas. And these figures do show something of what a single idea can accomplish. These people require food, clothing, shoes, houses, and so on. If they and their families were brought together in one place and those needed to supply their wants gathered around them, we should have a city larger than New York. All this has matured in less time than a child matures. What nonsense it is to think or speak of lack of opportunity! We do not know what opportunity is.

There are always two kinds of people in the world: those who pioneer and those who plod. The plodders always attack the pioneers. They say that the pioneers have gobbled up all the opportunity, when, as a plain matter of fact, the plodders would have nowhere to plod had not the pioneers first cleared the way.

Think about your work in the world. Did you make your place or did someone make it for you? Did you start the work you are in or did someone else? Have you ever found or made an opportunity for yourself or are you the beneficiary of opportunity which others have found or made?

We have seen the rise of a temper which does not want opportunities. It wants the full fruits of opportunity handed to it on a platter. This temper is not American. It is imported from lands and by races that have never been able to see or use opportunity – that have existed on what was given them.

Now the fact is that a generation ago there were a thousand men to every opportunity while today there are a thousand opportunities for every man. Affairs in this country have changed just that much.

However, when industry was growing up, opportunities were limited. Men saw along one track and all of them wanted to get on that one track. Naturally, some of them were shoved off; there were more men than opportunities. That is why we had so much fierceness and cruelty of competition in the old days. There were not enough of the big opportunities to go around.

But, with the maturing of industry, a whole new world of opportunity opened up. Think how many doors of creative activity every industrial advance has opened. It has turned out, through all the fierce competitive fights, that no man could succeed in his own opportunity without creating many times more opportunities than he could begin to grasp.

It is almost impossible to understand the rise of industry without recognizing the former scarcity of opportunity. Some forms of business seem to have gone onward, but our accounts of them mostly come from those who were beaten.

But there is enough of fact to indicate that, when industry was being evolved under the pressure of the people's needs (and that is the only force that brought it into being), some men had large vision while others had limited vision. The men of larger vision naturally bested the others. Their methods were sometimes immoral, but it was not their immoral methods that accounted for their success – it was their larger vision of needs, and ways and means to fulfill them. There must be a tremendous amount of right vision in anything if it is to survive dishonest or cruel methods. To attribute success to dishonesty is a common fallacy. We hear of men "too honest to succeed." That may be a comforting reflection to them, but it is never the reason for their failure.

Dishonest men do sometimes succeed. But only when they give a service which exceeds their dishonesty. Honest men sometimes fail because they lack other essential qualities to go with their honesty. It is safe to say that in the success of men who are dishonest, all that is touched by dishonesty sloughs off.

Those who do not believe in opportunity will still find places within the opportunities that others have created; those who cannot direct their work successfully will always find it possible to be directed by others.

But are we moving too fast – not merely in the making of automobiles, but in life generally? One hears a deal about the worker being ground down by hard labor, of what is called progress being made at the expense of something or other, and that efficiency is wrecking all the finer things of life.

It is quite true that life is out of balance – and always has been. Until lately, most people have had no leisure to use and, of course, they do not now know how to use it.

One of our large problems is to find some balance between work and play, between sleep and food, and eventually to discover why men grow ill and die. Of this more later.

Certainly we are moving faster than before. Or, more correctly, we are being moved faster. But is twenty minutes in a motor car easier or harder than four hours' solid trudging down a dirt road? Which mode of travel leaves the pilgrim fresher at the end? Which leaves him more time and more mental energy? And soon we shall be making in an hour by air what were days' journeys by motor. Shall we all then be nervous wrecks?

But does this state of nervous wreckage to which we are all said to be coming exist in life or in books? One hears of the workers' nervous exhaustion in books, but does one hear of it from the workers?

Go to the people who are working with the actual things of the world, from the laborer travelling to his work on the street car to the young man who hops across a continent in a day. You will find quite a different attitude. Instead of cringing away from what has come, they are looking with eager expectancy toward what is coming. Always they are willing to scrap today in favor of tomorrow. That is the blessedness of the active man, the man who is not sitting alone in a library trying to fit the new world into the old molds. Go to the laborer in the street car. He will tell you that just a few years ago he came home so late and so tired that he had no time to change his clothes, just got his supper and went to bed. Now he changes his clothes at the shop, goes home by daylight, has an early supper, and takes the family out for a drive. He will tell you that the killing pressure has let up. A man may have to be a little more businesslike on the job than formerly, but the old endless, exhausting drive has quit.

The men at the top, the men who are changing all these things, will tell you the same. They are not breaking down. They are marching the way progress is going and find it easier to go along with progress than to try to hold things back.

And just there is the secret: those who get headaches are trying to hold the world back, trying to wrap it up again in their small definitions. It cannot be done.

The very word "efficiency" is hated because so much that is not efficiency has masqueraded as such. Efficiency is merely the doing of work in the best way you know rather than in the worst way. It is the taking of a trunk up a hill on a truck rather than on one's back. It is the training of the worker and the giving to him of power so that he may earn more and have more and live more comfortably. The Chinese coolie *(as some ethnic hard laborers of the day were often called)* working through long hours for a few cents a day is not happier than the American workman with his own home and automobile. The one is a slave, the other is a free man.

In the organization of the Ford work we are continually reaching out for more and more developed power. We go to the coalfields, to the streams, and to the rivers, always seeking some cheap and convenient source of power which we can transform into electricity, take to the machine, increase the output of the workers, raise their wages, and lower the price to the public.

Into this train of events enter a great and ever-increasing number of factors. You must get the most out of the power, out of the material, and out of the time. This has taken us apparently far afield, as, for instance, into railroading, mining, lumbering, and shipping. We have spent many millions of dollars just to save a few hours' time here and there. Actually, however, we do nothing whatsoever which is not directly connected with our business, which is the making of motors.

The power which we use in manufacturing produces another power – the power of the motor that goes into the automobile. About fifty dollars' worth of raw material is transformed into twenty horsepower mounted on wheels. Up to December 1, 1925, we had, through cars and tractors, added to the world nearly three hundred million mobile horsepower, or about ninety-seven times the potential horsepower of Niagara Falls. The whole world uses only twenty-three million stationary horsepower, of which the United States uses more than nine million.

The effect of putting all this additional developed power into the country is something we do not yet know how to reckon with, but I am convinced that the remarkable prosperity of the United States is in a large part due to this added horsepower, which, by freeing the movements of men, also frees and awakens their thoughts.

The progress of the world has been in direct ratio to the convenience of communication. We have remade this country with automobiles. But we do not have these automobiles because we are prosperous. We are prosperous because we have them. You will remember that everyone did not buy them all at once. The buying has been gradual - in fact, we have never been able to keep up with orders, and with our present capacity of two million a year we are able to meet the needs only of our present owners if they should each buy a new car every six years.

That is an aside. The general prosperity of the country, in spite of bad farm years, is in direct proportion to the number of automobiles. That is inevitable, for you cannot introduce such a vast amount of developed power into a country without the effects being felt in every direction. What the motor car does among other things, quite apart from its own usefulness, is to familiarize people generally with the use of developed power - to teach what power is and to get them about and out of the shells in which they have been living. Before the motor car many a man lived and died without ever having been more than fifty miles from home. That is of the past in this country. It is still true of much of the world.

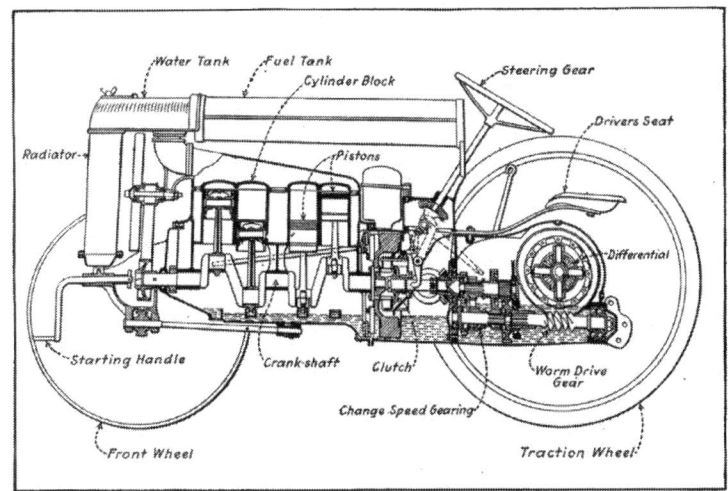

Schematics of the original Fordson tractor with principal parts circa 1919.

When the representatives of Russia came to buy tractors for their state farms, we told them:

"No, you first ought to buy automobiles and get your people used to machinery and power and to moving about with some freedom. The motor cars will bring roads, and then it will be possible to get the products of your farms to the cities."

They followed the advice and bought some thousands of automobiles. Now, after several years, they have bought some thousands of tractors.

The great point in all this, however, is not that an automobile or anything else may be well and cheaply made through planning and the use of power. We have known that for a long time. The automobile is particularly important for the reasons that have been given, but what overshadows all else in importance is that we have discovered a new motive for industry and abolished the meaningless terms "capital," "labor," and "public."

For many years we have heard the phrase "profit motive" which meant that someone called a capitalist provided tools and machinery, employed men - that is, labor - at the least possible wage, and then manufactured goods and sold them to some strange collection of people known as the "public." The capitalist sold to this public at the highest price he could get and pocketed his profits. Apparently, the public came out of the air and also got its money out of the air, and it had to be protected from the profiteering capitalist. The workman also had to be protected, and someone invented the "living-wage" notion, all of which grows out of a complete misconception of the entire industrial process.

It is true that petty business can work on the capital-labor-public mistake, but big business cannot, nor can little business grow big on the theory that it can grind down its employees. The plain fact is that the public which buys from you does not come from nowhere. The owner, the employees, and the buying public are all one and the same, and unless an industry can so manage itself as to keep wages high and prices low, it destroys itself, for otherwise it limits the number of its customers. One's own employees ought to be one's own best customers.

The real progress of our company dates from 1914, when we raised the minimum wage from somewhat more than two dollars to a flat five dollars a day, for then we increased the buying power of our own people, and they increased the buying power of other people, and so on and on. It is this thought of enlarging buying power by paying high wages and selling at low prices which is behind the prosperity of this country.

It is the fundamental motive of our company. We call it the "wage motive."

But, of course, high wages cannot be paid to any one just for the asking. If wages are raised without lowering costs, then buying power is not enlarged. There is no "living wage," for, unless an equivalent in work is returned, no wages can be high enough for a man to live on them. Also, there can be no "standard" wage. No one on this earth knows enough to fix a standard wage. The very idea of a standard wage presupposes that invention and management have reached their limit.

No greater injury can be done to a man than to pay him a high wage for a small amount of work, for then his high wage increases the prices of commodities and puts them beyond his reach. Also, it is untrue to say that profits or the benefit of inventions which bring lower costs belong to the worker. That grows out of another misconception of the industrial process. Profits belong primarily to the business and the workers are only a part of the business. If all the profits were given to the workers, then improvements, such as will hereafter be described, would not be possible. Prices would increase, and consumption would decline, and the business would gradually go out of existence. The profits have to go toward making lower costs, and the advantage of lower costs must in a large measure be given to the consumer. This, in effect, is the same as raising wages.

This may seem complex, but it has worked out rather simply with us.

To affect the economies, to bring in the power, to cut out the waste, and thus fully to realize the wage motive, we must have big business which does not, however, necessarily mean centralized business. We are decentralizing. Any business founded on the wage motive and animated solely with the thought of service must grow big. It cannot grow to a certain size and be held there – it must go forward or go back. Of course, what seems to be a big business may be created overnight by buying up a large number of small businesses. The result may be big business, or again, it may just be a museum of business, showing how many curious things may be bought with money. Big business is not money power: it is service power.

Big business happens to signify the means by which the people of the United States make their living. All our business, into however many pieces it may be broken, is inevitably big. This is a big country, with a big population having big needs and calling for big production and big supply. You cannot name the most trivial commodity that is not in this country an enormously big industry. Even more bicycles are being made than at the height of the bicycle craze. And business must grow bigger and bigger, else we shall have insufficient supplies and high prices.

Take the case of the farmers of Sudbury, Massachusetts, less than two hundred years ago. There is record of their meeting to approve the measures taken by the "merchants and other inhabitants of the town of Boston in order to reduce the exorbitant prices of the necessaries of life." Coffee was then counted reasonably priced at twenty dollars a pound; men's shoes at twenty dollars a pair (women's shoes are not mentioned, as perhaps being unnecessary); cotton cloth came high, and a bushel of salt cost a small fortune.

What accounts for the change in the price of those articles then and now? Business – which is the organization of supply.

Business began small and grew large. There is nothing mysterious about that. When transportation was difficult, and the community needed sap buckets, or hoes, it was easier to get them on the spot. They were not always the best buckets, but they were the most easily procurable. That represents one of the big elements of business – having the commodity near the person who needs it. In earlier times, the market spot was necessarily the manufacturing spot. Most of the stuff was made in the town. All the trades grew up around the post office. The blacksmith made most of the farming implements. The weaver made most of the textiles that the kitchen industries did not cover. A town was almost a self-supporting community.

It did not follow, however, that all this service was the best or the cheapest. Any grocer will tell you that "farm butter" does not mean anything. It all depends on what kind of a butter-maker the farmer's wife is. The best butter and the worst may come from home-made processes. The modern dairy approximates a higher average of quality. And so it was natural that, as the country expanded, as means of exchange between communities became more workable, and especially as transportation developed, the better type of suppliers obtained an increasingly wide range of territory.

In this way, many of the earliest of the biggest businesses grew up in the East, for there was the bulk of the increasing population. When industry came into the field it grew to its greatest proportions in those parts of the country that supplied its basic materials - ore and fuel. As the great food supply concerns arose they took their stand in a part of the country between the food-producing and the food-consuming sections of the population. These big service organizations all came into existence on a perfectly natural and logical plan. The people made them. One or more men may have developed the idea, but it was the support of the people that gave the idea its big place in the life of the world.

And now, as the country has grown larger, so has business, and we have learned a great deal. We now know that business is a science and that all other sciences are contributing to it. We are in the great age of transition from the drudgery of life to the enjoyment of life. And what we have learned about the ways and means of this transition will be told in the following chapters in terms of hard experience.

CHAPTER 2
IS THERE A LIMIT TO BIG BUSINESS?

If the worker is to be able to buy what he makes – that is, if the wage motive is fully to be carried out – then the large corporation is inevitable.

Putting the worker in a position to buy what he makes, of course, has its exceptions, and the thought applies principally to commodities. One would not expect the worker to buy a pipe organ, or a steamship, or a skyscraper. As a worker, he would have no use for any of these things. But he has use for good food, good clothing, good housing, and a reasonable amount of pleasure both for himself and for his family.

He cannot get these things by any political device or through any bargaining organization, such as a labor union, for goods are created neither by law nor by bargaining – which, strangely enough, does not seem generally to be recognized. Many foreign labor leaders have visited me during the past several years, and, without exception, they have talked politics, while the industrial leaders from abroad have talked politics only in a defensive way. Their chief interest, or, at least, so it has appeared, has been in finding ways and means to adjust the differences between labor and capital. Of course, when one thinks in terms of "labor and capital," one begins to think in a circle, but at least these men were groping for a way out through production, while the labor leaders seemed principally to want the opportunity to hold office and make speeches.

The people have been taught to fear the great corporation. They fear it partly because they do not understand it and partly because they are afraid of monopoly. Also, they have a fear of the money power, and confuse big business with big money power. Their thinking is many years behind the times. They are back in the days when a million dollars was a large sum of money, and when it was taken as a fact that no man could make or use a million dollars honestly. Whoever started that saying must have been a man of the narrowest vision, else he would have known that it is much easier to make money honestly than it is to make it dishonestly. The only important point in all this is that people think of business, and especially big business, as something of dollars instead of as something of service.

Now, let us remember that this is today and not yesterday or tomorrow. The world has always needed leadership. Yesterday that leadership was military and political. It made no difference what form of government any country had: it was successful when it had leadership and it failed when it did not. Neither military nor political leadership is creative. Business was called successful only when it took away something that someone else had already created. However, there is no use quarrelling with the past. The kind of leadership that the past got was undoubtedly the leadership it needed. But times have improved and today political and military leadership cannot serve the people as well as industrial leadership. Quite likely the political leadership everywhere is about up to the average. The reason why it seems to be below the average is that people have fallen into the habit of asking politics to do what only industry can do. The professional reformers do not understand this. They think that politics can do what only industry can do, and they propose regulations of prices and of this, that, and the other thing, on the ground that thus they can bring prosperity.

There is a craving for a prosperity ordained by law, and it is entirely natural that there should be. For the idea is rather general that the chief curse of life is to work for a living. Thinking men know that work is the salvation of the race, morally, physically, socially. Work does more than get us our living: it gets us our life. But somehow, prosperity - and everyone agrees that it is good to be prosperous - is mixed up with high prices and high wages, and since both prices and wages can apparently (though not actually) be raised by law, it would seem that some law could substitute for work.

Everyone should know by this time that true prosperity is marked by a reduction of prices, and that this is the only way by which prosperity can be made the normal condition and prevented from being merely spasmodic.

Consider a few fundamental principles. First, why should we ever have prosperity at all? Prosperity being the easy and uninterrupted supply of need, and the needs of our people being normal and varied, and the means to supply these needs being ample, with a surplus left over for those afar whose sources of supply have not been developed, the more logical question is, Why should we ever be without prosperity? Even in "hard times" we have every element of prosperity, so that the puzzle is that we ever should have to endure "hard times" except through bad management of our affairs. The economic basis of prosperity is always present.

But men must be led into prosperity. A mob is powerless except for destruction. All men are not voluntarily intelligent; they must be taught. All men do not see the high escape from drudgery in work by putting intelligence into work; they must be taught. All men do not see the wisdom of fitting means to ends, of conserving material (which is sacred as the result of others' labors), of saving that most precious commodity - time; they must be taught.

Industry must have generalship - and of a high order. The great corporation is the inevitable consequence of industrial leadership.

How great will corporations grow? Is there a limit to their size, and if so, what is that limit? Should they be regulated to serve the public interest? What are the dangers of monopoly? Should monopoly be restrained?

These questions will more or less answer themselves if we look at how a serving corporation comes into being. First of all, it has to be designed to furnish some service. The corporation has to follow the service. The service does not follow the corporation. The design is what counts. Everything in this world, to be made rightly, has to follow a design, and time spent in getting a thing right is never wasted. It is time saved in the end. But here someone may ask: "What am I going to design?" You may take something which people already know about and try to make a better design than is being offered. That might be the course to follow in commodities, but probably a better way is to judge the wants of the people by your own wants.

Then start from where you stand and let the public make your business for you. The public and only the public can make a business.

If we have good steel today, it is because the public bought steel when it was faulty, and thus helped the steel masters to perfect their science and production. If we have comfortable transportation today, it is because the people were willing to pay for uncomfortable transportation and let the system grow up. If we have swift, durable, and dependable motor cars today, it is because the people bought motor cars when they were largely in the experimental stage. If we have the varied products of petroleum today, it is because the people bought and burned "coal oil," and, by their confidence and patronage, set the oil industry on its way to world-wide service.

Since the public makes a business, the primary obligation of business is to the public. Those who work for and with the business are part of this public. And this settles one fundamental corporate policy: to whom shall the benefits of improvements accrue?

Suppose an industry, through efficiency and approved service, is able to reduce costs to the consumer. It gives the benefits of its improvements to its customers. If an article cost a dollar less to produce than formerly, a dollar comes off the price charged the consumer. By that process more people are able to buy. More buyers make a still larger business. A larger business still further reduces costs, which in turn increases the business still more.

Now, it is obvious that, however efficient the idea of economical production in that factory may have been, no such growth would have followed had the economy not been shared with the public. Suppose that the one dollar saved was added to profits, the price to the consumer remaining the same. There would have been no change in the volume of business. Suppose the dollar saved had been added to wages, there would have been no change in the volume of business. But by sharing the profits with the public comes an immediate and great public benefit, there is a stimulating reaction on the business; prices go lower, business increases, thousands of men are employed where but scores found work before, wages increase, profits mount. By starting at the right end prices go down, which is to say that, to the public, values go up, wages go up, and surplus goes up. The point is, this did not come by doing what is sometimes demanded, turning all the profits into wages. It is accomplishing more benefit for the wage-earner with a family of five, to reduce the cost of necessities for the members of his family, than to increase his pay without reducing his costs. Increased pay comes through increased business, and no increase in business is possible except by lowering prices to the public.

Labor is more of a buyer than a seller. The point at which to start the wheel a-rolling is the buying end. Make things easy for the plain people to buy. That makes work. That makes wages. That makes surplus for extension and greater service.

The burden of it all is on the shoulders of management. Labor works along under any system. There is little or no concern in the shop whether the best method is being used, whether the best results are being had from materials and from the motions of men; it is a day's work just the same. The difference in a day's work is in production value, and this is the business of management.

Suppose a business has grown and prospered under this policy of serving the public. It is not self-sufficient - it must buy on the outside. Its supplies are threatened. The mismanagement of businesses that supply the raw material causes strikes which delay it. Or the fast-passing policy of charging all that the traffic will bear is used to run up prices unreasonably, preventing the proprietor from selling his commodity to his customers at a price which is right for him and for them. He finds himself at the mercy of the misleaders of labor outside his business, and the profit-gougers who supply his raw material. Obviously, it is his duty to protect his customers. They need a certain commodity at a price they can afford to pay, and they are threatened with seeing this forced up to a price which they cannot afford to pay.

The business - the manufacturer - must at once decide whether he will have his service to his customers limited by forces beyond his control, or whether to the extent of his resources he will make his own supplies. If he decides, as we decided, that the quantity and quality of our service should be within our control, then gradually he will be drawn, at least to a protective degree, into the manufacturing of raw materials and into many ramifications such as later will be described in our own progress. And with the taking over of the very first source of raw materials comes the test of service.

In every one of the raw materials used there was a profit. A coal profit, a limestone profit, an ore and blast furnace profit, a lumber profit, a transportation profit, and so on. Is the manufacturer to collect for himself each of these profits, and add it to the profit he receives for turning these raw materials into an article of use? Not if he is a true business man operating on the principle of service and taking only a legitimate replacement and expansion surplus. He abolishes all subsidiary profits and gives the consumer the benefit of them.

The former profit which the public gave him to enable him to expand now comes back to the public in the form of a stabilized supply, a stabilized cost price, and a lower sales price. The number of the profits saddled on one commodity has been reduced.

The test of the service of a corporation is in how far its benefits are passed on to the consumer. The reduction of profits, in number and amount, on any commodity is an instant and general community benefit.

Is such a business a menace or a benefit to the public? It must be a benefit to the public else it would not grow. It has grown through serving the public, and the limit of its size is its ability to serve the public. That ability to serve may be limited by management or it may be limited by transportation. We have not found any difficulty in management largely because (as has been explained in a former book) we have no rigid management. We have just grown, and as each unit has been added, someone from the ranks has appeared to undertake the management.

The real limit to the size of a corporation is transportation. If it has to transport its commodity too far, then it cannot give service and it limits its own size. There is far too much transportation anyway - too much useless carting of goods to central points from there to be distributed to points of consumption.

If low prices and high wages are a menace, then the great industry is a menace. The corporation formed, not to give service, but only to sell its stock, is another matter which will be taken up subsequently.

There are people who think of big business as dangerous because it is big. They believe that the old way of each business being self-sufficient in its own town is the right idea. And one hundred years ago it was the right idea. Each cobbler in his little town made the shoes - and they were good shoes. The local wagon-maker made his wagons for the townsfolk.

The point to be remembered about the establishment of industry is that, while all these various new ideas were being developed, the people who paid for them were the people who bought. No tractor, no thresher, no motor car, no locomotive, no new industrial device has ever been developed unless the people paid the expenses.

The old idea of business, that it consists of one man getting the better of another man, is no longer acknowledged as businesslike even by those who practice it. The American idea of business is based on economic science and social morality - that is, it recognizes that all economic activity is under the check of natural law, and that no activity of man so continuously affects the well-being of others as does the daily activity of business. We do not have to ask for the public regulation of business. The public has always regulated business.

Monopoly or the super-control of commodities seems an impossibility among an enlightened and resourceful people. A people that would not stand a tax on tea - would they stand absolute despotic control of the things they need for life? A people that freed their slaves - would they turn slaves themselves? The pin-maker is permitted to make pins as long as they are good pins. If not, someone else will make them. The real controller is always the public.

Big or little business goes along in response to a demand, and the demand is created by the service rendered. Stop the service and the demand ceases. Stop the demand and where is big business? All the money in the world could not stop competition among Americans. To do one thing well stimulates others to do it better.

Business grows big by public demand. But it never gets bigger than the demand. It cannot control or force the demand. There is no super-control save that of the people reacting to the service they get. The only monopoly possible is based upon rendering the highest service. That sort of monopoly is a benefit. Any attempt artificially to monopolize is only a method of throwing away one's money.

But will not the growth of the great corporation shut off individual initiative? Where is a young man going to turn?

Is it better for a man to take employment with another or to go into business for himself? The question is legitimate when asked in full knowledge of two facts: that there are more doors into private business today than ever before, and that employment has come to compete with private business as a career for any man.

Men are constantly passing from one field into the other. In any large business may be found men who have been in business for themselves and have given it up. There may also be found men who hope someday to give up employment and set up for themselves.

The motives of those who leave business for employment are various. Some find themselves unable to bear the strain. They are fitted to serve, but not also to direct the services of others, or even adapt their own service to the changing needs of the time. So they take employment where they can serve under direction, certain of an income, and free to cultivate the other interests of their minds.

Some accept employment because they see in extensive modern business the widest and most inviting outlet for their powers. What would take them a lifetime to build, they find ready at hand, built by another, and needing their service.

That is the appeal of modern business to the young man: he can begin with an organization whose crude experimental days are over and which stands able to do the thing it was organized to do, and to do greater things, because increased experience leads to greater and more successful experiment.

In private business one enters an atmosphere of competition, whereas, in large employment, one enters an atmosphere of cooperation. A great modern industry progresses by the unified thought and energy of many men. Theirs is a cooperation based, not on emotional agreement or personal preference, but on common interest in the job to be done.

And the opportunities to acquire position and a competence are greater in employment than in private business, because there are more places to be filled and the rewards are larger. Salaries in this country are greater than profits. Those who feel that business is jealous of the employee's progress are behind the times. Business can live only as it develops within its corps of employees the talent and the force which will carry the business along. Business lives by the vigor and brains of the men it produces. And every big business needs more and bigger men than many, many small businesses could possibly need. With this larger need comes larger opportunity.

We have come to a point where there are more things to be done than we have men to do them. And it is big business which has brought all this about.

When there were more men than opportunities, there was struggle of a very fierce and often inhuman kind. But to assume that such is the essential law of business practice and business success in these days is nonsense. From a condition where it was believed that competition decreased business, we have advanced to a condition where we know that competition increases business. This is because opportunity exists in multitude where before it was scarce.

No, big business based on service regulates its own size and conduct. If it is based on money instead of service – then we have another matter.

CHAPTER 3
BIG BUSINESS AND THE MONEY POWER

Business – that is, the whole material side of life – is threatened by two classes of people who think they are in opposition, but who actually have a common cause – the professional financier and the professional reformer.

Both go about the destruction of business. That is what they have in common. Their ways are not alike. Their motives are not alike. But given a free hand, either can destroy business very quickly.

There is nothing to be said against the financier – the man who really understands the management of money and its place in life. There is nothing to be said against the reformer who knows what he is about and knows the effect of the changes he desires and who is willing to give the people to be reformed a chance.

But it is very different with the professional financier, who finances for the sake of financing and what he can get out of it in money, without a thought of the welfare of the people. The professional reformer likewise reforms for the sake of reforming and for his own satisfaction, and without a thought of the real welfare of the people.

These two classes are real menaces. The professional financiers wrecked Germany. The professional reformers wrecked Russia. You can take your choice as to who made the better job of it.

These two classes, working either directly or through politicians, are in control of Europe and are responsible for its poverty. The League of Nations and all its adjuncts, such as the World Court, are in their control, and under no system which they devise do the people have a chance. Especially are they opposed to any theory of industry which makes for the general welfare.

The people abroad are content to take sops in the form of resolutions and treaties, but presently people everywhere will learn to disregard the teachings of both professional financiers and professional reformers, just as we have learned to disregard them here in the United States.

They will go forward on principles of real economy and will learn that there is no connection between real business and the money power and that attacking business in order to reach the money power is merely playing into the hands of the financiers.

The notion that money is the life blood of business and that if you can control money you can control business has just enough foundation to make it seem real, because we have to express in dollars what are not dollars at all.

Take the Ford Industries. For accounting and tax purposes they have to be valued in dollars according to recognized modes of procedure. Thus the Ford Industries are supposed to be worth some large sums, and those figures are printed. Nine out of ten men think that we have that number of dollars somewhere on the premises. We have nothing of the kind. We have our power plants, furnaces, lathes, drill presses, coal mines, iron mines, and so on. We have the physical equipment to manufacture automobiles and tractors and some raw material to work with. As a going concern, the worth of all this equipment depends upon the skill of the management. Who can say what a chest of tools is worth to a carpenter on a job?

Take four furnaces, fifty stamping machines, a conveyor system, a dozen annealing ovens, a pile of coal, elevators, trucks, buildings, iron and wood and sand – the actual physical inventory of a place. You never see that inventory expressed as things. It is always in dollars. There are no dollars there, as dollars. There are furnaces, machinery, ovens, trucks, elevators, materials, and buildings. These things are valuable. They are intrinsically more valuable than dollars. That is, if you shoveled a building full of dollars, you would not have the same capacity for production and use as you would have if you filled that same building with machinery and an organization of human skill.

On a tax sheet, however, all this mechanical capacity is put down as "dollars," and on that basis a certain number of "dollars" are demanded of it. More than one business has been destroyed by taxes levied under the impression that its assets were in dollars.

That is only one of the collateral effects of thinking of things as dollars instead of as things. We must learn to drive through all our thinking the profound distinction between finance and business. This is the country of big business. But, as previously shown, big business controls nothing. It is entirely at the mercy of public demand. It is amazing how few seem able to distinguish between industry and finance.

In the violent period of the union labor movement, the employer was always referred to as the capitalist. The whole trouble was that the employer was not a capitalist, but was under the thumb of capitalists. In those years, most businesses were conducted on borrowed capital, which gave the capitalist a super-control of the industry. The manufacturer, standing between hostile labor and rapacious capital, had a hard time getting anything done. Pressed from above for interest and dividends, pushed from below to grant more money for less work, he had small chance to give service. And all the time he had to bear the abuse that was being heaped upon the capitalist.

But a change has come. Business does not minimize the service which the world of finance can render, but it has declared itself free from domination by that world. When finance exists to serve industry, which is its proper function, then finance is recognized as part of the service instrument of humanity.

Twenty-five years ago, we heard a great deal about big business. There was really no big business twenty-five years ago. What we had was our first mergers of money. Money is not business. Big money cannot make big business. Men of money, foreseeing the approach of the industrial era, sought to seize and control it by means of their pooled capital. And for a time, the country rang with their exploits. Money brokers are seldom good business men. Speculators cannot create values. However, the idea got abroad that "money" had grabbed everything and that "money" controlled everything.

Go back in mind twenty-five years - then count the big businesses existing now which did not exist then, which big money did not bring into existence, and which big money does not now control, to see how untrue is the assumption that we live under a super-control.

For centuries, with marvelous forethought, certain hereditary groups have manipulated a large part of the gold of the world, not all of it, but a controlling margin, especially in Europe, where they have used their power to make war or peace. Their power is not in their gold, because there is no power in gold; their power is in their control of people's ideas with regard to gold. It is not any enslavement to gold that menaces, but the enslavement of the people to a certain idea of gold. Money control does exist - not the control of mankind by money, but the control of money by a group of money-brokers. At one time, this meant the control of mankind by money. But now, with the growth of real industry, money is slowly receding to its proper place as one of the cogs in the wheel, not as the wheel itself.

No money trust today controls the American worker, or the creator - the men who with hand or brain serve society in a productive way.

This is not to say that money and profits are not necessary in business. Business must be run at a profit (this will be taken up in a subsequent chapter), else it will die. But when any one attempts to run a business solely for profit and thinks not at all of the service to the community, then also the business must die, for it no longer has a reason for existence.

The profit motive, although it is supposed to be hard-headed and practical, is really not practical at all, because, as has been explained, it has as its objectives the increasing of prices to the consumer and the decreasing of wages, and therefore it constantly narrows its markets and eventually strangles itself. That accounts for much of the difficulty abroad.

There business is largely controlled by professional financiers, and the men in actual charge of operations have little indeed to say about management. The worker is not expected to be able to buy what he makes, and he is further fooled by the reformers, who tell him that his way out is through higher wages and shorter hours. He wants exactly what the professional financier wants - that is, something for nothing - and thus, without knowing it, the financiers and reformers combine to destroy business as an instrument of service. That is why we hear so much talk in foreign countries of the necessity for export trade. The home market is not built up through the payment of high wages for well-managed work which will result in low price to the consumer. The worker is a consumer of only a few meager necessities of life.

This need not be so. We have demonstrated through our own industries in nearly every part of the world that it need not be so as will be later brought out. I have no doubt that the workers in the Ford Industries in the United States own more automobiles than are owned in the whole world outside of this country. There is no accident in this, nor is it due to the natural resources of the United States. Power can be made plentiful almost anywhere. Great Britain has plenty of coal and some water power. The Continental countries have either coal or water power or both. They all would have plenty of raw materials if the fences erected by the tools of the financiers were taken down. But raw material is not nearly as important a factor as it once was. We are every day learning to use less and less raw material by adding to its strength. One of these days steel and iron will no longer be on a tonnage basis but on a strength basis. This is one of the most important of our developments, and also we are learning that a great deal of material that has served its purpose can be reclaimed and reworked. But that, too, is a matter for another chapter.

The reason why Europe thinks that it cannot manage without export is that the professional reformers, coming from below, and the professional financiers, coming from above, have together squeezed the buying power out of the people, and the industries are forced to look abroad for markets - having exploited their own people, they seek to exploit other nations. There could easily be a healthy trading between nations. There need be no vicious competition - the kind of competition that brings on war. If the home market is built up (and everywhere in the world this can be done), then the export trade will be the natural and healthy exchange of commodities which one country can spare and another need. The present competition in the world markets is due largely to the exploitation of the people at home.

It becomes plain, therefore, that to confuse business with the money power is to make one thing of two and to unite elements which naturally oppose each other. A business cannot serve both the public and the money power. As a matter of fact, the money power has always lived more by exploiting or wrecking business than by the service of business. There are signs, however, that this may be on the mend.

Money put into business as a lien on its assets is dead money. When industry operates wholly by the permission of "dead" money, its main purpose becomes the production of payments for the owners of that money. The service of the public has to be secondary. If quality of goods jeopardizes these payments, then the quality is cut down. If full service cuts into the payments, then service is cut down. This kind of money does not serve business. It seeks to make business serve it.

Money that takes no risks in an industry, but demands its toll whether there be profit or loss, is not live money. It is not whole-heartedly in the business as a part of it; it is a dead weight, and the sooner the business is rid of it, the better. Dead money is not a working partner but an idle charge.

Live money goes into the business to work and to share with the. business. It is there to be used. It shares whatever losses there may be. It is asset to the last penny, and never a liability.

Live money in a business is usually accompanied by the active labor of the man or men who put it there. Dead money is a sucker plant.

The principle of the service of business to the people has gone far in the United States, and it will spread through and remake the world. It was not the war, but the seeming impossibility of restoring conditions as they were before the war, that gave men the first inkling of the lesson they are to learn. They would have accepted the war as an accident or as a mistake had they not been made to see that the war was but the symptom of a deeper malady. The old tricks have failed. The old wisdom has proved foolishness. The old motives are ineffective. If losing a false wisdom and finding a new beginning of learning is progress, then we may say that the world has progressed. Its old principles are disproved by experience. Progress is not marked by a definite boundary across which we step, but by an attitude and an atmosphere. Everything false does not vanish at a given moment, and everything true appear.

Some men know and many others feel that business is something more than money – that money is a commodity and not a power.

Any business is as good as finished when it begins to finance. It is sometimes necessary (although always dangerous) to get money for extensions except out of profits, and there may be emergencies when additional cash is required, but this is very different from financing for the sake of financing – using the business to make money through finance instead of through service.

The danger point of any business is not when it needs money, but when it becomes successful enough to be financed – to be a foundation for a great pile of stocks and bonds. The public is gullible and may easily be taken advantage of. For instance, a certain amount of the stock of the Ford Motor Company of Canada is on the market. It could be bought for about $485 a share. Some exploiters bought up a few shares, and against each share issued one hundred of what they called "bankers' shares" at $10 each. That is, they sold for $1,000 what they had bought for $485, and the strange part is that the public fell into the trap and freely paid two dollars for something which they could have bought themselves for a dollar!

That shows how easy it is to turn a successful business into a financial tool.

Thus, it is just when an industry becomes most widely useful that its strongest testing comes. The money power will point the way of large stock issues, of profits made out of paper instead of production, of easy gains by mixing water with true worth. This is a temptation to which many concerns succumb under the delusion that it is business. It is not business at all, but only a method of slow suicide. Think, if you can, of a single great industry operating today that was deliberately created and fostered by the money power. Every big business began lowly, grew because it filled a want, and if it attracted the attention of the money power at all, it was only after growth had been attained. A business which can bring itself to the point where it attracts the attention of money should be able to continue on its own feet without being financed.

Another rock on which business breaks is debt. Debt is nowadays an industry. Luring people into debt is an industry. The advantages of debt have become almost a philosophy. Possibly it is true that many people, if not most, would bestir themselves very little were it not for the pressure of debt obligations. If so, they are not free men and will not work from free motives. The debt motive is, basically, a slave motive.

When business goes into debt it owes a divided allegiance. The scavengers of finance, when they wish to put a business out of the running or secure it for themselves, always begin with the debt method. Once on that road, the business has two masters to serve, the public and the speculative financier. It will scrimp the one to serve the other, and the public will be hurt, for debt leaves no choice of allegiance.

Business has freed itself from domineering finance by keeping within itself its earnings. Business that exists to feed profits to people who are not engaged, and never will be engaged in it, stands on a false basis. This is being so well understood that it has become a part of the creed of commerce that the service of business is wholly to the public and that the profits of business are due, first, to the business itself as a serviceable instrument of humanity, and then to the people whose labor and contributions of energy make the business a going concern.

But neither business nor finance has power to compel the public to buy here or buy there. The record of financiers in business affairs is full of disaster. If finance had the far-flung power that alarmists say it has, America, like Europe, would be filled with ragged peasants.

But here the service of business always has controlled and always will control.

Money does not control wheat, coal, and other essentials of life. How can it? It does not create them. There are twice as many coal mines open as we can possibly use. Until a little while ago, wheat was a drug on the market.

Money does not own the coal in the United States. Money does not own the farms or the farmers. Money, following its traditional policy, would make coal scarce; here we have it plentifully. Money would make wheat scarce; the world is piled with wheat.

But while you can always go out and buy an automobile, you cannot always go out and buy a ton of coal; yet proportionate to the need, the ready supply of coal is greater than the ready supply of automobiles. It is not a matter of money control; it is a matter of wise method and system of business.

The true course of business is to follow the fortunes and pursue the service of those who had faith in it from the beginning - the public. If there is any saving in manufacturing cost, let it go to the public. If there is any increase in profits, let it be shared with the public in lowered prices. If there is any improvement in the commodity, let it be made without question, for whatever the capital cost, it was first the public that supplied the capital. That is the true course for good business to steer, and it is good business, for there is no better partnership a business can enter than a partnership of service with the people. It is far safer, far more durable and more profitable than partnership with a money power.

The best defense any people can have against their control by mere money is a business system that is strong and healthy through rendering wholesome service to the community.

Much publicity is given dishonest business, but this is not because there is more dishonest business than before, but because it has become such an out-of-date thing. The history of dishonesty in business in the United States begins, like the immoral methods of early competition, in the scarcity of opportunity. Dishonest business never had any excuse for existing, but there were times when it was at least understandable. Nowadays, it is not even understandable. The great swindles began in an age when opportunity was scarce. Swindling is out of date today because honest opportunity is unlimited.

The organization of industry to serve the people will not interfere with the profitableness of industry, as some seem to imagine. Putting right principles into our economic life will not decrease wealth, but increase it. The world as a whole is much poorer than it ought to be, because it has muddled along on one cylinder - the "get" cylinder - and has not grasped in any practical way the true law of service and increase.

For always builders want to build, bakers want to bake, manufacturers want to produce, railroads want to carry, workingmen want to work, merchants want to sell, and housewives want to buy. And why is it that sometimes all these operations seem to stop? Just because when things are going well some men will say:

"This is the time to make a big haul. People begin to want what we have to sell; therefore it is a good time to boost the price; they're in the mood to buy and they will pay more."

This is criminal, just as criminal as cashing in on a war. But it springs from ignorance. A part of industry understands so little of the essential laws of prosperity, that times of business revival appear like grab-bag periods in which the highest business wisdom is to get while the getting is good.

But enough men are becoming their own masters to know that bargaining and grabbing are not industry - that to grab is to kill. When all learn that profits have to be earned and not grabbed, we shall no longer have trouble with the money power or any other power. We can make prosperity continuous and universal.

CHAPTER 4
ARE PROFITS WRONG?

Last year, the Ford Industries paid directly, in wages, about two hundred and fifty million dollars; purchases were probably responsible for the payment of about five hundred million dollars more in wages; service stations and dealers paid about two hundred and fifty million dollars in wages. So the company last year generated about one thousand million dollars in wage money.

The 1896 Ford Quadricycle, the first automobile made by the Ford Company.

Beginning with the first car, it took us approximately twenty years to build a million cars - the millionth was turned out on December 10, 1915. On May 28, 1921, we turned out our five millionth car. On June 4, 1924, we turned out our ten millionth car. Since then our factories have reached a capacity in excess of two million cars a year.

In 1922, we bought three times as much as we made ourselves. Now it is only twice as much. We have raised the minimum wage from five dollars a day to six dollars a day. But our cars are being sold at 40 percent less than they were in 1914, when our average wage was $2.40 a day. The cars have steadily decreased in price, while almost all other commodities have increased in price. The touring car may be bought at about twenty cents a pound - a highly refined piece of machinery, built with the greatest care and of the best materials, costs less per pound than beef-steak.

The profits of the Ford Industries, other than a comparatively negligible amount, have gone back into the industries. The public built our industries through buying our product. The public subscribed, not through stock or bonds, but by purchasing the commodities which we manufacture and offer for sale. We have always sold to the public at a price higher than the cost of manufacturing - although often we have reduced prices to a point where no profit was visible and thus forced ourselves to find ways and means of reducing costs in order to earn a profit.

Each year has seen a profit. Nearly all of that profit has each year gone back into the business to provide facilities for still further lowering costs and raising wages. These profits put back into the business have not been invested in buildings, land, and machinery. We do not regard the public's money returned to the business as an investment on which interest should be charged. That money is the public's money, and the public, having confidence enough in our product to pay the money to us, is entitled to benefit by its confidence. We could have no right to charge the public with interest on its own money.

There are, however, profits and profits. Profits may be stupidly fixed and stupidly used. If so, they destroy their source and vanish. A business which charges too high a profit disappears about as quickly as one that operates at a loss.

However useful the commodity one may make, if it is produced and sold at a loss, its production ceases. There is nothing in quality of goods or quality of service that can overcome the economic error of selling at a loss. Profit is essential to business vitality. In proportion as a business increases, the cost of production decreases. A slack shop is costlier to maintain than a busy shop. The duty of every manager of industry is to encourage business by making it easy for people to obtain what they need at a price they can afford. A new revival of confidence and energy in the nation should be met halfway by a decrease in prices, a decrease that is in line with the decrease in cost.

To hold up prices is to tax the people more heavily than even a government could. Good management pays dividends in good wages, lower prices, and more business; it is very bad management that can see in a revival of national ambition only an opportunity to lay heavier burdens on the spirit of enterprise.

This ought to be self-evident. No one who gets rich quickly stays rich. Going into business just to get rich is a waste of effort. We do have a type of business whose only objective is the swelling of someone's personal fortune. A business which exists to make one man or one family rich, and whose existence is of no moment when this is achieved, is not solidly founded. Indeed, cupidity *(greed of money)* will usually force such decreases in the quality of goods, such curtailments of service, and such arbitrary charges to the public that the business will fade long before it has contributed to anybody's fortune.

One organization must have profit to pay the demand of those persons who have invested in the business but who have no hand in its operation. They are absentee dividend takers. What goes to them does not strengthen the business but is taken out of the business and may go to swell the sum of idleness outside. There is much justifiable idleness, of course. Looking over our country, we see millions of children in school; their leisure and education are made possible by the fact that men are at work. Likewise with the aged and infirm. But there is unjustifiable idleness, and that, too, is supported by men at work.

A business should pay everybody connected with it, and for every element used in it. It should pay for managerial brains, productive ability, contributive labor - but it should also pay the public whose patronage supports it. A business that does not make a profit for the buyer of a commodity, as well as for the seller, is not a good business. If a man is not better off for buying than he would be if he had kept his money in his pocket, there is something wrong. Buyer and seller must both be wealthier in some way as a result of a transaction, else the balance is broken. Pile up these breaks long enough, and you upset the world. We have yet to learn the anti-social nature of every business transaction that is not just and profitable all around.

The business itself, the organized entity that engages in production or service, needs a profit or a surplus to keep its vitality a little in advance of the drain upon it. This surplus is to prevent depletion under extraordinary strain, also to permit of expansion. Growth is necessary to life, and growth requires a surplus.

This statement is made of the business - not of the owner or director of the business. He is paid, like any other worker, out of the costs of the business. The profit belongs to the business to safeguard the business in its task of giving service and to permit natural growth. The main consideration is the business - this entity that gives employment to producers and gives useful commodities or needed service to the public.

The principle of service requires that profits be measured only by legitimate replacement and necessary expansion. Those are the limits - flexible limits, but still limits. Sometimes one hears a complaint against expansion as though it were potentially dangerous. If expansion is undertaken in the interest of service, quite the opposite is the case, as has been shown in a previous chapter. One need fear only the business which is not growing, for it is not rendering service.

Now, take our own company. How have we used our profits? What have we done with the public's money? What has been our stewardship?

Since 1921-22, when "My Life and Work" was written, we have more than doubled our productive capacity for cars and tractors. We are making hardly a single part in the same way or of precisely the same material as we made it then. We have, step by step, gone back to primary sources. We are in the motor business and in no other business. Everything that we do gets back to the motor. With the Ford Motor Company of Canada, there are now a total of eighty-eight plants, of which sixty are in the United States and twenty-eight in foreign countries. No one plant anywhere makes a complete automobile. Of the plants in the United States, twenty-four are exclusively manufacturing plants and thirty-six are assembling or partly manufacturing and partly assembling.

Our chief manufacturing plants abroad are at Cork, Ireland, and Manchester, England. We have assembly plants, some of which do or will do a little manufacturing, at Antwerp, Barcelona, Bordeaux, Buenos Aires, Copenhagen, Montevideo, Pernambuco, Rotterdam, Santiago (Chile), Sao Paulo, Stockholm, Trieste, Berlin, Mexico City, Yokohama, and Havana. The Ford Motor Company of Canada has plants or branches at Ford, Ontario, Calgary, Montreal, Regina, St. Johns, Toronto, Vancouver, Winnipeg, Port Elizabeth, South Africa, Geelong, Australia. The affiliated companies are Ford Motor Company, Australia; Proprietary Ltd., Manufacturing and Sales Branches, Geelong, Brisbane, Adelaide, Sydney, and Perth Australia, and Hobart, Tasmania; Ford Manufacturing Company, Proprietary Ltd., body plant at Geelong, Australia; and Ford Motor Company, South African Ltd., Port Elizabeth. Our plants in the United States are at Banner Fork, Dearborn, Duluth, Flat Rock, Glassmere, Green Island, Hamilton, Highland Park, Holden, Clayton Iron Mountain, L'Anse, Lincoln, Northville, Nuttallburg, Pequaming, Phoenix, Plymouth, Rouge, Stone, Twin Branch, Kearny, Waterford, Ypsilanti, and Chester. The branches are at Atlanta, Buffalo, Cambridge, Charlotte, Chicago, Cincinnati, Cleveland, Columbus, Dallas, Denver, Des Moines, Detroit, Fargo, Houston, Indianapolis, Jacksonville, Kansas City, Los Angeles, Louisville, Memphis, Milwaukee, Twin City, New Orleans, New York, Norfolk, Kearney, Oklahoma City, Omaha, Philadelphia, Pittsburgh, Portland, Oregon, St. Louis, Salt Lake City, San Francisco, Seattle, and Washington, D. C.

We are in the following lines of business, every one of which grows out of the making of motors: airplanes, coal mining, coke manufacture, by-products manufacture, lead mining, iron mining, foundry, steel manufacture, tool making, machinery manufacture, car truck and tractor manufacture, glass manufacture, artificial leather, copper wire, Fordite, textiles, batteries and generators, paper, cement, automobile bodies, Johansson gauges, electric power, filtered water, flour, motion pictures, hospital, farming and stock raising, radio, printing, photography, forging, flax growing, steam turbine, electric locomotives, logging, saw mills, body parts, dry kilns, wood distillation, products of hydro-electric power, grocery stores, shoe stores, clothing stores, butcher shop, railroads, educational, ocean transportation, lake transportation, tractors, and automobiles.

This rather extensive program, which has to do both with production and distribution, has been carried through because the public has found our products useful, and no step has been taken excepting in the interests of the public and the wage earners. We have built nothing for the sake of building. We have bought nothing for the sake of buying. We make nothing for the sake of making. Our operations all center about the manufacture of motors.

If those who sell to us will not manufacture at the prices which, upon investigation, we believe to be right, then we make the article ourselves. In many cases, we have gone back to the primary sources, and in other cases, we manufacture just enough of a product to get thoroughly familiar with it, so that in an emergency we may make it ourselves. Sometimes, also, we do this merely to test the price we are paying. In distribution, the same rule holds. We have lake ships, ocean-going ships, and a railroad, in order that we may measure transportation charges. All this is in the benefit of the public, for, excepting the railroad, which is a separate corporation, each new branch of industry merges into the industry and the savings which ensue are for the eventual benefit of the public.

For instance, we have made rubber tires, although we have no present intention of going into the tire business. The price of rubber may be forced inordinately high. In any event, we have to be prepared. It would never do to have to shut down our production for lack of tires.

We buy on cost and not on market price, and we believe we render a service in so doing; if we felt otherwise, we should not follow the practice. In our own production, we set ourselves tasks - sometimes we arbitrarily fix prices, and then invariably we are able to make them; whereas, if we merely accepted things as they are, we should never get anywhere. We follow exactly the same practice with those from whom we buy - and invariably they prosper.

Take a specific case. Before this policy was fully developed, a manufacturer was making a certain style of automobile body for us at a certain price each. He was not manufacturing in a large way, and his profits were insignificant. We calculated that those bodies ought to be made at exactly half the price, and that is the price we asked him to get down to. This was the first time that real pressure for a lower price had ever been put upon him, and of course he thought he could not do any better than he had been doing. His profits showed him that he could not; it is one of the oddities of business that a man will cite what he has done in the past as a proof of what he can do in the future. The past is only something to learn from.

This man finally consented to try to manufacture at exactly one half his former price. Then, for the first time in his life, he began to learn how to do business. He had to raise wages, for he had to have first-class men. Under the pressure of necessity, he found he could make cost reductions here, there, and everywhere, and the upshot of it was that he made more money out of the low price than he had ever made out of the high price, and his workmen have received a higher wage.

One frequently hears that wages have to be cut because of competition, but competition is never really met by lowering wages. Cutting wages does not reduce costs - it increases them. The only way to get a low-cost product is to pay a high price for a high grade of human service and to see to it through management that you get that service. We have had many experiences such as that with the body maker, and we believe that our policy is in the line of public service.

The most important basic developments have been in the use of more and more power, both from coal and from water, until now, with the completion of the Fordson power station, we shall have a unit producing half a million horsepower - of which more in a later chapter. (This is the plant on the River Rouge and which we formerly designated by the name of the river.) All our operations get back to the provision of power. The other developments of moment have been the coal and iron mines and the lumber camps, the extension of the Fordson plant as a converter of raw materials and waste, the building of a laboratory at Dearborn, the taking over of the Lincoln Motor Car Company, the extension of lake, ocean, land, and air transport, the building of new plants throughout the country and the world, and the going into the manufacture of glass, cement, flax, artificial leather, and a number of chemical compounds. But the necessity for all of these extensions into other lines is shown by the fact that of our by-products only two are sold outside of the company. All the others fit in somewhere into manufacture. For instance, we make cement from slag, but we have not been able to produce enough cement for even our own building needs. The two products which we have in part to sell outside are ammonium sulphate (which is sold easily in the amount that we produce for fertilizer) and benzol. We can use a deal of the benzol in the company motor-car transport, but not all, and hence we have to sell some of it on the outside as a motor fuel. The demand for this benzol is so much greater than our supply that the sales problem amounts to nothing at all. Eighty-eight stations now sell our benzol, and it is used quite extensively in airplanes. We do sell coal as a return cargo on our

Great Lakes ships through part of the year but this is just an aside to lessen the cost of transport.

Some of our extensions have been emergency measures. For instance, the making of glass. The automobile changed very quickly from an open summer vehicle to a closed year-round means of transportation, but few know what a strain this put upon the glass-making facilities of the country. We use about one quarter of all the plate glass produced in the United States.

But glass was getting scarce, and so we went out and bought the plant and equipment of the Allegheny Glass Company at Glassmere near Pittsburgh, which had a reputation for turning out first-class plate. At the time of our purchase three years ago, it was making six million square feet of glass a year, and 30 percent of its output was not fit for motor-car use. Now, with only a small amount of additional machinery and using most of the old machinery and the old staff of men, we are getting around eight million feet a year, and less than 10 percent is unfit for our use. The principal change we made was to put in the six-dollar-a-day minimum wage.

In this plant, in order not to avoid any interruption of production, we have kept the old way of making plate glass as against the new way which was finally achieved in the plant at the River Rouge. If you will compare these methods with the new methods described in the next chapter, you will gain some idea of the economies which may be had in almost any line of manufacturing, if only the will to get away from tradition be strong enough.

The batch or mixture is melted in clay pots, each of which will pour three hundred square feet of rough plate one-half inch thick. A furnace holds sixteen of these pots. When the glass is ready to pour, the pot is removed from the furnace by a crane and carried to the casting table, where its contents are poured and rolled to the desired thickness. The plate is then annealed, coming out at a temperature cool enough to handle. The next step is grinding and polishing.

This is done on circular decks on which sheets of glass are set in plaster, until the surface is completely covered with glass. The deck is then taken to the grinding machine. Seven different abrasives, ranging from coarse sand to fine emery, are used. After the grinding is done, the deck is washed free from abrasives and sent to the polishing table where a high gloss is put on by large revolving felt blocks. Liquid rouge is fed to the table at the center and the felt blocks spread it evenly. The plate is then reversed and sent back to the grinders, where the same process is gone through with again. It is all very slow and very wasteful.

The manufacture of the clay pots in which the glass is melted is the only archaic process to be found in the Ford Industries. It is all done by hand and by foot. The clay is first kneaded by the bare feet of the workmen until its consistency is uniform and all grit or foreign substances have been worked out. The pots are then built up by hand, layer by layer, until all the air holes have been closed - even a slight defect might cause the pot to crack in the furnace. No machinery has yet been devised which will make glass pots equal to those made by hand. In our new system, we have none of this hand work - we have no pots.

In order to make the Glassmere plant complete, we had also to buy a silica quarry at Cabot eighteen miles away. There, with forty men, we quarry, crush, and ship from eight to ten carloads of silica sand a day. We use the same men who worked off and on in the quarry before, but they are different men under the six-dollar-a-day wage and steady work. They are nearly all unskilled laborers, for we have arranged that nearly no skill need be used in any job; but they are not shiftless. They stay on the job, they work, they invest, and a number of them have moved out of the old shacks they used to live in and are building real homes. And the man effectiveness under the new methods is, we have been told, about double what it was under the old methods. Our costs of production are very low indeed, for nearly all the work is done by machinery.

The holes are sunk by a battery of rock drills. Holes are charged with dynamite which blasts off large quantities of sand rock. The rock is scooped up, put into small steel cars by steam shovels, and hauled by tractors fitted with steel wheels to the crushing plant. There the stone is crushed, sifted, and washed the requisite number of times to get the purity required for glass making, and finally flows through pipes by gravity into the cars which take it to the Glassmere plant.

And one more thing - this quarry is clean and the crushing plant is clean. That is another of our absolute rules every operation must be cleanly performed, and if some of the machines tend to create dust - and crushers do - then they must be made tight and apparatus provided for taking away dust. It is not right to expose men to dust, nor is it right to put a layer of dust over the surrounding country and spoil its trees and plants.

In order to have an independent supply of iron ore and to save transportation, we bought the Imperial Mine at Michigamme, eighty miles north of Iron Mountain, which is the center of our lumbering interests. The mine had not been producing for ten years, but we considered it a good mine and right in the line of our transport, so that there would be no waste in useless handling. This was our first venture in iron mining, but we followed our usual practice in putting at the head of the job a man who had thoroughly learned our methods and policies.

The first job was to clean up - that is always the first thing to do in order to find out what you are about. The place, having been abandoned for so long, was dirty and overgrown. There is a tradition that all kinds of mining have to be dirty. We cannot afford to have dirt around - it is too expensive. Then we began to work into mining, learning as we went.

The primary conditions were that the miners should have good wages, work and live under safe and comfortable conditions, and that we should have an ample supply of low-cost ore. This we have achieved.

This camp looks like a suburban colony - everything is painted and kept painted a light color, so that the least bit of dirt will show. We do not paint to cover up dirt - we paint white or light gray in order that cleanliness may be the order of things and not the exception. The housing was bad, and although we did not like to go into the housing business, in this case we had to, and we have also had to do the same in our coal mines and lumbering camps.

We put up a dormitory for single men, with a separate room for each man, and then we brought in portable houses for the married men, which have since been replaced by cottages. We rent them at twelve dollars a month, with electric lighting included - the whole mine and the camp are fully lighted by electricity. The only school was in a barn; we have built a good school and also a first-class store in which everything is sold at cost.

Of course, we put in our regular wage. That brought to us the best class of miners from all about, and although we cannot employ more than two hundred and twenty-five men at any one time, we have on file applications for several times that number of jobs. The men work eight hours without overtime, and the labor turnover is negligible. We are able to give practically steady work - and the men do work.

We do not pretend to know much about iron mining as yet - we have not been at it long enough to learn what can be done; but it seems to be a field in which machinery can be used in a much larger degree than it is generally used. We have gone slowly, for one thing, because we wanted to make the mining as nearly safe for the miners as is possible. Mining, working under the ground, is nasty work at the best, and the first effort has been to make everything safe. And it is safe; our list of accidents has been very small indeed.

Every part of the mine and the camp is kept in absolute order. The mining is on three levels about two hundred feet apart. The blasting of the ore is done at the end of each of the two eight-hour shifts to avoid danger to workers. The ore is then transferred by an electrified railway system. Ore at the different levels is dumped from the cars by compressed air into chutes which lead to a central pit at the bottom of the mine, where "Larry" cars drawn by cables pull it up the incline to the surface. A skip-hoist equipment takes care of ore mined at a deeper level.

The chief mine inspector tests walls and ceilings of all passages at frequent intervals. A wide-awake safety committee was organized and the cooperation of the entire camp has been secured in working constantly for safe conditions. In handling explosives, rigid precautions are observed. The safety lamps worn on miners' caps must be removed twenty-five feet from the explosives room, which is electrically lighted.

In the mine passages, an extensive pumping system clears the low points of seepage, while a steam-heating system aids in drying and warming passages. The miners wear specially protected clothes and rubber boots. After work, each man takes a bath in the company shower rooms and makes a complete change of clothing. Clothing worn in the mines is heated and dried during the time off duty. Mining operations are carried on the year around, the ore being transferred by rail to Marquette for shipment to the Fordson plant on the company's lake freighters. During the winter, when navigation is closed, it is stored near the shaft entrance, the handling being by special machinery – not a mule or horse is owned by the company.

The production of ore is now around two hundred thousand tons a year, and our costs are low – lower than those of any mine paying lower wages. In addition to this mine, we have taken over other ore properties in the range.

Such is the process – it will be developed in the following chapters – of putting the public's money at work. That money came to us as profits. Are profits wrong?

CHAPTER 5
IT CAN'T BE DONE

One of the surprising facts about industry is the tenacity with which people cling to methods which were used long before power and machinery entered the world. The only tradition we need bother about in industry is the tradition of good work. All else that is called tradition had better be classed as experiment.

In scrapping old ideas, one of the first that needs scrapping is the notion that because man power is cheap, developed power need not be used. Labor is not a commodity. The point has already been made that one's own workers ought to be one's own best customers, and until that is fully realized, it is quite impossible to make even a beginning on the application of the wage motive. It is not to be assumed that men are worth only what they will work for and that the manufacturer should adapt his wages and prices to what the traffic will bear - that is, pay his men the least that they can be had for and charge his customers all that they will stand for. A business ought not to drift. It ought to march ahead under leadership.

It seems hard for some minds to grasp this. The easy course is to follow the crowd, to accept conditions as they are, and, if one makes a good haul, to take it and plume one's self on being smart. But that is not the way of service. It is not the way of sound business. It is not even the way to make money. Of course, a man may, following this old line, fall into a bit of luck and make a million or two - just as a gambler sometimes wins heavily. In real business, there is no gambling. Real business creates its own customers.

Our own attitude is that we are charged with discovering the best way of doing everything, and that we must regard every process employed in manufacturing as purely experimental. If we reach a stage in production which seems remarkable as compared with what has gone before, then that is just a stage of production and nothing more. It is not and cannot be anything more than that. We know from the changes that have already been brought about that far greater changes are to come, and that therefore we are not performing a single operation as well as it ought to be performed.

We do not make changes for the sake of making them, but we never fail to make a change once it is demonstrated that the new way is better than the old way. We hold it our duty to permit nothing to stand in the way of progress - in the way of giving better service with all that follows in wages and prices.

It is not easy to get away from tradition. That is why all our new operations are always directed by men who have had no previous knowledge of the subject and therefore have not had a chance to get on really familiar terms with the impossible. We call in technical experts to aid whenever their aid seems necessary, but no operation is ever directed by a technician, for always he knows far too many things that can't be done. Our invariable reply to "It can't be done" is, "Go do it."

Take this matter of making plate glass. In the last chapter were described the methods in use at our Glassmere factory. Essentially those methods do not differ from the methods used centuries ago. Glass making is very old; it has traditions, and those traditions center around the clay pot in which the mixture is melted into glass. That pot, as has been said, must be made by hand.

The clay is tamped and kneaded by the bare feet of men and then the pot is built up by hand. Of course, machinery has come in to carry these pots to and from the furnace, there are conveyors to do the handling, and machine grinding and polishing has replaced the old hand work, but the operation itself has not been fundamentally changed. Machinery has been brought in to do, in so far as possible, what was formerly done by hand.

But the whole operation had never been thoroughly studied to discover what was really fundamental. The easy course is always to substitute machine effort for a hand effort, and the full value of power is not then realized. The hard course is to start at the beginning and evolve a method which, instead of substituting the machine for the hand, takes for granted that a method can be discovered by which the entirety may be done by machinery and the man considered only as an attendant upon the machine. This is the machine concept of industry as opposed to the hand concept.

It seemed to us that we ought to be able to manufacture plate glass continuously in a big ribbon and with no hand work at all. The glass experts of the world said all this had been tried and that it could not be done. We gave the task of doing it to men who had never been in a glass plant. They started experimenting at Highland Park. They ran up against every trouble that had been predicted and a number that had not been, but eventually they achieved their result. The little plant at Highland Park is producing two and a half million square feet a year, and the big plant at the River Rouge, which we built as soon as we knew that we could make first-class plate glass, is producing twelve million square feet a year. This big plant occupies about one half the space of the Glassmere plant, although it has nearly double its production, and also it employs only about one third as many men as Glassmere. Although we have not been able to expand our plants sufficiently to care for our needs, we are already saving about three million dollars a year on the glass that we do make as compared with what we have to pay outside.

Here is the new process. The batch is melted in huge furnaces, each with a capacity of 408 tons of molten glass. The temperature maintained is a melting heat of 2,500 degrees Fahrenheit and a refining heat of 2,300 degrees. The furnaces are charged every fifteen minutes with sand, soda ash, and other chemicals. The glass flows out in a continuous stream on to a slowly revolving iron drum, and passes under a roller which gives the right thickness, and rolls it into a sheet. From the drum it enters the lehr, moving at the rate of fifty inches a minute. The lehr is 442 feet long and anneals the glass under gradually diminishing heat.

The construction of the lehr was one of the hardest problems and the one on which all others had fallen down. We could not have constructed it without our experience in conveyors and accurate machine making. It is no small accomplishment to support a moving sheet of glass 442 feet long while it cools from a temperature of fourteen hundred degrees Fahrenheit at the roller to a point where it is cold enough to handle. The movement of the conveyor has to be absolutely even and the rollers on which the glass moves so perfectly lined and adjusted that at no point in the 442-foot journey will the glass be subjected to the slightest distortion. The diminishing temperature problem is solved by thermostatically controlled gas flames at varying intervals.

At the end of the lehr the glass is cut into 113-inch lengths, each sheet being the exact size required for six complete windshields, and then is carried by conveyors to the polishing machines.

The sheets are mounted in quick-setting stucco to hold them firmly in position and passed on conveyor tables under a series of grinding and polishing wheels. Sand mixed with water flows through a hole in the center of the cast-iron grinding disc and works its way out to the edge. Finer and finer sand is used as the glass moves on its way, each grinder taking a cut. Eight grades of sand and six grades of garnet are used in the grinding and smoothing.

The plate is then washed. The glass then goes to the polishing discs, which are felt-covered and which use a mixture of iron rouge and water. At the end of the line, the glass is turned over and proceeds back on another grinding and polishing line from which it leaves as completely finished and polished plate glass that has not been touched by human hand.

There is no handling of the sand, nor is there any handling of the various grades of polishing sand. The silica sand and other materials used in composing batches of glass are likewise untouched by hand. From a vacuum machine, a heavy rubber hose goes into the car of material. The material is drawn up through the hose and falls into a hopper. A conveyor of the elevator type carries it aloft and dumps it upon a belt conveyor equipped so as to permit the discharging of the material into the storage bin where it belongs.

The grinding sand has to be graded while being used. This is done in distribution by a process known technically as levigation.

As the sand arrives at the plant, it is received and stored in large tanks beside the railroad tracks. Then, as it is called into use, it is washed by a stream of water into a well. From here a pump forces it through pipe lines that carry it across the plant to the first supply tanks above the furnaces, and near to the grinding and polishing lines. From the first supply tanks the sand flows through inclined pipes to the first grinders in the line. As the rough grinding goes on, the used sand is edged off into gutters beneath the grinding machines, and a pump forces it from the gutters into the levigation system.

Floating now in a comparatively large volume of water, the sand begins to grade itself. The larger, heavier grains sink to the bottom of the second tank; the others float at depths that vary according to their size. The overflow from the second tank takes these smaller and lighter grains into the third tank in the supply line, where another settling takes place. The overflow from the third tank feeds in turn the fourth tank; and the same process is continued until the eighth and last tank holds the finest sand.

Sand supplied to the grinders by all tanks beyond the second is pumped from the gutters back to the second tank, from which it is again distributed in the same fashion as before. From the first to last, the overflow feed and gravity serve each successive tank with sand suited to the grinders it supplies. Garnet used in the last grinders is graded by this same method.

The process sounds simple enough, and it is. Every well-thought-out process is simple. And with the simplicity and the absence of hand labor has come a greater safety. Glass making used to be considered a dangerous occupation. It is no longer so with us. For two years past we have lost less than one hour per man due to accident. And that we shall cut down.

Spinning and weaving have come down to us through the ages and they have gathered about them traditions which have become almost sacred rules of conduct. The textile industry was one of the first to make use of power, but also it was one of the first to use the labor of children. Many textile manufacturers thoroughly believe that low-cost production is impossible without low-priced labor. The technical achievements of the industry have been remarkable, but whether it has been possible for anyone to approach the industry with an absolutely open mind, free from tradition, is another matter.

We use more than a hundred thousand yards of cotton cloth and more than twenty-five thousand yards of woolen cloth during every day of production, and even a very tiny saving per yard would mean a good deal to us in the course of a year. That is why, several years ago, we started our textile experiments, not with any thought of making over the textile industry - for we are manufacturers of motors - but with the thought of finding some way to avoid the fluctuations of the cotton market and to get our own requirements at a lower price.

At first, we took for granted that we had to have cotton cloth - we had never used anything but cotton cloth as a foundation material for tops and for artificial leather. We put in a unit of cotton machinery and began to experiment, but, not being bound by tradition, we had not gone far with these experiments before we began to ask ourselves:

"Is cotton the best material we can use here?"

And we discovered that we had been using cotton cloth, not because it was the best cloth, but because it was the easiest to get. A linen cloth would undoubtedly be stronger, because the strength of cloth depends upon the length of the fiber, and the flax fiber is one of the longest and strongest known. Cotton had to be grown thousands of miles from Detroit. We should have to pay transportation on the raw cotton, if we decided to go into cotton textiles, and we should also have to pay transportation on this cotton converted into its motor-car use very often back again to where it had been grown. Flax can be grown in Michigan and Wisconsin, and we could have a supply at hand practically ready for use. But linen making had even more traditions than cotton, and no one had been able to do much in linen making in this country because of the vast amount of hand labor considered essential.

Cotton goods were a luxury, and cotton growing was unimportant until Eli Whitney invented his gin, for until then, as everyone knows, the seeds had to be picked out of cotton by hand, which was not only a long and tiresome but an exceedingly wasteful and expensive process. The flax fiber has always been recovered by hand in Ireland, in Belgium, and in Russia - in fact, everywhere that flax is used. The methods are not much different from those used in the Egypt of the Pharaohs. That is why linen is expensive, and that is why so little flax is grown in the United States: we, fortunately, have not a sufficient supply of low-paid hand labor to make any crop which requires manual handling profitable.

We began to experiment at Dearborn, and these experiments have demonstrated that flax can be mechanically handled. The work has passed the experimental stage. It has proved its commercial feasibility.

To begin at the beginning. We put about six hundred acres into flax. We plowed and prepared the ground by machinery, we sowed by machinery, we harvested by machinery, we dried and threshed by machinery, and finally took out the fiber by machinery. That has never successfully been accomplished before.

Flax has always required a lot of cheap hand labor. We cannot use anything in our business which requires hand labor.

Flax grows very well in Michigan and also in Wisconsin, although in Wisconsin the attention has been given to growing a flax not for the fiber but for the seed, which is crushed into linseed oil. Flax growing for fiber has not gone far in this country, because almost the only market for flax is abroad, where cheap hand labor is available.

Flax is a peasant crop, and, before the war, the big producer was Russia: it had an abundance of people accustomed to living on nothing a year. Our own country has not been enough interested in flax growing to find out with exactness where it will grow. It seems to require a moist climate, but once the flax industry is established here, undoubtedly we shall be able to develop varieties so that nearly every section of the country will have a species which it can profitably raise.

The valuable fiber of the plant is on the outside of the stalk surrounding the woody core, and it has always been considered out of the question to mow flax as one would mow wheat, for it is essential to keep the stalks parallel, else the subsequent hand operations will be hampered. Also, cutting flax was supposed to leave too much valuable stalk attached to the root in the ground. Therefore, the foreign practice is to pull by hand and afterward, while the crop is on the ground, to comb out the seeds. A deal of the valuable seed is lost.

Thus, right at the beginning, under the old methods, we have two expensive and wasteful hand operations - the pulling and what is called the "rippling." We experimented with a rather intricate pulling machine, but found it was not worthwhile and that we could do better cutting very close to the ground. In our mechanical process, it is not necessary to keep the stalks parallel after they are cut, and it is cheaper to waste a few seeds than to use hand labor. Therefore, we harvested it by machinery, leaving the seeds on the stalks.

The next operation in the old style is what is called "retting"- that is, rotting. The usual method is to tie the stalks into sheaves and put them under water for some weeks with weights on top to keep them from drifting away. When the stalks have sufficiently rotted, the sheaves are taken out and dried in the sun. This is all hand work and extremely unpleasant, dirty work, because the rotting flax gives out an almost unbearable odor. It is a matter of great judgment to discover exactly the right kind of water for retting, and also to know when to stop the process. The next operation, under the old methods, is the most tedious, wasteful, and expensive of all. This is known as "scutching"- by which the fiber is separated from the woody core.

Under the method we have developed, all these expensive hand operations are done away with. After cutting, we leave the stalks on the ground for some weeks; then we gather them up and bale them, just as though they were hay. Instead of drying the retted flax in the sun, we pass it through an oven on a conveyor, and this conveyor delivers the conditioned flax to what we call a ginning machine, and which is the very heart of our process because it entirely replaces the old hand process of stripping the fiber. The gin has six sections running at various speeds with fluted rolls and combing rolls – there is no use going into the technical details. The upshot of it is that this machine mechanically takes out all of the seeds and stalks and leaves us a fiber which is, in part, what is called "line flax," and, in part, "tow."

There is a saving both in labor and in recovery. These gins do not care how the stalks feed into them, so it is no longer necessary to bother about keeping the stalks parallel. It is calculated that one machine working eight hours and tended by two men will scutch as much flax as ten men working by hand through a twelve-hour day.

This flax is now being spun into two grades of linen, one a coarse cloth and the other a fine cloth. This is done on standard equipment which we bought abroad, but our men have already managed to make some improvements on this machinery, and others will come as we get more fully into the work. For instance, the usual practice is to spin the flax on spools and then rewind on to bobbins for the filling yarn. We are spinning the flax directly to the filling bobbins. Eventually, we shall, by a continuous process, feed the flax in at one end of the line and have a dyed, all-linen backing cloth at the other. This will meet with the artificial leather, so that the whole process will be practically continuous.

We regard this work in flax as among the most important experiments which we are carrying on, for not only will it result in a better product than we have as yet been able to turn out, but also it will be another money crop for the farmer. We alone shall require the product of about fifty thousand acres annually and flax fits very nicely into the rotation of crops. Thus we shall have a cash crop for the farmer and perhaps a new industry for the country. And this is not counting the value of the flax by-products – the linseed oil, or the tow, which makes excellent stuffing for upholstery. Our chemists are experimenting with the "shives" or chaff, to the end of finding some satisfactory cellulose compounds. These might be used in a variety of ways – as liquids for the coating of the tops, or as solids for handles, and in connection with electrical equipment.

This flax growing, spinning, and weaving can and ought to be decentralized, so that it can be complementary to well-conducted farming – that is, grain farming as distinguished from dairying, stock raising, or truck farming. The place for the gins, the spindles, and the looms is out in the country where the flax is grown. It could be made a village industry manned by farmers, who can apportion their time between farm and factory.

We are also feeling our way into the manufacture of woolen cloth for our own requirements on our usual plan of making the process continuous. To start with, we took a young man out of a drafting room and for three months put him at work in a mill with instructions to learn all that he could about weaving excepting the traditions. We have as yet made only minor changes and improvements in the standard machinery, and the output of our experimental plant is negligible as compared with our needs, but we find that it will be possible to effect a saving of nearly 30 percent on our woolen cloth – which will mean a saving of many million dollars a year. Whenever one can line up machinery for the making of exactly one thing and study everything to the end of making only that thing, then the savings which come about are startling.

CHAPTER 6
LEARNING BY NECESSITY

We do nothing at all in what is sometimes ambitiously called research, excepting as it relates to our single objective. We believe that anything else would be outside our province and possibly done at the expense of our own particular function which, to repeat, is making motors and putting them on wheels. In the engineering laboratory at Dearborn we are now equipped to do almost anything that we care to do in the way of experiment, but our method is essentially the Edison method of trial and error.

As it is, our task is rather a large one, for we must look well ahead to the possible depletion of sources, to the saving of material, and to the finding of substitute materials and fuels. Quite often, we merely put the results of our experiments away for future use in case market conditions should change. For instance, if gasoline should go above a certain price, then it would be practical to bring in substitute fuels. But our principal duty, as we conceive it, is not to wander from our own path, but to learn to do one thing well. Learning to do that one thing well has taken us into many fields. We want to save material and we want to save labor and scarcely a week passes in which some change is not made. Some are of minor and others of major importance, but the method of procedure is always the same. Curiously enough, some of our largest savings come in the manufacture of parts where we thought we were doing rather well.

In one case we found that by using two cents more worth of material in a certain small part we were able to reduce the total cost of it by 40 percent That is, the amount of material under the new method cost about two cents per part more than under the old, but the labor was so much faster that, under the new method, the cost which was formerly $.2852 was now only $.1663 - we carry our costs out to four decimals. The new method required ten additional machines, but the saving was nearly twelve cents per part - that is, the cost was almost cut in two - which, on a 10,000 a day production, meant a saving of $1,200 a day.

From the beginning of manufacturing until several years ago we had used wood for the steering wheels. This seemed a great waste, for only the best quality of wood could be used and no wood-working operation can be carried through with absolute precision. At the same time, out on the farm at Dearborn, we had tons of straw yearly going to waste or being sold for next to nothing. Out of this straw we developed a substance which we call Fordite, which looks like hard rubber but is not. The steering wheel rim and, in all, about forty-five parts of the car, mostly having to do with the electrical work, are now made out of this straw, and the production is so large that the farm will produce only enough for about nine months. Then we have to buy straw. This is the process:

The straw, rubber base, sulphur, silica, and other ingredients are mixed in batches of 150 pounds each, which then go to the rubber mills, where they are mixed in heated rollers for forty-five minutes. Then the mass is fed into tubing machines in small strips and comes out through a round die, much as sausage from a grinding machine. As it comes out it is cut, on the bias, in lengths of fifty-two inches and then is ready to be rolled into an outside covering of fine rubber-like substance. This is then put into a mold under hydraulic pressure of 2,000 pounds to the square inch and heated by steam for nearly an hour. When they come out of the heat, the wheels are soft, but they soon take on a flint-like hardness that remains.

Next, these steering wheels go to the finishing rooms, where they are smoothly trimmed and polished. The pressed steel "spider," or cross piece, is then placed in the wheel and securely fastened by a machine which in one operation bores a small hole and in the next screws in the screw. The steering wheel is then ready for shipment and final assembly on the car.

We save about half the cost of wood – and we conserve wood.

The touring car uses about fifteen yards of artificial leather for the top, curtains, and upholstery, and we need altogether five grades. Using natural leather would be quite out of the question. In the first place, it would be too expensive, while, in the second place, not enough animals are slaughtered to begin to provide for our requirements. Our people had a hard time developing an entirely satisfactory artificial leather – it took them five or six years. First, they had to get the proper coating compound for the cloth which is the base of the leather, and then to make the operation continuous. Making our own leather not only renders us independent – which was the original purpose of the undertaking – but also saves us more than twelve thousand dollars a day. Essentially, these are the operations as we now perform them:

The cloth is fed into ovens. The ovens consist of a series of towers. At the base of each is a tank containing the coating compound. This is poured on the cloth as it travels through, a knife spreading it evenly and scraping off the surplus. After receiving the coating, the cloth ascends the tower to a height of thirty feet, at a temperature of about two hundred degrees. By the time it has descended, it is thoroughly dry. The second oven gives it another coat, dries it in the tower, and brings it down to the tank in No. 3 oven, and so on, until the first seven coats have been given.

It is then weighed to determine the amount of coating per running yard and sent to the embossing press, where it receives the graining under a pressure of 700 tons. One more oven gives it the finishing or sealing coat, adds luster, and keeps the material pliable.

The compound is a mixture of castor oil and drop black mixed with a preparation of nitrated cotton dissolved in ethyl acetate and thinned with benzol. This is highly volatile, which accounts for the easy drying. The fumes of the ethyl acetate, alcohol, and benzol are driven off in the ovens, but they are recovered by a special apparatus we developed. The fumes are drawn through charcoal made from coconut shells until the charcoal becomes saturated. Steam is then turned in, which drives the fumes into a condenser, from which they are separated into the original compounds. As much as 90 percent of the fumes have thus been recovered when the work of the condenser has been concentrated on one smokestack. The manufacturing is continuous. As soon as a roll of cloth is nearly used up, the end is unrolled by hand and sewn to a new bolt. Thus the coating continues without interruption – an important factor when one considers that even a brief delay would cause the compound to harden on the knives.

There are no lights within the building, all artificial illumination being furnished from the outside on account of the fire hazard. Every machine is grounded, and as many precautions against fire taken as in an explosive factory, and we have had no accidents at all.

The treating of steel by heat is of the highest possible importance, for it makes possible the use of lighter parts by increasing their strength. But it is a delicate process: a part must not be too soft or it will wear out, or again, if it is too hard, it will break. The exact state of hardness depends upon the use to which the part is to be put. This is elementary. But the treating of large quantities of parts so that each will be of the right hardness is far from elementary.

The old way was to guess. We cannot afford to guess. We cannot afford to leave any process to human judgment. In our former heat treat processes, we thought that we were fairly advanced. And we were advanced for the time, because the work could be done by men after only a little training and the results were uniform, owing to the mechanical regulation. But the heat treat departments involved hot, hard labor, and we do not like to have jobs of that sort in the shops. Hard labor is for machines, not for men. And also the straight parts, such as axles, did not cool evenly, and after treatment they had to be straightened, which added to the cost.

We set a young man the task of bettering all our heat treat operations. He felt his way for a year or two and then began to get results. He not only cut down the number of men, but he devised a centrifugal hardening machine which cools the shafts evenly all around. Thus, they do not bend, and the straightening operation is no more. The electric furnace replacing the gas furnace has been one of the large steps forward. Where four gas-fired furnaces, with six men and a foreman, did 1,000 connecting rods an hour for the drawing operation alone, now two electric furnaces will both harden and draw 1,300 rods an hour, with only two men - one to feed and the other to take off.

For the heat treat, the axle shaft department uses a large two-deck furnace. A walking-beam, working slowly, moves the shafts forward into the lower chamber of the furnace at intervals of one minute. It takes twenty-eight minutes for a shaft to move completely through the lower chamber of the furnace, and during those twenty-eight minutes it is in a constant heat of 1,480 degrees Fahrenheit, the temperature being regulated by instrument control.

As the shafts slowly come out at the far end of the furnace they are seized by an employee with tongs and placed one by one in a spinning machine. They are quenched in caustic solution at the rate of four per minute; the spinning motion given them by the machine makes the decrease in temperature practically instantaneous over the shaft's entire surface. This operation goes to insure a uniform hardness and avoids pulling them out of shape by uneven cooling.

The quenched shafts are carried by a conveyor to the upper chamber of the furnace, and move back toward the entrance end through a constant heat of 680 degrees Fahrenheit. It takes forty-five minutes for this treatment. Thoroughly drawn, they are sent by overhead conveyor to the final machining.

These changes may not seem important, but cutting out the item of straightening after the heat treat has saved us around thirty-six million dollars in four years!

We investigated the making of electric storage batteries and, after a period of trial - we always try out everything thoroughly before we go into it - we found that we could 1make batteries cheaper than we could buy them.

For the car and the truck 162 steel forgings are needed, and this has developed a forging department which daily uses more than a million pounds of steel, and in which, by constant change and experiment, we have saved many millions of dollars by combining in one operation complex forging operations which formerly required several, and also by extending the use of upsetting machines - that is, machines which press the steel into shape instead of hammering it. Our objective is always to minimize the subsequent machining.

In one of these upsetting machines, heavy dies placed in vertical order crash heavily together upon the heated steel bar. Three operation sets or more are needed, except in a few instances, thoroughly to shape a bar of steel to its required form. The bar is inserted between the top dies first. These do the actual upsetting - that is, strictly, the thickening and shortening of a portion of the steel bar to the degree required. In rare cases, two sets of upsetting dies are necessary. The remaining sets of dies shape, pierce - if necessary - trim, and cut off the shaped portion. The steam hammer group has ninety-six hammers. The smallest hammer in the group carries a ram and piston of 800 pounds weight, and the largest strikes a blow with a ram and piston weighing 5,600 pounds.

Dies are set in the anvils and hammer-faces. As in the case of the upsetting machines, each hammer is set with dies that enable it to perform a complete phase of the work of manufacture. There is no division of labor between hammers. In the forging of a crankshaft a bar of hot steel is placed across a bending die at the left of the anvil; a blow from the corresponding die on the hammer-face wrinkles the bar into the semblance of a crank shaft. The crank-bent bar is moved to the right; several blows from a second die complete the resemblance. The result is a crank shaft, in the rough, though the two ends are of equal size, and the whole forging is framed in a thin flashing of excess metal. The hammer work is complete. The flashing is removed on a trimming press, and the flange at the crank shafts end will be formed on an upsetting machine.

Some parts require only a portion of the bar for their manufacture. On the hammers where these are made, a small cutting block is placed, and a blow from the hammer separates the shaped portion from the remainder of the bar. Smaller forgings are made on hammers whose dies contain several exactly similar impressions, permitting a number to be forged at once.

The order in which forgings requiring both hammer and upset work are manufactured varies according to the peculiarities of the part to be formed. The axles go first to the upsetting machine, which shapes them roughly, spreads and divides their ends; from there they go to the hammers. Half their lengths are formed, made ready for machining, at a time, since they are too long to be put under the hammer entire.

To rid the forgings of the flashings that border them when they leave the hammers, eighty trimming presses are used. Most of these presses straddle a belt conveyor, so that the flashings that are trimmed from the forgings are carried away immediately. Small forgings are also allowed to fall to the conveyor. Near where the conveyor makes its exit from the building, these forgings are removed and sorted into boxes. The conveyor discharges the flashings into a car on the switch outside.

In the trimming presses, the punch contains the form of the forging in relief, while the die contains an opening exactly corresponding to it. The forging is thrust by the pressure through the opening, while the flashing is left lying on the surface of the die.

Special devices are used to make and keep the various longer forgings accurate in length. A separate mechanism is used for this purpose with the axles. The steering post, during its formation on an upsetting machine, is held to an accuracy never deviated from more than a thirty-second of an inch.

Thirteen upsetting machines are now used on the triple gear job. In making this detail it was once necessary to shape three separate forgings. It is now forged from a single billet of steel.

The most difficult upsetting job in the drop forge is the drive shaft roller bearing housing. This calls for a double upsetting and rather elaborate shaping at both upset ends. Nevertheless, it is being successfully accomplished on a single machine.

An interesting piece of equipment is the reclaiming steel rolling mill. In this mill, remnants of stock too short to be used are reduced in diameter and increased to usable length by successive trips between progressively smaller rollers. This salvaging is done on the spot to save transport.

The casting of aluminum in dies has made for considerable economy. It took us some years to devise a satisfactory method. For a long time die casting was looked upon as impossible. The old method of casting in sand molds lets the air exude through the sand as the hot metal is poured in, while pouring metal into dies or solid molds caused air bubbles to form, resulting in "blows" in the cast. Then the secret of feeding the molten metal into the dies from underneath was discovered.

The die is placed directly above the pot containing the molten metal. In fact, it takes the place of a lid. When a cast is to be made, the operator turns the air pressure into the hot metal. The pressure forces the metal up through a feeder into the die. As the metal goes in, the air is forced out through minute vents. As the top of the die is filled first, the cast naturally solidifies from that point downward. The air is forced out by the first rush of molten metal on the top of the mold, and as metal can enter only by the feeder, all danger of air bubbles is eliminated, and the cast is perfect.

Insulated copper wire - and we use large quantities - is expensive. So we set about making our own and now produce about one hundred miles a day. We use standard wire - making machinery, but with many improvements and simplifications made possible by using the machines for a single product. The process starts with 5/16-inch copper rod stock similar to that used for trolley wires. This is drawn through nine successively smaller chilled iron dies. Wire from the last die is about 3/32-inch diameter, travelling to the winding spool at a speed of 725 feet per minute.

The drawing process causes much heat, which is carried away by water flowing over the dies. It also tends to make the wire hard. To soften for further drawing, the wire is annealed in a water-sealed electric furnace. The wire is plunged into water on a turntable which is revolved until the load is under the furnace chamber. It is then raised into an airtight cylinder to be held at a temperature of 1,045 degrees Fahrenheit for one hour. Air is excluded to prevent oxidation.

Machines for the second drawing are fitted with eight pierced diamonds through which the wire is drawn, each reducing the size a few thousandths of an inch. These diamonds, which may cost $300 each, can be used six months without appreciable wear. The final die, .044, produces twelve-gauge bare wire ready for insulating.

This insulation consists of five coats of dielectric enamel and a wound cotton covering. Enameling is continuous and automatic. Four men easily take care of eighty rolls of wire at once, as they are unwound and rewound with each enamel coat baked on at 845 degrees Fahrenheit. The enameled wire, every inch inspected for roughness or breaks in enamel, is passed to the winding machines. Bad stretches of wire are cut out and the ends brazed and re-enameled.

Cotton-winding machines have prepared eighteen ply or "end" cotton wound on bobbins for the insulating machines. These bobbins whirl around the wire as it passes through them, winding an even coating of cotton at great tension over the enameled surface. Four men here take care of the work of seventy-two spindles. The machines are almost entirely automatic.

The screw driver is an ancient and valuable instrument, but one man with one screw driver is hardly in line with modern methods. He can scarcely do enough work to pay his way. We are trying to get away from the screw driver. For instance, we now have a sixteen-spindle screw driver, which drives home sixteen screws into the starter ring gear in a single operation.

As the transmission comes along, the conveyor bolts and washers are assembled through the sixteen magnet heels, and the bolts turned about, one thread into the flywheel holding the magnets in position. A white metal spool is placed under each magnet end, and a magnet clamp set on top. A brass screw is inserted through a hole in the magnet clamp, passing between the magnet ends, through the white metal spool and a small hole in the flywheel, and into the starter ring gear. All is now in position for tightening the screws and bolts.

The transmission slides under the spindle screw driver and, with a slight movement of the operating lever, the locating arm is dropped. The locating arm has a notched edge which fits over the four transmission bolts, bringing the screws on the rim of the flywheel directly under the screw drivers, which are suspended from a circular spindle guide plate held in position by a movable head. Each screw driver is encased in a thimble which drops over the screw head and guides the screw driver into the slot as the motion of the lever is completed. As the screw is driven in, the friction increases, more power being used for the last turn of the screw than for the first. When the screw has been driven home, a friction clutch, encased in the spindle arm, slips, action ceases, and the screw slots are prevented from being broken off.

From the spindle screw driver, the transmission passes to an eight-spindle bolt driver, which works on the same principle as the screw driver. The bolt driver tightens the bolts which pass through the heel of the magnet into the flywheel. Before the sixteen-spindle screw driver was placed in operation, six men were required to tighten the screws. Now. the work requires but one man, and the operation is completed in a few seconds.

Following the same thought is the use of rivets instead of screws in putting together the body parts. The rivets give better service than screws, and they can be put in faster. They will go in still faster when we have developed the magazine riveter which we are working on. We use 3,000,000 rivets a day.

The methods of casting bronze bushings have been constantly changed and bettered in order to get rid of hard hand labor; until now the department has almost nothing about it to suggest a foundry. The melting process is carried on chiefly by twelve electric furnaces, each taking a ton of metals at a charge and requiring about seventy minutes to the heat. The furnace is left motionless until the metals are thoroughly melted, then a gentle rocking to and fro gives a uniform mixture. When the molten metal reaches a temperature of 2,200 degrees Fahrenheit, a sample is sent to the testing laboratories to be analyzed, while the remainder is emptied into small buckets lined with fire clay which are trundled by an overhead supporting tram to the pouring line.

The patterns used for casting small bushings resemble several bushings united by gates with four or five gates united at one end to form a good-sized cluster. By using such a pattern, only one mold and one pouring operation are necessary to produce a larger number of bushings.

The molders are provided with all possible aids to rapid and efficient work. Instead of sifting the sand by hand over the pattern, electric riddles are used – a press on a button does the work. The sand must be shaken and packed down to make a solid, dependable mold. Here, again, machines do a far better job than any workman could do. Electric coils under the metal table heat the mold that is being made without producing unnecessary warmth for the worker on a hot day. In line with this idea is the system of cold air blowers which furnish streams of cool air near each workman. Finally, in order to remove the pattern, the mold must be in two parts fitting closely together and yet easily separable. Between the two halves, it was once customary to spread lycopodium, a fine powder made from the pollen of flowers found only in Russia. This was very expensive, but now we have a cheaper preparation which is just as effective. An air vibrator and a simple gear arrangement make it possible to lift the upper half of the mold evenly, so that it will not be damaged in the process.

The finished mold is carried by a continuous conveyor to the pouring line and filled with the liquid metal. There is a tendency at this time for the mold to separate, allowing the metal to seep in between the halves. Formerly it was necessary to place heavy weights on the molds, which was an occupation for husky workers. Now, however, a simple clamp, revolving on the spindle supporting the platform on which the mold is riding, does the same work with a single stroke of the hand. Farther along, the molds are broken and the hardened castings removed, while the steel flasks used to support the outside of the molds are returned by the same conveyor to the molders.

The clusters of bushings are broken apart and the connecting gates sent to the charging room. The bushings are then placed in large cylindrical mills and tumbled about until the sand is cleaned off, and finally they are placed in the notched rim of a wheel which carries them against a grinding disc to smooth off the knob left by the gates. The castings are now ready for the finishing rooms, but are not sent through until the fracture test results come from the laboratory. The castings made from each heat of metal are kept separate from one another until this test has been made. Transportation costs and delays are lessened by locating the three finishing departments directly above the foundry. Practically all of the machinery for finishing is automatic and foolproof. Double automatic lathes turn our six thousand piston pin bushings every eight hours with such accuracy that only 1.3 percent fail to pass the inspection requirements; automatic punch broachers finish the bore directly from the rough castings for these piston pin bushings as well as the larger ones: automatic drills handle a few types that cannot be easily broached; even the inspection is automatic.

The automatic lathe needs but one speed and one size of arbor. Instead of being thrown out of gear every few seconds, the direction of the feed is reversed, and rather than have the machine run idle while the finished bushing is being replaced by one in the rough, two arbors are supplied, the cutting tool operating between them like a shuttle.

The broaching machines have their most dangerous feature – that of mistaking the workman's hand for a piece of metal–eliminated. Instead of its being necessary for the operator to reach under the punch, a metal channel is provided which is kept filled with castings. As the broach rises, a push on the end of the line moves the first one into place. The broached bushing drops into a chute while the next one is fed in through the channel in a fraction of the time required by the hand method of feeding. The automatic drill presses are in duplicates like the lathes, but in this case there are two drills, one rising while the other is cutting.

For sorting or inspecting as to length of the bushings, there is a machine with three sets of discs, so arranged that the first pair will take up the bushings which are too long, the second pair will remove only those which are within the limits of the specified length, while the third pair will take the undersized. This is all regulated by the distance between the discs, and this may be adjusted by ten thousandths of an inch. The bushings slide into notches in the rim of a large wheel that holds the pieces in line for the sorting discs.

The outside diameter sorter is even simpler. Two ground and polished rollers are set parallel to each other and on an incline, the diameters of the rollers decreasing by steps toward the lower ends, so that the space between them increases. Bushings are fed on to the rollers by gravity and are revolved. As they travel down the incline, they fall through into the space underneath which is so divided that the undersized ones go into one chute and the good ones into another. Those which remain on top are dropped from the end of the rollers into the over-size chute.

What does all this mean? This: in 1918 this entire department averaged 350 finished pieces per man per day of eight hours, with a machine scrap of about 3.0 percent. At present 830 completed pieces is the daily man average, while only about 1.3 percent of the product is scrapped.

In the making of springs, a similar advance has come, both in accuracy and man saving. In shaping the leaves, the forms used keep them so exact that they are interchangeable with corresponding leaves on other springs. The leaves are formed and hardened in oil in one operation. Next, they are tempered in nitrate at 875 degrees Fahrenheit, after which they are graphitized and used.

In 1915, the department employed four men to make fifty springs a day; at present, 600 men make 18,000 springs a day.

We must have inspectors at every stage of the work; otherwise, faulty parts might get into the assembly. Our inspectors in only a few cases are required to use judgment – mostly they apply a gauge, but, as was shown with the bushings, we are working toward mechanical inspection. For instance, electricity at 20,000 volts now tests the timing of the eight cams on the Model T Ford camshaft, not only more precisely than was possible by the former method, but seven times faster. Operated by one man, the new electrical gauge displaces seven of the old type gauges and their operators. The electrical test takes ten seconds.

In the new gauge, the camshaft is inserted in bearings, so that the cams operate push rods just as they do in the assembled motor. Instead of operating against valves, however, the push rods in the gauge close and open electrical contacts as the shaft is revolved. These electrical circuits are supplied with current only when the opening and closing points on the contour of each cam are in contact with the push rods, a distributor in the handwheel by which the shaft is revolved taking care of this.

If, at a critical position of the cam, the contour is too high or low within very close limits, an electrical contact is made completing a circuit which causes an electrical indicator to flash. There are two of these indicators, one for high and one for low cams. On the hand wheel is an index; the position of which at the time of the flash indicates which cam is faulty. If the cams are all accurate within specifications, the electrical indicator does not flash at any point during the revolution. The electric gauge may be set to detect errors of two ten thousandths of an inch.

But this is the sort of thing which is going on every day – we take it as our duty to use the public's money to the advantage of the public by pressing always for a better and cheaper product.

CHAPTER 7
WHAT ARE STANDARDS?

One has to go rather slowly on fixing standards, for it is considerably easier to fix a wrong standard than a right one. There is the standardizing which marks inertia, and the standardizing which marks progress. Therein lies the danger in loosely talking about standardization.

There are two points of view - the producer's and the consumer's. Suppose, for instance, a committee or a department of the government examined each section of industry to discover how many styles and varieties of the same thing were being produced, and then eliminated what they believed to be useless duplication and set up what might be called standards. Would the public benefit? Not in the least - excepting in war time, when the whole nation has to be considered as a productive unit. In the first place, no body of men could possibly have the knowledge to set up standards, for that knowledge must come from the inside of each manufacturing unit and not at all from the outside. In the second place, presuming that they did have the knowledge, then these standards, although perhaps effecting a transient economy, would in the end bar progress, because manufacturers would be satisfied to make to the standards instead of making to the public, and human ingenuity would be dulled instead of sharpened.

Some standards, of course, are necessary. An inch must always be an inch. When we buy by weight or by measurement, we ought to know what we are buying. Every Number 9 shoe in the country ought to be of the same length. A quart ought to be a quart, and a pound ought to be a pound. To that extent standardization is a convenience and a help to progress. And likewise with description. A certain grade of cement ought always to be of the same grade, so as to relieve the careful buyer from the necessity of testing. "All wool" ought to be all wool. "Silk" ought to be silk. The small buyer who has no facilities for testing should be able to rely on a published description of any article. All this, to repeat, is a matter of convenience, and also it prevents the unfair competition which permits an inferior article and a superior article both to be sold under exactly the same description.

But when we come to styles, we have an entirely different matter. Those who are unacquainted with the processes and the problems of industry are given to picturing a standardized world in which we should all live in the same sort of houses, wear the same sort of clothing, eat the same sort of food, and all think and act in the same way. That would be a prison world, and such a world is not possible until all the human beings in the world stop thinking. It is hard to imagine how such a world would get along, for with everyone thinking or not thinking in exactly the same way, leadership would vanish.

The eventuality of industry is not a standardized, automatic world in which people will not need brains. The eventuality is a world in which people will have a chance to use their brains, for they will not be occupied from early morning until late at night with the business of gaining a livelihood. The true end of industry is not the bringing of people into one mold; it is not the elevating of the working man to a false position of supremacy - industry exists to serve the public of which the working man is a part. The true end of industry is to liberate mind and body from the drudgery of existence by filling the world with well-made, low-priced products. How far these products may be standardized is a question, not for the state, but for the individual manufacturer.

The strongest objection to large numbers of styles and designs is that they are incompatible with economical production by any one concern. But when concerns specialize, each on its own design, economy and variety are both attainable. And both are necessary.

Standardization in its true sense is the union of all the best points of commodities with all the best points of production, to the end that the best commodity may be produced in sufficient quantity and at the least cost to the consumer.

To standardize a method is to choose out of many methods the best one, and use it. Standardization means nothing unless it means standardizing upward.

What is the best way to do a thing? It is the sum of all the good ways we have discovered up to the present. It therefore becomes the standard. To decree that today's standard shall be tomorrow's is to exceed our power and authority. Such a decree cannot stand. We see all around us yesterday's standards, but no one mistakes them for today's. Today's best, which superseded yesterday's, will be superseded by tomorrow's best. That is a fact which theorists overlook. They assume that a standard is a steel mold by which it is expected to shape and confine all effort for an indefinite time. If that were possible, we should today be using the standards of one hundred years ago, for certainly there was then no lack of resistance to adopting what goes to make up the present standards.

Industry today, under the impulse of engineering ability and engineering conscience, is rapidly improving the standards. Today's standardization, instead of being a barricade against improvement, is the necessary foundation on which tomorrow's improvement will be based.

If you think of "standardization" as the best that you know today, but which is to be improved tomorrow, you get somewhere. But if you think of standards as confining, then progress stops.

We believe (as was fully developed in "My Life and Work") that no factory is large enough to make two kinds of products. Our organization is not large enough to make two kinds of motor cars under the same roof. Several years ago, we bought the plant of the Lincoln Motor Car Company, more for personal reasons than because we wanted it. Our Model T - the "Ford "- is our principal business, and we have made it a commodity. We have no desire to make a commodity out of the Lincoln. Its standards are no higher than those of Model T, but they are different. Both cars are what might be called "standardized" in that every improvement has to be so arranged that it will fit on an existing car without machine work. Of course, all parts are interchangeable - which is one of the advantages of machine work over hand work which is not generally appreciated. It is always possible to devise a machine which will do better and more accurate work than can be done by hand.

But the point is that though the one company makes these two types of cars, they are not made under one roof, and they are made from different motives. The Model T is low-priced and serviceable. The man who makes it can buy it. The Lincoln effort is not in the direction of prices at all and the man who makes it cannot buy it. It is not a luxury car in the sense that it performs no service; it gives supreme service, but it is not a commodity. There must be grades of service, just as there are grades of human beings; one man's effort will bring him a return sufficient to buy one kind of article, while another man's effort will bring him a return sufficient to buy something higher in price. This is not violating the principle of the wage motive; it is extending that principle through all grades of service. We must level upward and not downward. And keeping that principle will prevent standardization from ever becoming a menace.

It is essential to economical manufacturing that parts be interchangeable. We do not make Ford cars in any one place. We turn out only a few completed cars in Detroit, and those only for the local market. We make parts, and the cars are assembled where they are to be used. And this involves an accuracy in manufacturing beyond anything thought of in the old days. Unless parts fit accurately, the resulting assembly will have lost motion, and much of the economy of design will be lost. That took us into the necessity for absolute precision in manufacturing - a precision extending in some cases to a ten thousandth of an inch. Under ordinary circumstances gauges cannot be kept so accurate - of course, only in exceptional cases do we work so accurately, but in many, perhaps most of our tolerances, we work to one thousandth of an inch. And to gain this accuracy we sought out the one man in the world who had made a business of absolute accuracy and brought him into the organization - Carl E. Johansson. As

a foreman in the Swedish Government Arsenal at Eskilstuna, he conceived the id\
gauges used in the production of accurately finished rifle parts, so that a greater r\
obtained from a small number of blocks. The first set was produced in 1897. To\
recognized throughout the world as the most accurate precision instruments kn\
manufacturing rights for Johansson gauges, as well as the plant at Poughkeeps\
Johansson joined the organization as a member of our engineering staff \
instruments.

Johansson combination gauge blocks are rectangular pieces of tool steel, hardened, ground, an\
surfaces are absolutely flat and parallel, one of the most remarkable achievements in mechanics, as the diffic\
making one steel surface truly parallel to another is a universally recognized problem. Professor J. Hjelsley, head of the Department of Mathematics at the University of Copenhagen, states that the surfaces of these blocks more nearly approach the perfect theoretical plane than any other produced by the hand of man.

These surfaces possess extraordinary qualities when rubbed across the palm of the hand and brought in contact with one another, sticking together with a force equivalent to thirty-three atmospheres. Scientists have offered various theories in explanation of this phenomenon – atmospheric pressure, molecular attraction, and the presence of a very minute liquid film on the contacting surfaces. Possibly it is a combination of all three. Two blocks wiped across the skin and pressed or "wrung" together with a slight sliding movement have resisted a direct pull of two hundred and ten pounds, which proves that there is something besides air pressure that makes them stick.

Some of the sets differ in steps of one ten thousandth of an inch, while others differ by as low as one-one-hundred-thousandth of an inch. A ten thousandth is about the lowest limit of accuracy in fine tool making, but this seems almost crude when measured with Johansson gauges. The ultimate, however, has been reached in a set which differs in steps of a millionth of an inch. This is so delicate that even the heat of the user's body several feet away influences the results. It is the only set in the world.

While we have a monopoly on these gauges, our first move after acquiring the American rights was to improve the manufacturing processes to increase the output and decrease the prices, so that these gauges would be within the reach of every machine shop and tool maker – which incidentally proves that there is nothing incompatible between quality and mass production.

At the Highland Park, we have 25,000 machines and at Fordson, 10,000 more. Scattered throughout our various plants, we probably have an additional 10,000. From time to time we are called on to fit out new branches in various parts of this country and of the world, and also to have at hand spare parts for these machines. That brought us into an important division of standardization. An operation in our plant at Barcelona has to be carried through exactly as in Detroit – the benefit of our experience cannot be thrown away.

Model T assembly line at the Ford plant of Highland Park, Michigan circa 1913.

on the assembly line at Detroit ought to be able to step into the assembly line at Oklahoma City or Sao [Paulo, B]razil. We use single-purpose machinery - that is, a machine is called on to do only one operation, although [in the] case of an automatic machine that operation may consist of several parts. The tendency is always for tool [des]igners to make each machine from the ground up without reference to any other machine. About 90 percent of [o]ur equipment is standard, and the conversion into a single purpose machine is a matter of detail. For instance, one operation calls for the piercing of a steel billet with hole seven eighths of an inch in diameter. Formerly this had been done by drilling, which was slow and costly, using many men and thirty drill presses, and wasting a lot of material. Then we substituted a standard disc piercing mill for which our men designed a new set of tools and made it do an entirely different job from the one for which it was originally intended. It is estimated that more than five hundred miles of boring was done before this time and labor-saving machine was developed.

We have 800 special machines designed to meet our own conditions of work. The major classifications of the standard machines are under 250 different headings, each of which is divided and subdivided into types and varieties until the list runs into the thousands. Under headings like Lathes, Millers, Grinders, Presses, Saws, Drills, etc., come lists of hundreds of different varieties, each of which is different in design and size. Yet with production standing at more than eight thousand cars a day, there is less money tied up in perishable tools than when the company's productive limit was 3,000 cars a day. The reason for this is standardization.

These tool standards are the result of twenty years' work. Today the system has been developed to such a stage that our manufacturing tools are as easily obtained as commercial hardware. This also applies to the tools and equipment used in making productive machinery. Gears, keys, shafting, levers, pedals, and other elements that make up a machine are all standardized, and out of various combinations of these standardized parts even highly specialized machinery is built.

Some of the most intricate designs have been built with no other special work than the frame casting. The glass grinding machinery illustrates this. Here the disc driving mechanism consists of the standard worm and gear, and the disc elevating mechanism of the standard ring gear pinion, axle shaft, and steering wheel. This simplification of the equipment problem is the basis on which the manufacturing program rests.

This system is carried out in every branch and manufacturing unit, not only in equipment but in shop methods. The conveyors used at the various branches and the chains used in their construction all are standard. All stock comes in standard sizes. Blue prints are made in a certain standard form with the various information always listed in the same location on the sheet, so that no time need be wasted in hunting for it. A series of books entitled "Ford Tool Standards" contains all the necessary data and gives the complete story of our standard practice with all its ramifications, down to the last detail. These books have saved thousands of dollars in the training of new men, but their real importance cannot be estimated, for they are primarily responsible in keeping the work uniform throughout the entire organization.

The advantages of this system of standardization of machine tools and equipment are numerous. The machine tool problem is reduced to a simple hardware affair and is hardly more expensive. Immense savings are possible in the construction of standard and special machinery, and if a design proves unsatisfactory, its major parts may be salvaged. The equipping of branches and manufacturing units becomes greatly simplified, and emergencies can be met without special effort. Furthermore, the maintenance and repair of machinery and tools is made simpler and easier. How much a year this saves for us can only be guessed at.

The advantages of standardization are apparent in production. The disadvantage is the expense incurred when changing from the standard. But the cost of changes is usually more than compensated by the improvements which a change gives opportunity to make. We have made many improvements in design and materials and, of course, in manufacturing methods, but the benefit of every improvement had been passed on to the public. The design has been as good looking as we knew how to make it, considering that each part had to be made in the light of these three principles, given in the order of their importance:

(1) Strength and lightness; (2) Economy in manufacture; (3) Appearance.

It may be asked: "Is it not better to sacrifice the artistic to the utilitarian than the utilitarian to the artistic?" What, for instance, would be the use of a teapot that would not pour because of the ornate design of its spout? Of what use would be a spade which cut one's hands because the handle was richly carved? As soon as the decoration on an object of utility interferes with its functioning, it ceases to be an object of art and had better be discarded as a nuisance.

It has been said that trade and industry are fatal to art, but that is not true. When art is divorced from utility something is wrong. Industry and art are not incompatible, but sound judgment is necessary in preserving the true balance between them. An automobile is a modern product and has to be designed, not to represent something which it is not, but to do the work for which it was intended.

Last year we made certain changes to the end of turning out somewhat better cars. The engine we did not touch – that is, the heart of the car.

In all, eighty-one changes, major and minor, were involved. None of these changes was made lightly. The new designs were thoroughly tried out all over the country in actual service for many months.

After we had decided to make the changes, the next step was to plan how it could be done.

We set a date to begin changing over. The planning department had to calculate on just the amount of material which would keep production going at full speed until that date and then permit production to stop without having any material over. It had to make the same calculations for our thirty-two associated plants and for the forty-two branches.

In the meantime, hundreds of drawings had to be made by the engineers for the building of the new dies and tools. We arranged to make this change without a wholesale shut down. We "staggered" the process, changing one department at a time, so that by the time the last change was made production had caught up to the last department involved.

All of this sounds simple enough, but here is what it meant to make only eighty-one changes. We had to design 4,759 punch and dies and 4,243 jigs and fixtures. We had to build 5,622 punch and dies and 6,990 jigs and fixtures. The labor cost of this amounted to $5,682,387, while the material ran to $1,395,596. Installing new enamel ovens at thirteen branches cost $371,000, and changing the equipment in twenty-nine branches cost $145,650. That is to say, these changes cost us upward of eight million dollars, not estimating time lost from production.

CHAPTER 8
LEARNING FROM WASTE

If one used nothing then one would waste nothing. That seems plain enough. But look at it from another angle. If we use nothing at all, is not then the waste total? Is it conservation or waste to withdraw a public resource wholly from use? If a man skimps himself through all the best years of his life in order to provide for his old age, has he conserved his resources or has he wasted them? Has he been constructively or destructively thrifty?

How are we to reckon waste? Usually, we count waste in terms of materials. If a housewife buys twice as much food as her family eats and throws the rest a way, she is considered wasteful. But on the other hand, is the housewife who gives her family only half enough to eat thrifty? Not at all. She is even more wasteful than the first housewife, for she is wasting human lives. She is withdrawing from her family the strength which they need to do their work in the world.

Materials are less important than human beings - although we have not yet come quite around to thinking in that fashion. Once upon a time, society hung a man for stealing a loaf of bread. Now society treats such an offence differently. It takes that man, puts him in a prison, withdraws the benefit of an amount of labor which might make thousands of loaves of bread, and then actually feeds him many times as much bread as he stole! We not only waste this man's productive power, but also we call on our other producers to give up a part of their production to support him. That is flagrant waste.

It is necessary and will be necessary to put men in jail until the news gets about that the profits of dishonesty do not compare with the profits of honesty, but there is no reason for thinking of a jail as a tomb for the living. Under first-class, non-political management, every jail in the country could be turned into an industrial unit, pay higher wages to the men than they could earn in outside industry, provide them with good food and reasonable hours of labor, and then turn over an excellent profit to the State. We already have prison labor, but most of it is ill-directed, degrading labor.

A criminal is a non-producer, but when he has been caught and sentenced, it is very wasteful to continue him as a non-producer. He can surely be turned into a producer and probably into a man. Yet, because we value human time so lightly and materials so highly, we do not hear much about the waste of man power in prisons, nor do we hear much of the terrible waste of withdrawing support from the families of the convicts and throwing them on the community.

Conserving our natural resources by withdrawing them from use is not a service to the community. That is holding to the old theory that a thing is more important than a man. Our natural resources are ample for all our present needs. We do not have to bother about them as resources. What we do have to bother about is the waste of human labor.

Take a vein of coal in a mine. As long as it remains in the mine, it is of no importance, but when a chunk of that coal has been mined and set down in Detroit, it becomes a thing of importance, because then it represents a certain amount of the labor of men used in its mining and transportation. If we waste that bit of coal - which is another way of saying if we do not put it to its full use - then we waste the time and energy of men. A man cannot be paid much for producing something which is to be wasted.

My theory of waste goes back of the thing itself into the labor of producing it. We want to get full value out of labor so that we may be able to pay it full value. It is use - not conservation - that interests us. We want to use material to its utmost in order that the time of men may not be lost. Material costs nothing. It is of no account until it comes into the hands of management.

Saving material because it is material, and saving material because it represents labor might seem to amount to the same thing. But the approach makes a deal of difference. We will use material more carefully if we think of it as labor. For instance, we will not so lightly waste material simply because we can reclaim it - for salvage involves labor. The ideal is to have nothing to salvage.

We have a large salvage department, which apparently earns for us twenty or more million dollars a year. Something of it will be told later in this chapter. But as that department grew and became more important and more strikingly valuable, we began to ask ourselves:

"Why should we have so much to salvage? Are we not giving more attention to reclaiming than to not wasting?"

And with that thought in mind, we set out to examine all our processes. A little of what we do in the way of saving man power by extending machinery has already been told, and what we are doing with coal, wood, power, and transportation will be told in later chapters This has to do only with what was waste. Our studies and investigations up to date have resulted in the saving of 80,000,000 pounds of steel a year that formerly went into scrap and had to be reworked with the expenditure of labor. This amounts to about three million dollars a year, or, to put it in a better way, to the unnecessary labor on our scale of wages of upward of two thousand men. And all of that saving was accomplished so simply that our present wonder is why we did not do it before.

Here are a few examples: We formerly cut our crank cases out of trimmed steel plate exactly the width and length of the case. That steel cost $.0335 per pound because it had in it a good deal of labor. Now we buy an untrimmed sheet 150 inches long at $.028 per pound, shear it to 109 inches - the sheared portion going to make another part - and on the remaining plate we can lay our five crank cases, which are cut in one operation. This saves four million pounds of steel scrap a year, and the whole saving amounts to nearly half a million dollars. The windshield bracket is somewhat irregularly shaped, and we formerly cut it from 18 x 32½ inch rectangular steel sheets. A sheet gave us six brackets and a quantity of scrap. Now, by taking stock 15½ x 32½ inches cut at a seven-degree angle, we get six windshield brackets as before, but also in the same operation we get ten other blanks for small parts. This saves a million and a half pounds of steel a year. The oil-can holder is in the shape of a cross, and we formerly stamped it out of steel with great waste at a cost of $.0635 each. Now we cut the two parts of the cross separately with almost no scrap and weld them together, and they now cost $.0478 each. The bushing on the steering gear, which is made of bronze, was formerly .128 inches thick. We found that it could be half as thick and do its work quite as well which saves us 130,000 pounds of bronze a year, or more than thirty thousand dollars. The head lamp bracket pad is a cross, measuring 7½ x 3½ inches, and we used to cut fourteen of them out of a sheet 6½ x 35 inches. We reduced the size of the bracket to 7½ x 3½ inches and now get the same number as before out of a sheet 5⅞ x 35 inches which saves more than a hundred thousand pounds of steel a year.

We formerly cut the fan-drive pulley out of new stock. Now we cut it out of the salvage from the hand door stock which saves nearly three hundred thousand pounds of steel a year. By making very slight changes in twelve small brass items, we are saving nearly half a million pounds of brass a year. On nineteen items cut from bars or tubing we have, by changing the cutting tools and multiples and the length of the stock, saved more than a million pounds of steel a year. For instance, on one part we used a bar 143 inches long and got eighteen pieces per bar; we found that we could get the same number of pieces out of a bar 140 9/82 inches long-thus saving more than two inches per bar. On many small parts which were formerly cold rolled, we have changed to hot rolling. This, on sixteen little items, saves about three hundred thousand dollars a year.

This general policy has been extended in a great number of directions. We found that in many plates and bars, bought according to standard sizes or to specifications, we were not only paying for the shearing and the scrap at the steel mill, but we were actually losing serviceable metal both in getting fewer parts out of the steel and also increasing our own scrap. Thus, there was a waste all around. We have been working on this only a year and have hardly had a start on what can be done.

Scrap, we take it, is something to be avoided and not to be remelted until no other course remains. We had considered the worn steel rails from the railroad as scrap steel to be remelted. Now we pass them through a roll which separates the head, the web, and the foot - which gives us excellent steel bars which can be used for a number of purposes. This idea also is going to be carried further. On the other hand, such steel as we at present must consider as scrap amounts to a thousand tons or more a day. We had been selling this scrap to Pittsburgh and buying it back again as steel-paying transportation charges both ways. Now we have erected at the River Rouge a series of electric furnaces and a large rolling mill, so that we can convert the scrap ourselves and save this item of double transportation. If we cannot avoid all of this scrap - and some of it is hardly avoidable - we can at least save the waste of human labor in handling and transportation.

The salvage of materials about the shops has developed into a large industry, which is uncommonly important because it employs sub-standard men - men who could not work in production. We can use men otherwise unemployable to salvage the labor of other men. The simplification and classification of tools and machinery described in the last chapter have greatly aided in the salvage - every part of an industry should fit into every other part.

Thousands of broken tools and damaged plant equipment come in for reclamation every twenty-four hours. The value of the belting sent to the salvage department amounts to more than a thousand dollars a day. This is all repaired and reworked, the smaller scraps going to make life belts for window washers or to the cobbler shop to be used for soles or patches. Broken tools of all kinds - pliers, wrenches, shears, braces, bits, hammers, drills, gauges, chucks, planes, saws, dies, jigs, and fixtures are repaired and returned to stock. These repairs are not patchwork. The tools are actually rebuilt according to the original blue print and come up to specifications in every particular.

The department has a record of every machine operation in the industry and just what kind and size of tools are required. It can instantly tell what can be done with a damaged tool. Generally, it can be profitably reworked to smaller size, there being several machines which can use a drill even less than an inch in length. If a drill, a broach, or a reamer is worn out, it is cut down to a smaller size, always in accordance with the original blue print. Cold-heading dies are all reworked to the next size, and so on down through the entire list of tools. All tool steel is classified and sorted before reworking. Tool handles of all kinds are salvaged; a broken shovel handle may make several screw driver or chisel handles. Picks, rakes, spades, crowbars, mops, brooms, and similar implements are all salvaged as long as it is profitable. Two men spend most of their time in repairing mop pails.

Pipes, valves, joints, and other steam-fitting apparatus are reconditioned. Old paint is reclaimed to the extent of 500 gallons a day and is used for rough work. The salvage of oil and cutting compounds from steel shavings amounts to 2,100 gallons a day.

Metal scrap, such as copper, brass, lead, aluminum, babbitt metal, solder, steel, and iron are remelted. Since all our cast iron is classified under heads according to analysis, it is a simple matter to sort iron scrap and return it to the proper cupola for remelting.

Molding sand is salvaged for its intrinsic value, and because of the saving in freight and handling. Scrap oil is salvaged, and what is unfit for either lubrication or rust-proofing is burned for fuel. A process by which the cyanide used in heat treating can be diluted has been developed and the cyanide bills cut in halves. The laboratories have developed a cement by which canvas facing may be stuck to pulleys, thereby reducing slippage of belts and the consequent waste of power. Old fire brick is broken up and reworked. Dross from the melting pots gives a yield. In the Photographic Department the silver salts are recovered from the developing solutions and the saving amounts to nearly ten thousand dollars a year.

The great amount of paper and rags gathered in a day throughout the plants bothered us, and so did the hardwood scrap from the body plant. Since we have swung over to all-steel bodies for most of the styles, the wood scrap has been much reduced. Having developed a salvage department, we at once start to make it unnecessary.

The first thought with the hardwood scrap was to make it into paper, but we were told that only soft wood could be used in paper making. But we went ahead with our plans for a mill and proved that it could be successfully done. The paper plant now uses 20 tons of scrap paper a day and produces 14 tons of binder board and 8 tons of special waterproof board which is the result of a process developed in our laboratories. The board is of such great tensile strength that a ten-inch strip can bear the entire suspended weight of a Ford car.

We use standard machinery with some improvements and adaptations of our own in order to make the process continuous and to cut down labor. Only thirty-seven men are required to operate the mill, which contains more than seventy-five separate units of apparatus.

Part of the product is used in backing the upholstery and the remainder for containers in which to ship parts - which saves wood.

The blast furnaces produce five hundred tons of slag a day, 225 tons of which go into the making of cement, the rest being crushed for roads.

The conversion of blast furnace slag into cement is quite common, but we could not afford to have the dust of the usual cement plant, and so we worked on a new process known as the "wet," which is now being experimented with by other American manufacturers.

As the molten slag runs from the blast furnace, it is met by a stream of cold water which granulates it to the size of coarse salt. The wet mass, of which the wet slag comprises sometimes as much as 40 percent, though usually only 10 to 25 percent is pumped through a 1,300-foot pipe to the cement plant, where it pours into constantly moving de-watering elevators which permit all the water to be drained off before it reaches the belt conveyors at the top. These carry the granulated slag to the storage bins from which it is drawn as needed. Inasmuch as this slag contains about 1 percent iron, the conveyors pass under powerful magnets which pick up the iron particles, a considerable amount being recovered in a day. This is sent back to the blast furnace for reclamation.

From the storage bins the slag is carried to the mill where, mixed with crushed limestone and 30 percent or more water, it is ground to powder. Before the mixture leaves the mill, it is so fine that 90 percent will pass through a 200-mesh screen. This mixture, of the consistency of cream, is called "slurry," and is forced by air pressure into huge storage vats. The analysis of this mixture is taken hourly and corrections in the proportioning are made accordingly.

The slurry then goes to rotary kilns 150 feet long where, under intense heat, the cement is fused to clinker form, after which, with the addition of a small amount of gypsum, it is ground to powder, in which form it is ready for use. Gypsum is added to regulate the setting of the finished cement.

The plant gives us about two thousand barrels a day. We sell a little of it to our men for their own use - just so that they can buy cement below the market price.

The point, to repeat, in all of this is the saving of human labor so that it may be made more effective and more valuable. It was to save the human labor that had gone into their making that we bought two hundred ships from the government. They had been built by the Emergency Fleet Corporation for use during the war, and there was no commercial demand for them. We are now breaking them up at our plant at Kearney, New Jersey. We can use some of the engines in our smaller plants, for many of the engines are first class. We do not expect to make any money out of the salvage of these ships - we did not go into it to make money. We simply did not like to see such a mass of fine material and so much labor go to waste when we might reclaim it. We bought with the wage, not the profit, motive in our minds.

Industry owes it to society to conserve material in every possible way. Not only for the element of cost in the manufactured article, although that is important, but mostly for the conservation of those materials whose production and transportation are laying an increasing burden on society.

As it is now, every manufacturing concern exists only to make its own products. It has not been linked up with the community.

But it is becoming apparent that manufacturing concerns of size can be much more useful to the community than they now are, for example. in the matter of supplying fuel and power. Under the present system, coal hauled to a factory is just burned under its boilers, and a small fraction of its content utilized. Deliver a thousand cars of coal to the shops of a great manufacturing district, and that is the end. In a time of coal shortage, the job of keeping the factories supplied with fuel and the job of keeping the homes supplied with fuel are distinct, requiring two great supplies of coal.

Some day – in order to save human labor – we shall link all of this together. All phases of life should be and can be complementary.

CHAPTER 9
REACHING BACK TO THE SOURCES

We look upon industry largely as a matter of management, and to us management and leadership are quite the same. We have no patience with the kind of management that shouts orders and interferes with instead of directing the men at their work. Real leadership is unobtrusive, and our aim is always to arrange the material and machinery and to simplify the operations so that practically no orders are necessary. Unless management begins on the drawing board, it will never get into the shop.

It is the work, not the man, that manages. That work is planned on the drawing board and the operations subdivided so that each man and each machine do only one thing. This is a general rule, but it is flexible and has to be applied with common sense. If a machine can be devised to perform several operations at once, then it would be waste to have several machines. A man may sometimes as easily perform two operations as one - in which case he performs two operations.

It is often imagined that our system of production is founded on moving platforms and conveyors. We use moving platforms and conveyors only when they aid in the work. For instance, in making headlights we do not use conveyors, because the nature of the parts is such that they can more easily be moved on in boxes than by a conveyor. On the other hand, in many departments we find conveyors extremely useful, and especially so in assemblies - that is, bringing the component parts of a unit together - for then the assembly can start at one end of the moving platform or belt conveyor and have its various parts added as it moves along.

The thing is to keep everything in motion and take the work to the man and not the man to the work. That is the real principle of our production, and conveyors are only one of many means to an end.

The key of our production is inspection. More than 3 percent of our entire force are inspectors. This simplifies management. Every part in every stage of its production is inspected.

If a machine breaks down, a repair squad will be on hand in a few minutes. The men do not leave their work to get tools - new tools are brought to them, but they do not often need new tools, and machines do not often break down, for there is continuous cleaning and repair work on every bit of machinery in the place. When new tools are needed, there is no delay. Tool rooms are provided for every department. Once we had large supply rooms, and men lined up at the windows to get their tools. That was waste. We found it often cost us twenty-five cents worth of a man's time (not counting overhead) to get a thirty-cent tool. With that, we abolished the central tool room - a man cannot be paid high wages for standing around waiting for tools. Nor, which amounts to the same thing, can the public be served.

Stooping to the floor to pick up a tool or a part is not productive labor - therefore, all material is delivered waist high.

Our system of management is not a system at all; it consists of planning the methods of doing the work as well as the work. All that we ask of the men is that they do the work which is set before them. This work is never more than a man can do without undue fatigue in eight hours. He is well paid - and he works. When management becomes a " problem," the fault will be found to be with the planning of the work.

Of course, if men are under some outside influence or control by which the amount of work which they do in a day is limited - if they have to answer to an outside authority, then management is impossible, and consequently, high wages cannot be paid for the production of low-priced products. The whole wage motive fails.

It was in order to eliminate lost motion - which is just as fatal in a factory as in a bearing - that we began, some years ago, the plant which we call Fordson and which has now become the heart of our industries. Four years ago, it had a blast furnace, several shops, and about three thousand men. We had taken over the ground and put up some buildings to manufacture Eagle boats for the government during the war - fast little boats to go after the submarines. Now the plant covers more than a thousand acres, has a mile of river frontage, and employs upward of seventy thousand men.

It is not in the line of our thought to build many large plants. We believe that smaller plants have a function, too, and we have made some interesting experiments along that line. But Fordson handles raw materials and in order to avoid unnecessary transport we have had to group around the raw materials the heavier assemblies, such as the motors, and also the entirety of the making of the tractor.

Aerial view of the Ford River Rouge plant near Dearborn, Michigan circa 1927.

The reason for Fordson is transport. The Rouge is not much of a river - although we have managed to use its power almost from its source. But now the river is dredged so that Great Lakes boats and the smaller ocean liners can come into our docks, and we have dug a good-sized turning basin. This opens the plant to water transport, and the ore and lumber boats can come directly into the plant from our mines and forests in Upper Michigan. Then also it is the terminus of the Detroit, Toledo & Ironton Railroad, which we own. This road connects with our coal fields and also crosses nine main trunk lines. Therefore, not only can all our essential raw materials meet at this plant with no extra handling, but also finished automobile parts can leave with equal ease for any part of the country or the world.

The whole plant has been built with the single thought of simplifying the handling of material, and the backbone of its transportation is what we call the "High Line." The High Line is a concrete structure forty feet high and three quarters of a mile long, with five railroad tracks and two protected footpaths across its top. The outer track, nearest the storage bins, is of open-girder construction and permits bottom-dumping cars to discharge their loads directly into the bins.

Underneath the tracks are the active storage bins which supply the blast furnaces and other units. Every bit of space under the tracks is utilized for the full three quarters of a mile. Here are machine shops for making locomotive parts and other equipment, stock rooms, tool rooms, conduits, conveyors, and blacksmith shop. There are eighty-five miles of railroad track in the plant supplementing the High Line. This permits the transportation of car loads and even train loads of material to any part of the plant.

Most of the coal, iron ore, limestone, and lumber arrive by boat, and enormous storage facilities have been provided to carry the plant through the period when navigation is closed on account of ice. The primary storage bins extend for half a mile in length, and their total capacity is more than two million tons.

Cargoes are removed from incoming ships at the rate of 1,050 tons an hour by two mechanical unloaders, which can lift twelve tons at a dip. The primary storage bins are spanned by travelling bridges 520 feet long which transfer material from one bin to another or to the High Line, where the secondary or active storage bins are located, convenient to the blast furnaces.

The moment a vessel docks, the unloaders get to work and the record is the discharge of 11,500 tons of ore in ten and a half hours. The average time is around eleven hours, but this is being cut down by dropping a tractor into the hold when it is almost empty and scraping the ore into piles to be more easily picked up by the big unloaders.

Now see what all this means from the standpoint of production. (Neglecting for the moment the power house - which will be taken up later - it is enough to say that we are centralizing our power at Fordson for Highland Park, Fordson, the Dearborn laboratory, the Lincoln plant, the Flat Rock plant, and the railroad, and that we are getting 40 percent of this power practically as a by-product of our blast furnaces.) Trace the operations. Coal comes up from our mines in Kentucky and is stored in bins under the High Line or goes directly to the coking ovens, being pulverized on the way. We have one hundred and twenty "high temperature" ovens with a capacity of 2,500 tons a day. These are all by-product ovens and beside them is the by-product plant in which we recover such of the products as may be used within the organization, excepting the ammonium sulphate which we sell outside, and we also sell our surplus of benzol - as was said before. The coal delivered at the plant costs us about five dollars a ton, but when converted into coke and by-products, it is worth about twelve dollars a ton. We have erected an experimental paint and varnish plant further to utilize by-products. Part of the gas produced in distillation is used to heat the ovens so as to make the process continuous, another part is piped to Highland Park while what remains is sold to the local gas company - which is an indication of how eventually the industries of community and the community itself may be linked together. The tar and oil we use in our own industries. At no point in the coking process is hand labor used.

Nearby the coking ovens are the blast furnaces. They are charged with iron ore, coke, and limestone from the bins along the High Line. The blast furnace charge is made in the ratio of two tons of ore, one ton of coke, half a ton of limestone, and three and a half tons of air. The products taken out are in the ratio of a ton of high silicon iron, half a ton of slag, and five and a half tons of gas, equal to 200,000 cubic feet. None of these products is wasted.

The gas is cleaned and filtered to remove blast furnace dust and part of it used in the stoves to pre-heat the blast. The balance is piped to the power house, where it forms the principal fuel. The blast furnace dust is also saved. Formerly, this dust, which is nearly 50 percent pure iron, was regarded as waste, and was either dumped or sold as scrap, for it was too fine to be melted in the furnaces or cupolas. This dust is caught up in collectors, unloaded in cars by gravity, and carried directly to the sintering plant, where it is mixed with steel or iron borings and agglomerated into heavy lumps, which will melt easily. This process not only reclaims a great amount of iron, but it also avoids the former labor of hauling it away. At the time the sintering plant was first put into operation, we had accumulated enough blast furnace dust to furnish material for more than six hundred-thousand-cylinder block castings. A comparatively small force of men is required to operate the blast furnaces, all the heavy work being done by machines. Electric drills cut the clay plugs when the furnaces are tapped, and a compressed air gun shoots in clay balls to close it again. As has already been explained, a large portion of the slag goes directly to the cement plant.

Formerly the foundry operations were at Highland Park, but now all our iron casting is in the Fordson foundry to avoid transportation and the reheating of the metal. This foundry now extends over thirty acres and is entirely operated on the conveyor system. The foundry is paved, the floors are kept spotlessly clean, and a system of suction pipes, ventilators, and dust collectors keeps the place cool and free from dust - in fact, there is nothing but the castings being made and the hot metal to suggest that the place is a foundry.

The foundry is not segregated into departments. Instead, every department is coordinated into a continuous system of manufacture by the use of conveyors.

Core making takes place on an endless chain which feeds the conveyors carrying the molds to the pouring stations at the cupolas. Molds are also made on moving conveyors and reach completion only a few yards away from the hot metal ladles. The return trip allows the castings to cool before they reach the shake-out station, where they are removed from the flasks and the sand shaken out. After the fins and rough edges are chipped off, another conveyor carries the still hot castings to the tumbling barrels, where they are revolved until the surfaces are smoothed.

The motor block is the heaviest casting used in the car. It was formerly manufactured at Highland Park, but it was a waste to transport these castings to Highland Park and then ship the completed motors out by rail to the branches past the very gates of Fordson. Therefore, we transferred the motor assembly to Fordson, putting it in a building 800 feet long by 600 feet wide. There are four main assembly lines or conveyors, and now the process of making the motors is continuous.

We start with the blast furnace and end with a completed motor stacked in a freight car. The casting leaves the foundry on a moving platform or conveyor to one of the assembly lines, it is machined, the other parts are added as it moves along, and when it reaches the end of its line, it is a completed and tested motor - and all of this without a stop.

Out of the same foundry come the tractor castings. They pass into the tractor division, and the tractors leave the final assembly under their own power and pass into the freight cars for shipment.

The processes all differ in detail from those described in "My Life and Work," but the principles are the same. By bringing everything together in the Fordson, we have been able to cut very largely into the time of making -so much so that it is said we deliver our tractors before they have had time to cool! Unlike the motor car, we ship the tractor complete from the factory. The tractor is so compact that it does not pay to ship it in parts for assembly at a branch.

For several years we have had large electric furnaces - one a fifty-ton furnace - for the salvage of steel scrap - as has been noted. And now we are adding more furnaces and a rolling mill, so that we shall be in a position not only to cast but to roll all our steel scrap and, if we find it advisable, to make our own steel. I have great faith in steel; Model T came into being because of vanadium steel - no other steel up to that time gave the necessary strength without bulk. We are working on many special kinds of steel, and I believe that the lightness and strength necessary for the all-metal airplane will eventually be found in steel. We must be prepared to make the special steels exactly suited to our uses.

The real age of steel - when we begin to realize something of its possibilities - is only approaching. Tonnage still predominates, and not only are we transporting too much metal about the country as metal, but also nearly every steel product that we use is far too heavy. Every time one uses two pounds of steel when one pound of special steel would do the work, one puts an unnecessary burden on the public which reflects in higher prices, less consumption, and lower wages. Steel has more possibilities than any other metal.

An interesting side development of putting the work on the machines instead of on the man is the increased necessity for skilled workmen to repair machinery and tools and now to construct new machinery. Many people thought that machine production would destroy craftsmanship. Exactly the reverse has come about: we now need more expert machinists than ever we needed – we can always use more tool makers. Making and repairing machinery is now a large industry with us, employing several thousand men.

As we increase our fund of mechanical knowledge, productive machinery will steadily require less attention from its operators, and the shift will be to the making of this machinery. We are not as yet equipped to make more than a small part of the machinery that we use and have thus far confined ourselves almost wholly to special machinery on our own designs. We have made some large machinery in connection with our new power plant. The condenser casting for the turbo-generators weighed ninety-six tons. We made the generators partly because we wanted to put into them some of our own ideas and partly because we could not get delivery from outside manufacturers as quickly as we needed.

The savings brought about at Fordson have been enormous – we do not know how great they are, because we have no method of comparing the savings on our present large production with the former cost of production.

CHAPTER 10
THE MEANING OF TIME

Ordinarily, money put into raw materials or into finished stock is thought of as live money. It is money in the business, it is true, but having a stock of raw material or finished goods in excess of requirements is waste – which, like every other waste, turns up in high prices and low wages.

The time element in manufacturing stretches from the moment the raw material is separated from the earth to the moment when the finished product is delivered to the ultimate consumer. It involves all forms of transportation and has to be considered in every national scheme of service. It is a method of saving and serving which ranks with the application of power and the division of labor.

If we were operating today under the methods of 1921, we should have on hand raw materials to the value of about one hundred and twenty million dollars, and we should have unnecessarily in transit finished products to the value of about fifty million dollars. That is, we should have an investment in raw material and finished goods of not far from two hundred million dollars. Instead of that, we have an average investment of only about fifty million dollars, or, to put it another way, our inventory, raw and finished, is less than it was when our production was only half as great.

The extension of our business since 1921 has been very great, yet, in a way, all this great expansion has been paid for out of money which, under our old methods, would have lain idle in piles of iron, steel, coal, or in finished automobiles stored in warehouses. We do not own or use a single warehouse!

How we do this will be explained later in this chapter, but the point now is to direct thought to the time factor in service. Having on hand twice as much material as is needed – which is only another way of saying twice as much stored human labor as is needed – is precisely the same as hiring two men to do the job that one man ought to do. Hiring two men to do the job of one is a crime against society. Also, to carry a product 500 miles to the consumer, if that product can be found within 250 miles, is a crime. For a railroad to deliver in ten days when it might deliver in five is grand larceny.

This country was built by transportation. The big through trunk lines made us a nation – we had no political barriers to trade, and the railroads removed the natural barriers. Manufacturing naturally centered in the East because the known deposits of coal and iron were in the East, and so, also, were most of the consumers of the finished products, but now we have great cities from coast to coast – too great a population for our railroads to serve, following the old way of doing nearly all the manufacturing in the East.

A big factory unit sometimes pays. Our Fordson plant pays because it brings raw materials together economically. Our finished product, in the way we ship and assemble, goes out with a minimum transportation charge. But if Fordson did not deal in heavy, bulky raw materials it would not pay. It pays because it combines quick transportation both inward and outward. As a general rule, a large plant is not economical. A small plant making only one part is with cheap power more economical than a large plant with equally cheap power making all the parts – even in separate departments. At least, that has been our experience, as will be told in a later chapter. The cost of power and transportation is controlling.

It is not possible to repeat too often that waste is not something which comes after the fact. Restoring an ill body to health is an achievement, but preventing illness is a much higher achievement. Picking up and reclaiming the scrap left over after production is a public service but planning so that there will be no scrap is a higher public service.

Time waste differs from material waste in that there can be no salvage. The easiest of all wastes, and the hardest to correct, is this waste of time, because wasted time does not litter the floor like wasted material. In our industries, we think of time as human energy. If we buy more material than we need for production, then we are storing human energy – and probably depreciating its value. One may buy ahead on speculation in the hope of realizing an unearned profit. That is both poor service and poor business, because, over a term of years, the profits of speculation will not exceed the losses, and the net result to the speculator is zero, while the community itself has lost by having to make detours from the ordinary highways of trade. On the other hand, it is a waste to carry so small a stock of materials that an accident will tie up production. The balance has to be found, and that balance largely depends upon the ease of transportation.

There can be no ease in transportation unless the unnecessary shipment of goods is avoided. The country has railroad facilities enough to carry all the goods that need carrying, but it has not facilities enough to provide for unnecessary transportation. To have a surplus of facilities would only be waste. We should do better to look to the necessity of the transportation than to extend the railroads. For instance, when we wholly manufactured our motor cars at Highland Park and shipped them out complete, the day we went into the production of 1,000 cars a day brought on one of the worst freight jams ever known. That jam might have been broken by spending some millions of dollars in extending the railroads and building new box cars. But a much better way was to ship our cars in a different fashion. It would scarcely be possible to ship our present 8,000 cars a day production in the old fashion, and, if we did, our cars would cost the buyers much more than they now do.

Modern business is on a different basis from the old business. In the days when opportunities were few, it is not surprising that making work for someone was regarded as a worthy act, but now, if the principle of the wage motive be followed, there is more work to do than there are men to do the work. Making a job for a man is merely asking him to assist in lowering wages and raising prices. It would seem that the more traffic given to the railroads the more prosperous they would be, and through buying new equipment they would share their prosperity with the steel makers, the locomotive builders, the car builders, and everyone in the long line of industries which the railroads support.

This is true if the transport be necessary, but not at all true if the transport be unnecessary. If we carry wheat 500 miles to the mill and then carry the flour back over that same 500 miles, then there is a waste, unless the economy of milling at the central point exceeds the extra cost of double transportation. If the carriage is waste, it will find its way into the price of bread, and people will eat less bread, and the farmer will get less for his wheat, and the traffic of the railroad will decrease, and it will be less prosperous and so will all those who depend on it.

Exactly the same principle goes through every kind of business that depends on transportation – and the number of businesses which are not dependent on transportation are so few that they do not have to be considered.

The speed of the transportation is itself a factor, and its importance depends on the value of the commodity carried. If a railroad does not insist that its freight cars go through on time, and allows them to pile up and be forgotten on sidings, then, regardless of the value of the commodity carried, that railroad will have a lot of dead money in surplus equipment.

Handling freight roughly is another source of great waste. It is absurd that an article for shipment has to be protected against other than the ordinary jarrings of travel. The function of the carrier is to receive goods and transport them to their destination with the utmost care. This function seems to have been forgotten. Ordinarily, goods have to be packed, not merely to resist jar and ordinary handling, but to resist any attack that may be made on them. This is especially true of goods for overseas. The labor and material involved in packing are enormous, and most of it is sheer waste – waste of human labor and of valuable lumber.

All of these problems we have had to meet in our industries, and we have shaped our industries with transport always in mind. Instead of shipping complete cars, we have thirty-one assembly plants located at trade centers throughout the United States to receive standard parts from the manufacturing plants and assemble them into finished cars and trucks. This calls for chassis assembly, body building, and all the paint, trim, and upholstery work. Some of the branches manufacture cushions, springs, and closed bodies. They all operate under the same system, use the same standard tools, and build cars in the same way. Together they furnish employment for around twenty-six thousand men.

Recently, a new type of assembly plant building has been worked out, and all new branches are being built to these specifications. This calls for a one-story structure with the conveyor lines laid out in such a way that trucking and handling are practically eliminated. The new one-story design permits the greatest efficiency. Production may be greatly increased without additional labor. In the Chicago plant, the greatest distance any material has to be trucked is twenty feet, this being the distance from the incoming freight car to the first conveyor. After this it is mechanically handled during the entire process of assembling the units into a finished car.

The location of a new plant is largely determined by the cost of its power and the price at which it may make and ship goods to a given territory. The saving in freight rates of a fraction of a cent per part often decides the location. The St. Paul plant is able to supply all the country west of the Mississippi River at a lower freight rate than any plant east of it. St. Paul, therefore, makes all the parts that cannot be made elsewhere at a cost to offset the freight-rate advantage. Different parts of a motor car come under separate freight classifications, each with a different tariff. A single first-class part in a case of fifth-class parts may bring the whole shipment under the first-class rate. Packing and shipping are watched in the interest of economy. The amount of machining done on a part sometimes affects its freight classification. In such cases, the lower rate is taken advantage of by having only part of the machining done at the factory and the remainder at the branch to which it is shipped.

Only a few years ago, seven touring car bodies made a full load for a standard thirty-six-foot freight car. Now the bodies are shipped knocked-down to be assembled and finished in the branches, and we ship 130 touring car bodies in the same sized car - that is, we use one freight car where we should formerly have used eighteen.

Our finished inventory is all in transit. So is most of our raw material inventory. When production stands at 8,000 a day, this means that our various factories manufacture and ship enough to make 8,000 complete cars. We know just how many machines and employees it will take to reach a given figure at a given time, and how to take care of seasonal demands without the danger of becoming overstocked. A thirty-day supply of any one material is the maximum carried by a department, with the single exception of the blast furnaces, which carry enough iron ore in storage to last them through the winter. The average department inventory is less than ten days' supply.

The average shipping time between the factory and the branches is 6.16 days, which means that there is an average of a little more than six days' supply of parts in transit. This is called the "float." If production is at the rate of 8,000 cars a day, there are parts enough in transit to make more than forty-eight thousand complete cars. Thus, the traffic and production departments must work closely together to see that all the proper parts reach the branches at the same time - the shortage of a single kind of bolt would hold up the whole assembly at a branch. The exact status of the float may be determined at any hour of the day.

The problem of coordination is simplified by standard carloads - of which we have twenty-five. The standard carload for front axles, for example, contains exactly 400 sets. Limited quantities of smaller parts, such as spring hangers, are always included with the shipment of larger parts, but these, too, are standardized. This is worked out in a manner that will take advantage of the lowest freight classification.

This method does away with filling out shipping orders. Instead, they are printed and books are kept on one master part only. The only time it is necessary to specify quantities is when special shipments are made.

Whenever a shipment starts, the car number is wired to the branch. The factory traffic department traces all shipments and sees that they are kept moving until they are in the branch's territory, where the branch stock traffic man picks them up and follows them through to the unloading platform. We take no chances with the ordinary flow of traffic. Men are stationed at junctions and other points throughout the country to see that the cars are not delayed. The traffic department knows the exact transit time between different points, and if a car is overdue more than an hour, the fact is known at headquarters.

Our production cycle is about eighty-one hours from the mine to the finished machine in the freight car, or three days and nine hours instead of the fourteen days which we used to think was record breaking. Counting the storage of iron ore in winter and various other storages of parts or equipment made necessary from time to time for one reason or another, our average production cycle will not exceed five days.

Take the usual procedure. Let us say one of our ore boats docks at Fordson at 8am on Monday. It has taken forty-eight hours for the boat to come from Marquette to the docks. Ten minutes after the boat is docked, its cargo will be moving toward the High Line and become part of a charge for the blast furnace. By noon Tuesday, the ore has been reduced to iron, mixed with other iron in the foundry cupolas, and cast. There-upon follow fifty-eight operations which are performed in fifty-five minutes. By three o'clock in the afternoon the motor has been finished and tested and started off in a freight car to a branch for assembly into a finished car. Say that it reaches the branch plant so that it may be put into the assembly line at eight o'clock Wednesday morning. By noon the car will be on the road in the possession of its owner. If the motor, instead of being sent to a branch, goes into the assembly line for the Detroit district, then the completed car will be delivered before five o'clock Tuesday afternoon instead of at noon on Wednesday.

All of this is made possible by the transportation within the plant, the development of the Detroit, Toledo & Ironton Railroad, the dredging of the River Rouge, and the development of water transportation with our own ships. A few years ago, the River Rouge (which flows into the Detroit River and through the Detroit River connects with the Great Lakes) was only a shallow, winding stream from seventy-five to a hundred feet in width and not more than a nine-hundred-ton barge could come up to the factory docks. It was then necessary to transfer the cargoes of the Great Lakes steamers to barges at the mouth of the River Rouge and tow them up. Now we have a shortcut canal, reducing the distance from the lake to our turning basin from nearly five miles to three miles. The canal and river have a surface width of 300 feet and an average depth of twenty-two feet - which is sufficient for all of our purposes.

Since the completion of the dredging, we have been building a Great Lakes fleet and now have four vessels, two of which, the Henry Ford II and the Benson Ford, are somewhat unusual in that they are driven by Diesel engines and are designed not only to carry the greatest possible amount of ore, but also to give the officers and crew what are practically first-class hotel accommodations. These boats are each 612 feet long and will carry 13,000 tons of coal or ore. As with everything in our industries, these boats are designed to operate with the smallest possible number of men and are kept spotlessly clean.

The engine rooms, for instance, are finished in gray and white enamel, with nickel-plated trimmings. Both the officers' and the crew's quarters are finished in hardwood, with shower baths enough for everyone. The heat is electrical, and all the auxiliary machinery, such as pumps, windlasses, and winches, is electrically driven. These boats are used only on the Great Lakes, but, as far as possible, we are locating our branches on navigable waterways. The Memphis and the St. Paul plants are on the banks of the Mississippi River; the Jacksonville plant is on the St. Johns River, with docks for ocean freighters; and the Chicago plant is on the Calumet River, which flows into Lake Michigan. Our Green Island plant is at Troy, near the confluence of the Hudson and the Mohawk rivers. This plant connects with the Kearny, New Jersey, plant by boats on the Hudson. It is less expensive to load boats than freight cars, and the transportation by water in this case is not only faster than by rail but also is cheaper.

A further development has been serving the Atlantic Coast plants at Norfolk, Virginia; Jacksonville, Florida; New Orleans, Louisiana; and Houston, Texas, directly by steamships going out through the Great Lakes and the canals. These vessels deliver on the coast about as quickly as do the railroads, and we have the added advantage of providing special racks and the like aboard the ships, so that our engines and larger parts do not have to be crated. This is applying the single purpose machine idea to the ocean steamship - just as we have applied it to the freight car.

Carrying out the same thought, we are organizing an ocean fleet, a part of which has been in operation for more than a year, to our European branches, to our South American branches, and to our Pacific Coast branches. Loading "loose" on these steamers saves us about twenty thousand dollars in crating alone on each trip, in addition to a large saving in cargo space. On two shipments to the Pacific Coast, we saved more than seventy thousand dollars as against shipping by rail. We now have five units in the ocean service and will add as many more as necessary. On all of them we are using Diesel engines. For transatlantic shipments we mostly load at our plants at Kearny, New Jersey, and Norfolk, Virginia, and for the care of these vessels, as well as for the establishment of a new branch, we bought a shipbuilding plant at Chester, Pennsylvania.

On the ships on the high seas, as well as on the lakes, we have put into effect our wage and cleanliness policies and also our labor-saving devices. On our ships, we pay a minimum of $100 a month with board and room - and we board them well. The inclusion of board and lodging makes the rate higher than the shore rate - which is as it should be. We pay the captain and the engineers wages commensurate with the responsibilities they assume. On the whole, our wages will run considerably higher than the highest wages elsewhere paid. We make money on these wages, for really, the whole total of wages paid on a ship is not very important - the important thing is to see that you get the full use out of the big investment, which is the ship.

If a ship is held a couple of weeks in port unloading and loading, the loss will probably be greater than the total wages for a year. Low-priced, irresponsible men will not care what happens to a ship or how long it stays in port. Our men are on their toes to see that our ships are kept moving. They know they must do that to hold their jobs, for every one of our ships, no matter in what part of the world it may be, is held to schedule just as closely as a railroad train. We keep a constant check on every movement of every ship, and any delay has to be explained, and so it is a rare thing for one of our ships to be in port more than twenty-four hours.

There are a thousand economies to be brought about in ocean transportation. We are so new at shipping that we are only beginning to appreciate the vast savings which are so easily possible. These savings lie in every direction. There are too many men ashore getting commissions and brokerage fees and what-nots; there is almost no attempt at the scientific buying of supplies; the loading and unloading are about the same as they were a hundred years ago, and the element of time to the shipper is almost totally disregarded. A job at sea is as important as a job on shore - which will have to be recognized by the pay.

Modern business - modern life - cannot afford slow transportation.

CHAPTER 11
SAVING THE TIMBER

Getting something for nothing is the ideal of a common type of social reformer. But he does not go about it in the right way. It is not possible long to continue to get something for nothing, but it is possible to get something from what was once considered nothing. That is at the root of our efforts to save timber. We are trying to use as little lumber as we can. We use less wood each year, in spite of our ever-growing production, but still we use a great deal of wood, so we try to get the utmost out of every tree we cut. We treat each tree as wood until nothing remains which is serviceable as wood, and then we treat what remains as a chemical compound to be broken down into other chemical compounds which we can use in our business.

We save, not only lumber, but also we save transport by the carriage of wood instead of wood mixed with water - green wood. More than that, we carry only finished wood - parts all ready to go into assembly. Instead of paying freight on waste, we keep the waste and earn money from it.

Our work began six years ago in a small way - which is always the way we start. Already we are saving nearly one hundred million feet of wood a year by the salvage of old lumber - we buy only four tenths of one percent of the lumber used in our crates and packing. And in our forests and sawmills we have discovered that, instead of wasting at least half of the tree - which is usual - we need waste not a bit of the tree. Also we have discovered that lumbering need not be rough, ill-paid work. We have our minimum wage scale, and instead of lumberjacks, we have sober, self-respecting citizens working for us.

The tradition of lumbering is of waste - that is why wages are so low and the prices of lumber so high. The standing timber is cut ruthlessly and the brush is left to lie and invite forest fires. When the log finally gets to the sawmill, it is cut into commercial sizes of lumber regardless of the waste. There are two wastes here - the waste of the log and the waste of the finished lumber, for our commercial sizes are based, not on use, but on custom.

The whole lumbering industry lacks coordination. Why should one have to buy a ten-foot plank if only five feet are to be used? Why should not crating be done with the smallest instead of the largest amount of lumber, and above all, why cannot large users of lumber - whose needs are not large enough to justify going into the lumber business themselves - at least arrange with mills for special sizes instead of taking the commercial sizes? Why should a crate or a packing box once used be considered only as so much waste to be smashed and burned?

Saving timber is as much a matter for the shop as for the forest. We are now using much less lumber in our cars than we did before. We have shifted to steel whenever and wherever possible, just to save wood. The supply of steel is inexhaustible, while at the present rate of consumption the country's wood will hardly last beyond fifty years. Our own supply will easily last us a hundred years in the manner we are using it.

Not so many years ago, we looked at wood simply as wood, but, abhorring waste, we soon began digging in to find out what we were doing with wood. We had made arrangements for burning the sawdust and scraps from our wood-working department as fuel, and on the surface it seemed as though we were getting the utmost out of what was considered waste, and that, as usual, brought us to asking the question: "Why should there be so much waste to dispose of?"

Answering that question has taken us into the salvage of all the wood that comes into our plants in crates and boxes, it has taken us into the buying of large tracts of forest land, into logging, into sawmills, into wood distillation, and finally into removing all our woodworking departments from Detroit to the forests in order to save transportation.

First take the salvage of wood at the plant. Only six years ago, we used around six hundred different size boxes and crates for shipping. We studied the shipments and the boxes, and today, instead of six hundred sizes, we have fourteen sizes, for each of which a standard method of packing has been devised. We are cutting farther into wood by using wherever possible burlap bags and cardboard boxes - the latter made from waste and in our own paper mill. We now need, under this simplified plan and because of the burlap and cardboard, only about one third as much wood as when our daily production was one half of what it is today.

We have a positive rule in every factory and branch that each crate and box must be opened carefully without breaking the wood. Crowbars are not permitted, and at any point where the incoming freight is heavy, we have a kind of hoist which clutches and pulls the top off a box without damaging the wood. All scrap wood eventually gets back to the wood salvage department at Highland Park - even old box cars from the railroad, rotted logs, and piling must go to this department, which has developed a rather interesting salvage technique.

The lumber arrives in all shapes and sizes and mostly studded with nails and spikes. It is sorted into heavy lumber and light lumber. Heavy stuff - one to two inches and over - is placed on the south conveyor; the lighter stuff - one half to an inch - goes to the conveyor on the north.

Just inside the swinging doors of the south conveyor entrance stands an ordinary punch press, mounted, however, with tool-steel cutters which meet at an angle of forty-five degrees. Heavy planks and boards which contain crooked nails are removed from the conveyor at this point and turned over to the operator. To hammer those nails straight would take time. Unless they are made straight, they will not come out. Unless they are pulled out, a sizable portion of the lumber is fit only for the furnace. The operator feeds the boards to the press, which bites the nails off sharply close to the board. A claw-hammer or gooseneck bar does the rest, and the entire board- barring serious flaws - is saved for sawing, re-sawing, and planing to box size.

A smaller press does the same for the lighter boards that enter on the north conveyor. Much of the lighter stuff needs no further treatment, and is simply sent on to where the boxes are being constructed; for the close-clipped nails will not in the least interfere with its use. Where it is desirable to have the nails completely removed, we have a simple device. This is a hook-shaped band of tool steel, five inches wide and a quarter inch thick, bolted through the shank to the surface of a table, with the hook end curling upward. Where the barb should be, if it were really a hook, are projecting teeth about an inch in length chamfered on the underside. A few blows with a hammer loosen the nails. The board is drawn across the teeth, the nail heads catching in the narrow tooth intervals. A little pry, and the nails fall, six or eight at once, from between the teeth. After being thoroughly cleaned, the lumber moves on to the sawyers' tables to be cut into standard thicknesses, widths, and lengths. As the sawing progresses, flawed boards are separated from the sound. In a given lot of lumber, not a few long planks are usually found. Their surfaces are often in bad condition, and always they are too thick for box factory use. Such planks are cut twice across their thickness on the band saw, and the resulting boards of standard thickness are put through a planer which turns them out with new surfaces.

The lumber moves forward always by conveyors and eventually comes through ready cut for size to the box factory. Other conveyors take the lumber which may be used for cleats, blocks, and mats to their proper departments.

What is left is carried on a conveyor to a chute, which leads to a sawdust machine below. The sawdust which results is drawn by suction into two accumulators on the roof. From here a blower forces it through a large pipe that carries it into the furnace room.

The box factory also supplies, over and above its quota of containers, any amount of specially shaped blocks and cleats for shipping and packing automobile parts, such as radiators and generators; tiny wooden forms used in the coil unit assembly; and joined wooden mats for the whole organization. In addition, it manufactures new shipping lumber, whenever this becomes necessary.

The short pieces of heavy lumber are used in many ways. For instance, a standard carload of one hundred motors requires 750 feet of heavy lumber for packing and bracing. A number of these planks have to be exactly 8 feet 6 inches long. We have devised metal splice plates to make up these big timbers out of shorter pieces.

And not the least interesting feature of this whole department is that many of the men are sub-standard and would be unable to do hard, exacting work. They are salvaged in the process of salvaging.

Our lumbering activities have gone far afield from lumbering and have developed into a big industry. It is truly remarkable how far afield the pursuit of waste will take one and equally surprising are the results, for by following out the by-products, one gets the original material sought for next to nothing. It is really hard to say which is the product and which is the by-product. That has happened to us in wood. In order not to be a party to wood waste - for we use about a million feet of lumber a day - we bought nearly half a million acres of timber land in northern Michigan, in addition to 120,000 acres in Kentucky. The Kentucky property is as yet undeveloped. Incidentally, most of the land we bought had not proved profitable to its owners because of transport troubles. We always prefer - as in iron - to take abandoned property and make something of it.

The original purchase was an old government land grant to the Michigan Land & Iron Company. Later, an English syndicate took this over, and it was from them that we bought. Most of the timber lies in alternating sections though there are large and scattered miscellaneous holdings, including considerable iron-bearing property. The next purchase was 70,000 acres of timber land at L'Anse. This included a large sawmill, thirty houses, and a narrow-gauge railway to the logging section. We have rebuilt this line as a standard-gauge system and connected it with the main line. About the same time, 30,000 acres were taken over at Pequaming, a town nine miles east of L'Anse. This also included a modern mill with excellent docks, two tug boats, twenty miles of standard-gauge railroad, and the entire town of Pequaming. Both of these towns are on the shore of Keweenaw Bay, Lake Superior, and have the advantage of shipping by water.

Our work centers about Iron Mountain, which was a typical Northern lumber and mining town that had all but passed away after the country had been cleared of timber. An iron mine and a sawmill were the only industries before we put up our plants, and there were many vacant stores and dwellings. The whole country was done. Now we have 5,000 men up there and it is a new country again. Long-closed shops reopened their doors, and the young men have stopped going to the cities - they can earn six dollars a day at home.

In other words, this whole region has been brought to life, not by the discovery of anything new, but by using what was already on hand-and considered worthless.

Start at the beginning and trace the operations. Start with the forest and the lumber camps. We cut no trees under twelve inches, the young ones being allowed to grow and provide the future supply. We cut with a band saw driven by a little gasoline motor. This will fell a tree twenty-six inches in diameter in forty seconds, or one twentieth of the time required by hand. Also, it will cut close to the ground, saving a deal of lumber that formerly was left in the stump.

The greatest cause of deforestation is forest fires. Most of these are caused by accumulated brush - the dried limbs and branches left from logging operations. Our lumberjacks bum the brush as fast as it is cut, although the old-timers swore that green brush could not be burned. This is the best method of fire protection yet devised. Nature will provide the second crop of timber if given half a chance. It costs about $1.25 per thousand feet to burn the brush, but it makes it so much easier to skid logs out of the woods that seventy-five cents of this is recovered, making the net cost only fifty cents, which is not too much to pay for fire protection and the speeding up of the remaining growth.

We use tractors almost exclusively. At the Sidnaw camp the tractors are six times as efficient as horses, hauling twice as large loads and making three times as many trips per day. These tractors are generally equipped with crawlers, this type of equipment being very efficient in the snow. The sleds are built with exceptionally wide tracks, and the tractor runs between these. The tracks are iced every night, and a road gang keeps them in good repair.

At L'Anse and Pequaming, railroads run far into the woods and connect the camps with the mills or the main line. More than thirty miles of new track have already been laid, some of the rails having been salvaged from the D. T. & I. equipment when heavier rails were put down. The logging camps are just as clean as our other plants. Living conditions are healthful and sanitary, and while this cleanliness was considered outrageous by some of the old lumberjacks, the class of young men the company is now getting appreciates it. Running water, steam heat, and electric lights are in all the larger camps. The old built-in bunks have been abolished. At some of the camps there is a housekeeper, usually the wife of one of the men, who makes the beds and does the washing and mending. A recreation hall or clubhouse is provided for the men during their leisure, it being understood that the bunk houses are places to sleep in. Moving pictures and the radio offer diversion that was impossible a few years ago.

The lumberjack is paid at the rate of six dollars a day for eight hours' work, and he is charged a moderate amount for his board and lodging. This brings him at least four dollars a day net, which is very high pay for the woods, particularly when the employment is steady for seven or eight months of the year. The pay and the conditions of work have attracted the best men from everywhere. Although our wages are supposed to be high, our logging costs are very low.

The logs come in to Iron Mountain by rail or by water, and it is there that we have made our largest developments in the direction of eliminating waste.

We have several sawmills, but the largest is at Iron Mountain, which cuts as much as 300,000 feet of lumber a day when running at capacity speed.

In January, 1924, we introduced a new method of sawing which made all previous records for economy look ridiculous, for the new system reduced waste and scrap to negligible quantities. This consists of sawing the body parts direct from un-edged planks as they come from the log. Heretofore, body parts were made from kiln-dried boards which had been sawed to uniform size and graded. These boards had been produced at a sacrifice of much of the youngest and best wood in the log, and if the log happened to be curved or irregularly shaped, the scrap often exceeded the merchantable lumber obtained.

The new system is to saw the log into parallel planks, leaving the bark on. These planks are cut without regard to the shape of the log. In fact, the shape of the log or the plank is of no consequence. The plank is then taken to the layout table, where patterns of various shapes are marked out until the plank is completely covered right up to the bark. Any irregularities, such as the swell of the butt, are taken advantage of. Instead of trimming the board to avoid a knot or check, the layout man simply goes around it. This method permits the utilization of nearly all the wood, and very little scrap remains. The various parts are then sawed from the board with a high-speed band saw. From 25 to 35 per cent. more body parts may be obtained from logs than under the old method where the log was "squared" and the boards edged and trimmed. In addition to that, branches not under four inches in diameter may be cut up into body parts. Heretofore, the branches, on account of their irregularity, were useful only as fuel or for wood distillation.

We calculate that this method will make our forests last one third longer than under the old way of sawing, and perhaps they will last forever if we learn how properly to reforest. The present savings are about twenty thousand dollars a day.

Once sawed, the parts are sent to the dry kilns. We have 52 kilns. Body parts are loaded on special trucks, each with a capacity of 1,122 cubic feet. A kiln holds 36 of these trucks, making the total capacity of each kiln 40,392 cubic feet of body parts. The kilns are kept full all the time and every time a truck is taken out, another is pushed in. Accurate records are kept of each truck load and it is not removed until an analysis shows the moisture content. Green wood contains about 40 percent water, which is dried down to 7 percent before it leaves the kiln. About twenty days is allowed for drying, the exact time depending upon the thickness of the cellular structure of the wood. There is less end-checking and warping by drying shaped parts than there was when the boards were first dried and then sawed into parts. The time required for proper drying has also been reduced by approximately ten days.

Clear lumber is dried in the open air. This is not used for small body parts. It would be waste to cut up clear lumber when smaller lumber is just as strong.

Precedent had it that parts could not be cut from green lumber and afterward kiln dried. It was declared they would warp and crack. We have had no trouble. We found that what was supposed to be trouble was due to improper stacking and the uneven introduction of the steam.

The savings in lumber to this point through cutting close to the ground, through sawing the log directly into the shapes required, and by improved kiln drying amount to about 50 percent. But now we have gone still further by manufacturing the parts completely at Iron Mountain, and not only do we cut out the transport of waste wood and water, but also we use the waste.

The central feature of Iron Mountain is the power house which coordinates with the sawmill, the dry kilns, the body making plant, and the wood-distillation plant, and we get a deal of our power as a by-product. The power house was put up, by the way, in the dead of winter with the thermometer sometimes going as low as thirty degrees below zero.

Steam is required for heating the wood-drying kilns at five pounds per square inch pressure. Steam at 225 pounds pressure suitable for operating turbines can be produced at only 10 percent greater cost than that for the heating pressure. Thus, by developing steam in the power-house boilers at 225 pounds per square inch, passing it through turbines and "bleeding" low pressure heating steam from the turbines after a part of its available energy has been obtained, the steam is practically serving a double duty - supplying both power and heat.

The power house has several unusual features. The furnaces are designed to burn almost anything - refuse, sawdust, oil, tar, or powdered coal may be used as fuel.

Smoke from the power plant is delivered through a horizontal duct to the carbonization and distillation buildings of the wood-distillation plant, where the heat is used in drying wood previous to distillation and also in some of the chemical processes. Thus, much of the heat ordinarily wasted is recovered. The horizontal smokestack is ten feet in diameter in its main section, branching into nine-foot and five-foot diameter ducts which lead respectively to the carbonization building and the distillation building. The pipe is thirty-five feet above ground and is supported on steel towers. It is built of heavy steel plates and lined with magnesia and asbestos fire brick as heat insulators.

In addition to the power obtained from steam, we have introduced into the group of plants an additional 9,000 horsepower by damming the Menominee River two miles away. Three vertical water turbines are connected with the electric generators. This is one of the finest of our smaller power houses, being marble lined. All the fittings are nickeled.

The body plant is not unusual - little that we have is unusual. Our results come from coordination. But we save every scrap of wood and particle of sawdust. The plant is as clean as an office - but all our plants are that way.

The end of our lumbering comes in the wood-distillation plant. We chose the Stafford process instead of the old-fashioned oven process. The latter requires good-sized pieces of wood, while the Stafford process can use anything with a cellulose structure. Sawdust, shavings, chips, bark, corncobs, nutshells, or straw may be converted into charcoal and its by-products.

The first step in the distillation of wood is the transfer of chemical wood from the hot pond, which washes off all dirt and grit, to the chemical sawmill. The mill salvages all merchantable lumber, and only the refuse, combined with blocks sawed from branches and other unworkable timber, is sent to the drying department. The small branches and limbs have few commercial uses except as fuel, and the chemical plant therefore converts into valuable products great quantities of wood hitherto considered worthless, for transportation charges make its use as fuel too expensive.

The wood driers are cylindrical shells a hundred feet long and ten feet in diameter. They have an internal flue through which hot gas from the power-house stacks is forced, the gas passing down the flue, radiating its heat through the walls, and then passing back through the surrounding jacket, which is filled with wood. This is known as the counter-current method of wood drying and it thoroughly removes the water. The driers are set on a slight incline and rotate constantly. The dry wood leaves the shells heated to a temperature of 300 degrees Fahrenheit and is carried by a system of asbestos-covered conveyors to the retorts, where it enters through a gas-tight barrel valve.

The retort is a shell fifty feet high and ten feet in diameter, lined with fire brick. When the retort is started for the first time, a fire is built in it and the brick lining heated to 1,000 degrees Fahrenheit. The retort is then closed and the barrel valve turns the dry wood in. The heat retained by the fire-brick lining is sufficient to start the reaction which produces pyroligneous acid and charcoal. This reaction generates sufficient heat to make the process continuous. Meanwhile, the mass of wood moves slowly toward the bottom of the retort, the volatile substances being driven off. What gets to the bottom is pure charcoal, which is removed through another barrel valve.

The vapor is condensed, but the gas is not. All the gas goes to the scrubber, a tower fifty feet high, where it is thoroughly scrubbed and the condensable portion recovered as pyroligneous acid. The remainder goes to the power plant to be burned as fuel.

When the charcoal leaves the retort it drops from the barrel valve into a gas-tight conveyor which takes it to a rotating water cooler. This is a shell six feet in diameter with a ring of tubes through which water circulates, cooling the charcoal. From the coolers the charcoal goes to a set of conditioners, which stabilize it to prevent spontaneous combustion. It is then screened, the larger lumps being conveyed to storage bins while the smaller particles are pulverized and carried to the charcoal bins, which supply the briquetting department. Mixed with a special binder, this charcoal is briquetted for fuel. All briquette drying is done with waste gas from the power-house flues.

From the pyroligneous acid in the condensers, a wide variety of by-products may be recovered. The first step is the transfer of the acid from the condensers to storage tanks in the primary room of the distillation building, and into the primary stills. There it is broken up into tar, methyl alcohol, acids, and light oils.

The tar, upon further distillation, yields pitch, wood creosote, and flotation oils, all of which we use in our industries. The pitch is used for sealing batteries and insulating coils; the creosote as a preservative for poles, posts, and railroad ties, and the flotation oils for mining purposes.

The group of by-products containing the methyl alcohol and acid is first neutralized with lime and then passed to the stills which drive off the alcohol, the lime combining with the acetic acid to make calcium acetate. This is taken to the acetate drying room in semi-fluid form, partially dried on atmospheric drum driers, and finally dried to solid form in large wire belt driers. From there it goes to the acetate storage bins, and thence to the ethyl acetate department where it is mixed with ethyl alcohol and sulphuric acid to form ethyl acetate. Great quantities of this product are used in the manufacture of leather cloth for tops and upholstery.

The methyl alcohol coming off goes to the refinery and emerges as pure methyl alcohol and methyl acetone, useful as solvents or denaturing agents. The remaining oils are used as fuel.

Under this treatment, each ton of waste wood yields 135 pounds of acetate of lime, 61 gallons of 82 percent methyl alcohol, 610 pounds of charcoal, 15 gallons of tar, heavy oils, light oils, and creosote, and 600 cubic feet of fuel gas.

And these products of distillation, at the moment of writing, give a daily recovery which, in dollars and cents, amounts to around twelve thousand dollars.

And eventually we shall go much farther. There is wood enough in this country for everyone - when we learn to use it.

CHAPTER 12
TURNING BACK TO VILLAGE INDUSTRY

It has always been taken for granted that big business brings in its wake big buildings and great numbers of men working in these big buildings and going home at night to slums or hovels. And many well-meaning people have opposed big business because they saw in it only the slum with all that the slum means.

Big business animated only by the profit motive makes all this inevitable. The plants are concentrated, and they open up and shut down according to whether the getting is good or bad. Under these conditions the workman never has enough ahead in money to choose where he may live. And also he has been compelled for lack of transportation to live within walking distance of his work, or to spend a sizable part of his income and energy riding on crowded cars. He has had to take what he could get in the way of housing. And as long as industry believes in concentration and does not follow the wage motive, just so long will this condition continue.

But the remedy is not to be found in any charitable housing schemes. If you apply the wage theory to the building of houses, then it will be easily possible to build good houses which self-respecting people can live in at a rental they can pay. And the owners of those houses can earn a profit - any sort of operation well conducted will earn a profit. If it does not, something is fundamentally wrong with the plan. Turning to charity is always bad, but especially when applied to conditions brought about by industry. Industry, properly managed, can take care of itself and everyone connected with it. Charity merely covers up ills that ought to be and can be cured.

Big business, however, did not concentrate because there was anything in big business which made for concentration. Really big business cannot concentrate in one place, for the reason that transportation charges, aside from all other factors, discourage it. A great business has to have far-flung markets, and in these days it does not pay to transport heavy products, raw or finished, over long distances. But what, some years ago, was thought to be big business did concentrate.

Similar sorts of industries have always tended to group in neighborhoods. And big business simply followed little business because no one stopped to think that little business and big business have more important differences than size. There is a kind of business which just swells and becomes cumbersome and which is sometimes thought to be big business, but it is only little business suffering from elephantiasis. The big business which is worthwhile grows to power. It is not size without strength. It is great and quick and strong. Any business which truly serves must grow in resource and might - though that resource and might will quickly dwindle when the service which built it ceases.

There is now no reason at all for building a factory in a large city or near a "labor market," and there are many compelling reasons for not doing so. We started, as has been told in "My Life and Work," in a small brick building in Detroit, and some years later moved to a larger building, also in the city. When the time came for greater expansion, we moved out into what was then a suburb of Detroit - Highland Park - and there for years we made our automobiles. We grew so quickly that we followed the perfectly natural course of expanding Highland Park. We then were buying far more of the automobile than we made, and although Highland Park grew to be a factory, it was for a long time essentially an assembling plant. It was when we reached a production of one thousand cars a day and jammed the freight facilities of Detroit that we began seriously to examine into the wisdom of having so large a plant.

We approached the subject from several directions. First, it did not seem to be in the best interests of business in general to concentrate so much wage-purchasing power in a single locality, both because the people who bought our product ought to have some of the advantages of the sums disbursed in the making and also because our own men were becoming crowded and being profiteered upon. They were not getting value for the money they earned.

Second, the number of men became so large that the hours had to be so arranged that not too many men would get through or come on at the one time - otherwise transportation could not be provided. And having men going and coming all the while is not good for production. We have not for years been able to have a single pay day because of the general inconvenience it would cause, not only to ourselves and to our workmen, but to the community in general. To pay out some millions of dollars on a certain day each week would have made it necessary for the stores to carry idle stock against the payday rush; it would have been an invitation to crooks of all kinds to gather around on the one day when everyone had money, and it would have made local banking exceedingly difficult. On our own part, it would have made necessary a large payroll force, and even at the best, the men would have lost hours waiting for their pay. So now we pay in groups. Almost every hour of the day is pay day somewhere in the plants.

We have overcome the difficulties of handling large bodies of men, but that is not enough. It is better to avoid difficulties than to overcome them, and not only do we find it easier to manage smaller plants but also - which is most important - the costs of production in the smaller plants are lower. Any change in method which results in higher costs - no matter how public spirited it may, on the surface, seem to be, is bad if it increases costs. But that we do not have to bother about, for every change of real merit results in decreased costs.

Now, to go back a bit and start with the whole theory of manufacturing and big business and how inevitably it leads one away from the great cities.

Management is not something in an office building miles away from the product. It starts with the product itself, and then, step by step, works back. A fine machine is a good thing to look upon of itself, but in a factory no machine is worth giving floor space to unless it contributes exactly and according to a plan to the doing of whatever it is you have started out to do. There need be no guess-work about a machine. People used to talk about hand work as though it were better than machine work, but now the proper kind of machine will not only work to a thousandth of an inch, or to whatever degree of accuracy is necessary, but will do it every time. It is the fault of management if a machine or a series of machines leaves anything to be done by hand.

We used to think of a machine as a machine - as a thing which the employer owned and which could be used to make money for him. Now we know that a machine tool is a method for the application of power. A man can hit a harder blow with a hammer than he can with his bare fist - the man's power is increased by the extra force of the leverage of the hammer handle, and the wear and tear on the hammer head is substituted for wear and tear on his hand. The power hammer goes much farther than the hand hammer; it puts more power at the service of the worker. Therefore, the operator on a power hammer can do so much more, in a day than can a man with a hand hammer that he can earn for himself a larger wage than can the hand worker and at the same time produce a cheaper product.

A machine does not belong to the man who buys it or to the man who operates it, but to the public, and it advantages the worker and the proprietor only as they use it to the advantage of the public. It benefits the public when and only when it is used to turn out cheap, well made, well-designed articles that satisfy a public need. The workmen and the owner cannot expect to derive a benefit from the operation or from the ownership of the machine excepting as it benefits the public. We are learning that a machine is a public servant - that it is useful only as it serves.

A place which has power and which subdivides it through whatever number of machines may be necessary to accomplish a given object is a factory and it, too, pays only as it serves. The factory may generate its own power and perform within its own walls all the operations necessary for a complete product, or, again, it may buy its power and perform only a part of the necessary operations. Its course is surely determined by the measure of service which it has adopted. It means nothing to say that you carry your product from the raw material stage to the finished article unless, under your control, this process results in a cheaper product and a better one than you could achieve by assembling instead of manufacturing. The product alone governs - that is, the public governs. And seeing that it does govern is management.

We, all of us do many useless things solely through custom. Years ago the finished car was taken out and "tested," and then taken down for crating and shipping. Testing was something that could not be dispensed with. As a matter of fact, if all the parts are made accurately and inspected as they go through, then the assembly of those parts is bound to result in machines that are exactly alike, and there is no reason at all for making a final test. Silver dollars come from the mint all alike; so should it be with cars which are made according to our system.

The business of making parts to be assembled into an automobile brought up the question of whether these parts had all to be made under one roof. There seemed to be no escape from the big factory, and there could have been no escape if our main factory had to turn out a completely assembled product. But, having found that it was wasteful completely to assemble at the factory, the reason for complete construction in a single great factory or group of factories vanished.

It has been more or less taken for granted that a factory ought to be near what is called the labor market, because it has also been taken for granted that industry had to be intermittent. If a plant is continually shutting down and opening up again, it saves money to have at hand a fund of unemployed, skilled workers who can be put into operation without the delay and expense of training. A labor market means at the least a small city or some densely populated district. A district of this character, where a majority of people take unemployment as a natural condition, certainly cannot be prosperous, and the living conditions cannot approach those necessary for a decent standard of health. The workman receiving wages this month and none next month will be most of the time in debt to his grocer, butcher, and landlord - which means that his living costs him more than it should. A man who has to buy on credit because he is unable to pay cash is not in a position to question prices. The upkeep of a city is expensive and, therefore, taxes are high and land values are high.

Therefore, to get rid of the overhead of the big city, to try to find the balance between industry and agriculture, and more widely to distribute the purchasing power of the wages we pay among the people who buy our products, we began to decentralize.

We began our experiments in village industries seven years ago by taking over an old mill at Northville, about a dozen miles up the River Rouge, and turning it into a valve shop. The Rouge is only a little stream at Northville - scarcely more than a small creek - and, though we planned to use water power at the beginning, we are only now getting around to installing a turbine which will furnish a part of the power. We took the mill as it stood and sent thirty - five production men and the necessary machinery from Highland Park. Our idea was to draw the men from the surrounding country, but we had to make a start with more experienced workers, especially to set up the machinery.

The making of a valve is divided by us into 21 operations, and 300 men are now employed. Those valves cost us 8 cents each to make at Highland Park, and that was thought to be a low cost. Northville is turning out 150,000 a day at a cost of $3\frac{1}{2}$ cents a valve.

That is one part of the story. Here is a more important part. All the men live within a few miles of the plant and come to work by automobile. Many of them own farms or homes. We have not drawn men from the farms - we have added industry to farming. One worker operates a farm which requires him to have two trucks, a tractor, and a small closed car. Another man, with the aid of his wife, clears more than five hundred dollars a season on flowers. We give any man a leave of absence to work on his farm, but with the aid of machinery these farmers are out of the shops a surprisingly short while - they spend no time at all sitting around waiting for crops to come up. They have the industrial idea and are not content to be setting hens.

Now that the plant is well in operation, we take only employees from the district and none at all from Detroit.

The change in the country has been remarkable. With the added purchasing power of our wages, the stores have been made larger and better, the streets have been improved, and the whole town has taken on a new life. That is one of the ways in which the wage motive inevitably works out.

Years ago the Rouge River operated many little mills along its banks, but when we began at Northville, only a little flour mill at Nankin was operating. The power of the stream had simply been allowed to go to waste, and all the villages were dwindling. The best men had gone off to Detroit for higher wages. We took the stream in hand.

At Waterford, a few miles from Northville, we put up a one-story factory which employs fifty men making the measuring instruments and gauges used by the inspectors throughout our plants in testing parts for size. The water comes a half mile through an underground tunnel which we constructed. This water goes through a turbine directly connected with an electric generator and gives forty-seven horsepower. The turbine, as in all our new hydraulic plants, is in a glass case outside the factory just to exhibit to the public what water power can do.

Next down the river is the plant at Phoenix where there is a twenty-one-foot head of water and one hundred horsepower, although only twenty-seven horsepower is used. Here we make generator cutouts and in the operation make use of what would otherwise be scrap material from the Fordson plant and the Flat Rock plant - which is another little factory on the Huron River. The work is light and, excepting for a few operations and for repairs where mechanics are necessary, we employ only women from the surrounding country. There are at the time of writing one hundred and forty-five women and nine men, and we like to employ only those living within a radius of ten miles of the plant, although in a meritorious case we will stretch the distance. We do not take married women unless their husbands are unable to work, and we prefer the older to the younger women merely because it is usually harder for an older woman to get a job than it is for a young girl. One woman travels about fifteen miles a day to her work and rarely misses a day - she has a sick husband and four young children. Working eight hours a day, five days a week, she provides the family with a larger income than when her husband was able to work, and she still has time over for housekeeping. She. is unskilled in other than household duties, but our jobs do not require much training.

In this factory there is not a task which cannot be learned by any one of ordinary intelligence within a week. Some thirty of the women operate farms, and these women may have leave of absence at any time to attend to their farms. Forty percent of them have dependents. Most of the work is performed sitting in front of belt conveyors, and there are 18 operations. These women turn out 8,900 complete units every 8 hours, and they can go to 10,000 with the present staff and equipment if necessary, and while these pieces cost us 36 cents each when made at Highland Park, they cost only 28 cents in this factory. The women seem to like the work - we always have a long waiting list, and practically no one ever leaves excepting to get married. The women are paid at the same rate as men would be, and of course, the $6 a day minimum rate is in force.

Next down the river comes Plymouth, which is on the site of an old flour mill. It has a 15½ foot head of water and generates 26 horsepower, of which the plant uses 19 horsepower. It began making generator cut-outs, but that work was shifted to Phoenix, and now the factory turns out small taps used in threading operations in making car parts. We use about four thousand small taps a day and the factory now is up to a production of 2,000 and at a cost 10 percent less than we have to pay outside. Not only that, but we make better taps here of special steel chosen for the work the tap is to do, and there is thus another saving in the longer life of the tap. We employ 35 men and they make 40 different sizes of taps. As in all the village industries, no city men are employed; these men are from the farms and villages and while some of them have farms all at least have vegetable gardens. One man operates a farm of 13 acres, another a farm of 17, another a farm of 22 acres, and so on.

Nankin is our smallest plant. We took the old flour mill which had been standing for a century or more and converted it into a factory, at the same time preserving the old beams and all the features of the old mill excepting the dust and dirt. It is on a branch of the Rouge and we get about sixty horsepower from the turbine, of which we now use thirty. The machinery in this plant is wholly automatic, and it needs only eleven men to attend it. The parts made are very small - a day's production may be carried on a bicycle. But the number of parts made is enormous. For instance, the machines have turned out 124,000 little rivets used in the coil unit in a single day. The men all live nearby, and the plant furnishes electricity for their homes. Our costs of production are about 15 percent lower than when these same parts were made at Highland Park.

The river passing through my farm is dammed again and gives the power for my house and farm. We have, in all, nine sites on the Rouge for little water-power plants, and in the course of time we shall use all of them, for the production has proved to be economical, and we hope that we are finding the way to put industry and agriculture in the balance they should have.

The bookkeeping and management of these plants is very simple. The records show how much material goes in, how many finished articles come out, and how many people are employed. That gives all we need to know. In the smaller plants, the manager attends to the records as part of his duties, while where more men are employed, the manager has an assistant who, in addition to other duties, keeps the records. None of the plants have offices or clerical staffs. There is no need for them – and that is a saving in expense.

It is far from impossible that with automatic machinery and widespread power the manufacture of some articles may be carried on at home. The world has proceeded from hand work in the home to hand work in the shop, to power work in the shop, and now we may be around to power work in the home. Who knows?

On the Huron River we have two more hydroelectric plants bearing out the same idea of putting our factories in the country. At Flat Rock, twenty miles from Dearborn, is a dam which also serves as a railroad bridge, and a factory which we originally intended as a glass plant; but we turned it into a headlight factory. This little plant right out in the country employs an average of around five hundred men in two shifts, and it makes 500,000 headlights a month. Two men make up the whole managerial and office force.

Twenty miles up the Huron at Ypsilanti we have a larger plant developing 700 horsepower. The dam here backs up a lake covering 1,000 acres and also serves as a highway bridge.

At Hamilton, Ohio, we brought into control about five thousand horsepower through our hydroelectric generators, and gradually that plant is growing in importance, until now it employs around twenty-five hundred men and is passing out of the class of village industries. It manufactures wheels and a variety of small parts – the production of wheels has reached around fourteen thousand a day, owing to the improved machinery and methods which concentration on one kind of work inevitably brings about.

At Green Island, on the Hudson River, we have another large electrical development with upward of ten thousand horsepower, and the plant employs 1,000 men recruited from the neighborhood. We have found it most economical to put the whole of a plant under one roof, and at Green Island the building is more than a thousand feet long. It connects by canal with Detroit and by the Hudson River with the seaboard.

All of the above are plants, but in addition we have branches which also do a deal of manufacturing. The largest of these is at St. Paul. It completes a project undertaken by the government. During the war, work was begun on a dam 574 feet long to impound waters of the Mississippi above St. Paul so that the river would be navigable for grain carriers and other shipping bound up-stream. When the dam was built, the power possibilities of the site were recognized and the foundations for a power house were incorporated in the St. Paul end of the dam.

The power project lay idle until it was leased by the government to us. It is the second government power site developed by the Ford interests, for the dam at Green Island was also built by the government. In both instances we pay substantial rentals for the use of the dams.

The dam, which is about one city block long, provides for a head of 34 feet. On the Minneapolis side are locks to pass large river barges. On the St. Paul end the water enters the power house through "trash racks" extending the whole length of the upstream side. These racks prevent logs, trash, and ice from getting into the water wheels and other mechanism. The water, dropping 34 feet and controlled by wicket gates, actuated by automatic oil-operated governors, drives 4 horizontal water wheels of 4,500 horsepower capacity each. Each wheel is 20 feet in diameter. The water emerges under a platform 33 feet wide on the downstream side into a tailrace channel 150 feet wide excavated for 1,500 feet where it has a broad connection with the navigation channel, thus returning the water to this channel without high velocities that would interfere with navigation.

The water turbines are directly connected to electric generators by vertical shafts and are 28 feet below the main generator room floor level. The generators are 60-cycle, 3-phase, 13,200 volts. Each generator is about 20 feet in diameter and 18 feet high above the floor. They are located in a room 160 feet long by 35 feet wide and 36 feet high. All mechanical equipment is finished in enamel with polished nickeled trimmings. The floor is of red tile with black tile border. Walls are of pressed face brick. Large plate-glass windows flood the room with daylight. All power transmission lines on the property are underground.

The manufacturing and assembly building is of one-story construction and 1,400 feet long and 600 feet wide, having a floor area of more than nineteen acres.

Two underground tunnels lead from the 650-foot dock along the river, under the boulevard to the center of the plant, allowing river freight to be brought in and sent out without the least interference with boulevard traffic or damage to the natural scenery. Farther south, a third tunnel leads from the steam plant at the river's edge to a coal receiving platform beside the railway track east of the plant. Through this tunnel coal is brought by conveyor to the steam plant, and steam and water are carried to the assembly building.

Current for light and power is distributed from a central substation inside the plant. This substation is completely enclosed in steel and glass partitions. The motor generators contained in this unit draw their power from the hydroelectric and steam plants, which together can supply 28,000 horsepower. Exhaust steam is led into the building through the tunnel to an underground pump chamber. Here it is converted into hot water and in this form is pumped through the heating system of the plant. A separate hot water line extends around the building behind the roof gutters, to thaw ice and snow.

Oils for the painting and enameling departments are pumped from an outside oil house through pipes housed in a concrete tunnel terminating near the center of the building. From here the pipes run overhead to their destination.

At Los Angeles the branch plant makes bodies and as many parts as can be made more cheaply there than at St. Paul or Detroit. For cushions, the plant consumes cotton from the Imperial Valley and from Arizona at the rate of the yield of fifteen acres a day or the yield of about forty-five hundred acres in a working year - which is another example of the many directions in which carrying out the wage motive benefits the community.

It is this wage motive that has been behind all of our domestic and foreign extensions. As a matter of course, it results in lower costs. But it all goes to prove that big business, keeping service to the public always in mind, must scatter through the country not only to obtain the lowest costs but also to spend the money of production among the people who purchase the product.

We have never put in a plant anywhere without raising the purchasing power and standard of living of the community, nor without increasing our own sales in that community.

One cannot hope to live on a community - one must live in a community. And the results abroad in low wage countries have been even more noteworthy than at home - which will be told about in another chapter.

CHAPTER 13
WAGES, HOURS, AND THE WAGE MOTIVE

We are, as a matter of policy, against hard work. We will not put on the back of a man what we can put on the back of a machine. There is a difference in a man working hard and hard work. A man working hard will produce something, whereas hard work is the least productive sort of labor. It is not possible, except in the crafts which approach the arts, for a man to earn a really good living with his hands. It is management which has so to arrange work that it can be productive of high wages. But the starting point of high wages is the willingness to work. Without that willingness, management is powerless.

Somehow a deal of confusion has crept into wages, hours of work, profits, and prices. Most of this confusion traces back to an unwillingness on the part of someone to work - that someone may be a money broker, a manager, or a workman. Or again, all three may be trying to do the impossible - that is, to live without work. Nearly every social theory, when stripped of its emotional trimmings, gets down to a formula for living without work. And the world being what it is, none of these formulas can operate. They can only bring on poverty, for they are not productive.

The man who possesses health, strength, and skill is a capitalist. If he can use his health, strength, and skill to the best advantage, he becomes a "boss." If he uses himself to still better advantage, he becomes a boss of bosses - that is, the head of an industry.

And now take wages. An unemployed man is an out-of-work customer. He cannot buy. An underpaid man is a customer reduced in purchasing power. He cannot buy. Business depression is caused by weakened purchasing power. Purchasing power is weakened by uncertainty or insufficiency of income. The cure of business depression is through purchasing power, and the source of purchasing power is wages.

This country could not last any time on the purchasing power of those whose income is independent of what they receive from their work. This country is maintained by work. The evidence of work is wages. The effect of wages is the continuity of work. Reduce wages and you reduce work because you reduce the demand upon which work depends.

Wages is more of a question for business than it is for labor. It is more important to business than it is to labor. Low wages will break business far more quickly than it will labor.

The old theory, which still persists in business, is that the rate of wages depends on the bargaining power of the worker as against the monopoly power of the employer. Under that theory, both sides lost. Under that theory, labor unions rose and organized war began, with boycott and lookout as the weapons. Nothing more is needed than these results to prove the theory false. Yet it is clung to by old-line management and old-line labor with equal tenacity. They both are wrong.

It needs to be driven home to men's minds that such a theory represents nothing but the accommodation of their logic to their errors. The theory of wages in the past has been merely a description of the predatory spirit that once actuated money-making. There is no standard wage except that set by the energy, ability, and character of all who are engaged in the business. The basic fact is that the standard wage is what management and industry can make it. Upon managers more than upon political economists rests the responsibility of furnishing data for the new theory of wages.

A business that does not include a steady and profitable wage scale among the good things it produces is not a productive business. A business where the dividends are out of all proportion to the wages is perilously lopsided. Yet a business which should divide every last surplus dollar into wages would be in danger of extinction.

There are three factors in the situation: the manager, the employee, and the business. The business as a going concern must always be considered. It provides the worker with an outlet for his activity and the public with commodities and utilities.

The right kind of wage increase comes as a result of management having the wage motive. The way to check a threatened depression is to cut the price and increase the wage. High wages with high prices do not help anyone - it just means that everything has been marked up. But higher wages and lower prices mean greater buying power - more customers. Cutting wages is no cure for low consumption - it only makes the consumption still, lower, by reducing the number of possible consumers. One of the objects of industry is to create as well as to supply consumers. And customers are created by finding out what people want, making it at a reasonable price, and then paying high enough wages in the making so that they can afford to buy.

The payment of high wages, however, is not just a matter of wishing to pay them. Neither has the rate of wages much to do with the scale that workmen may ask for. It goes back much farther than that - it goes back to the very structure of the business itself and the idea on which it is founded.

We have heard a great deal about the profit motive being wrong. We have heard nothing at all about what might be called the wage motive. That is the only motive of any importance, for it brings in the whole of service, and when we have real service, the profits have a way of looking after themselves. It is the new modern motive that can control all industry for the public good.

The wage question does not start with the workman. It stops with him. It starts back on the drawing board of the employer. And before a pencil is put to paper the draughtsman - the employer - has to know what he wants to do. Is he going to create a thing which will help people or is he only going to create something to sell to people? There is a vast difference in the approach.

If you set out to make something which will help people, then you have to plan slowly and surely, trying out as you go along, until you have what you believe is right. Then, and not until then, have you anything worthwhile making.

The next step is to find out how to make it, and that is a job which is never finished. For this brings in quality, price, and wages. Your design - speaking of commodities - has to be such that it can be made by machinery. High wages can be paid in the making of luxuries and added into the price. If what has been thought to be a luxury can be manufactured in quantities at a low price, then it may become a commodity and a necessity - that is what has happened with automobiles.

If we set ourselves to the payment of wages, then we can find methods of manufacturing which will make high wages the cheapest of wages. And that keeps us always on the drawing board, finding ways and means to improve methods in every direction - in buying, in making, in selling, in transportation - so that prices may be lowered and wages paid.

The right price is not what the traffic will hear. The right wage is not the lowest sum a man will work for. The right price is the lowest price an article can steadily be sold for. The right wage is the highest wage the employer can steadily pay. That is where the ingenuity of the employer comes in. He has to create customers, and if he is making a commodity, then his own workers are among his best customers. We have about two hundred thousand first-class customers in our own company - in the people we directly pay wages to. And we are creating more customers every day in the workmen of the people we buy from. For every dollar we pay in wages, we pay two for materials and parts made on the outside. It is an ever-widening circle of buying - paying a high wage has the same effect as throwing a stone into a still pond.

There can be no true prosperity until the worker upon an ordinary commodity can buy what he makes. Your own employees are part of your public. The same ought to be true everywhere, but one of the difficulties in Europe is that the workman is not expected to buy what he makes. A part of Europe's trouble is that so much of its goods has gone abroad in the past that there is little thought of really having a home market.

If you cut wages, you just cut the number of your own customers. If an employer does not share prosperity with those who make him prosperous, then pretty soon there will be no prosperity to share. That is why we think it is good business always to raise wages and never to lower them. We like to have plenty of customers.

But buying labor is just like buying anything else - you have to make sure that you get your money's worth. Every time you let a man give you less than full value for the wage you pay him, you help to lower his wage and to make it harder for him to earn a living. You can do a man no greater injury than to allow him to "soldier" on his job. The reason ought to be plain. The less work a man does, the less purchasing power he creates, which means a lessened number of people to ask for his services.

Thus there can be no "standard wage." A wage based on a standard of living is destructive, for it implies that all men are alike and can agree on how they want to live. Fortunately, all men are not alike, and fortunately, only a few care to live this year the way they did last year. Any attempt to fix a "living wage" is an insult to the intelligence of both managers and workers. We do not know what the right wage is, and perhaps we shall never know. But certainly it only clogs progress to try to fix wages without the facts. The world has never approached industry with the wage motive - from the angle of seeing how high wages may be - and until we have had some experience in that line we shall not know much about wages.

Trade union limitations on production can never come up in a well-managed business. They are an answer to bad management. If an employer sells his product at too high a price, with his eye on profits instead of on costs, he will pay low wages, for he will not know what kind of men he needs. He limits his market by his price, and there is no reason why the men who work for him should not also limit their output. Why should men work for an employer who will not so manage his business as to pay proper wages?

We have been steadily cutting down the number of men employed per unit of output. If we can arrange the work or the machinery so that one man can do the work formerly done by three, then, of course, we put the change into effect at once. But that does not mean that two men are thrown out of work. Nobody with us ever thinks about improvements lessening the number of jobs, for we all know that exactly the contrary happens. We know that these improvements will lessen costs and therefore widen markets and make more jobs at higher wages. All of our efforts to reduce the number of men on the single job have resulted in more jobs for more men.

There is more to giving service than just the designing of machinery; there is more to management than merely the handling of men. Service is the low-cost production of high-grade goods, made by well-paid labor, and manufactured and distributed at a profit. No man can really claim to be in business until he has equipped himself to attain these objectives.

The theory that efficiency and better methods make for unemployment is pernicious, but it is widespread. It is widespread because so many men make their livings out of preaching it to workmen. It all goes on the theory that there is only so much work in the world to do and it must be strung out. The professional agitators insist that efficiency makes less work, fewer jobs, and decreases employment. They say that where two men conduct a process that formerly used eight, six men are thus left without work.

The fallacy of this has been proved over and over again and nowhere more effectively than in our own industries. Take England at the present time. Hand-in-hand with unemployment goes the preaching of the make-work theory. The British bricklayer, with kind intent toward his fellow bricklayer who is out of a job, is easily persuaded that if he will lay only half the number of bricks that he formerly laid, the bosses will have to hire his out-of-work friend to lay the other half. That is, he thinks he is creating two jobs where only one existed before, and so decreasing the evils of unemployment. But he does not make a job. He only increases unemployment by making bricklaying so expensive that few can afford to build houses. Instead of making a job for his friend, he more than likely loses his own job through "slackness in the building trade." Though England cries for houses, few houses go up. Working men's houses do not go up at all, the reason being that bricklayers will not lay bricks enough to make an honest day's work, and thus double costs are imposed upon a house, with the result that the workingman who should inhabit it with his family cannot afford to. Holding back in any service decreases opportunity. The way for the English bricklayer to make work for all his fellows in the trade is to do so much work in a day that house-building will be cheap - and since the country needs cheap housing, bricklayers will be needed.

Exactly the same principles apply to management. It is clear what the bricklayer should do. But we have had so much talk about the duties of workmen that we forget to talk about the duties of managers. Really, the slack workman is a product of slack management. The workman did not invent the scheme of getting something for nothing. He only copied those who employed him.

The manufacturer who gives his workmen as little as he can for their labor and the public as little as he can for its money is in like case with the bricklayer who will handle only half as many bricks as he can.

But many a manufacturer sincerely believes that he is paying the highest wages his business will stand. Perhaps he is. But no one knows what he can afford to pay until he tries. In 1915, we raised our wage from an average of two dollars and forty cents to a minimum of five dollars a day. Then we really started our business, for on that day we first created a lot of customers for our cars, and second, began to find so many ways to save that soon we were able to start our program of price reduction. If you set yourself a task, it is really remarkable how many other things grow out of doing that task. You simply cannot make a thing cheaply and well with cheap men. You have to get good men in order to keep the cost of production down.

We have no fixed scale of wages excepting that no wages must be less than six dollars a day - our present minimum - after a man has been broken in. We have that minimum because we set ourselves to paying it - in order to increase our business through making lower costs. We began with a five-dollar minimum and later we found that we could add a dollar more. But we have no rule as to what any job is worth. We pay according to the man, and more than 60 percent of the men earn above the minimum.

We have settled on the eight-hour day, not because eight hours is one third of a day, but because it so happens this is the length of time which we find gives the best service from men, day in and day out. Only caretakers work on Sundays anywhere in our industries. Sometimes the rule against Sunday work is violated by superintendents at distant points, but when called to account, we have yet to find one of these superintendents who could justify his Sunday work.

As with wages, hours are a matter for management.

Another point which we make is that no man can be allowed to consider himself as belonging to a particular craft and therefore barred from doing work outside his craft. We have an immense fund of men to draw on, and we do draw on them. We have on our payrolls men from nearly every nation on the globe and from every trade and profession, from accountants and aviators to zoologists and zincographers.

We place new employees where they are most needed, not always according to their previous training. We prefer to have men working in their trades rather than out of them, and so we keep a card index record of a man's previous training, if he cares to submit it, and from this source we constantly draw men. For instance, when the Dearborn flour mills were opened, the original millers came from Highland Park, where they had been working at something else. Experienced greens-keepers for the Dearborn Golf Course also came from the shop. Once, a man skilled in bas-relief work was needed, and the card index turned up a talented sculptor who was working on a drill press.

We do not believe in paternalism. When first we raised the wages to five dollars a day, we had to exercise some supervision over the living of the men because so many of them, being foreign born, did not raise their standards of living in accord with their higher incomes. That we entirely gave up when the need had passed.

We feel that a man ought to have savings enough to tide him over any crisis, but there are times when illness wipes out the savings, and then we arrange for loans. We have legal and real estate departments and stand ready, in fact, to render any reasonable service that is asked for.

We had to branch into store-keeping at Highland Park in 1919 because rents and prices were everywhere being forced up on our men, and it seemed useless to pay good wages if the men could not get value for them. At first, we went in only for groceries and drugs, but now we have butcher, clothing, and shoe shops, and also sell fuel. We have ten stores in all and they do a business of ten million a year at prices on an average of 25 percent below the market. The stores are restricted to our employees and executives and are on the cash-and-carry basis. We sell only first-class products, and some of them come from our own lands. A deal of the bread is made from flour raised on our land and ground in our mills. The coal, coke, and briquettes are all from our own properties.

Arranging to have the employees share in the profits of the business up to a degree presents many difficulties. We have devised a plan of investment certificates which seems to work out. These certificates are issued in denominations of $100 and are non-negotiable and non-assignable. They are paid for by the employees on the installment plan and have a guaranteed return of 6 percent, but additional payments may be made at the discretion of the Board of Directors. We have voted returns as high as 14 percent. The men's investments have reached as high as $22,000,000.

These are only details – things over and above wages. No service to employees will take the place of wages. The wage motive requires that the highest wages be paid, for not otherwise will the cycle of purchasing power be started.

Of necessity, the work of an individual workman must be repetitive – not otherwise can he gain the effortless speed which makes low prices and earns high wages. Some of our tasks are exceedingly monotonous, as was outlined in "My Life and Work," but then, also, many minds are very monotonous – many men want to earn a living without thinking, and for these men a task which demands no brains is a boon. We have jobs in plenty which need brains – we are always looking for brains – and men with brains do not long stay in repetitive work.

Highland Park plant assembly line fabricating magnetos and flywheels circa 1913.

After many years of experience in our factories we have failed to discover that repetitive work injures the workman. In fact, it seems to produce better physical and mental health than non-repetitive work. If the men did not like the work, they would leave. In 1913, in the Highland Park plant, we had an average monthly turnover of 31.9 percent. In 1915, we introduced the five-dollar-a-day minimum and the turnover dropped to 1.4 percent. In 1919, when labor was floating everywhere, the rate rose to 5.2 percent and now it is at 2 percent. Out of 60,000 men at the River Rouge plant, only about eighty men are in and out each day. Our turnover now is mostly due to illness or discharge for wanton and repeated disobedience.

Fully to carry out the wage motive, society must be relieved of non-producers. Big business, well organized, cannot serve without repetitive work, and that sort of work, instead of being a menace to society, permits the coming into production of the aged, the blind, and the halt. It takes away the terrors of old age and illness. And it makes new and better places for those whose mentality lifts them above repetitive work.

We need more creators than ever we did – not fewer.

And that the system is universal, we have proved by our plants and branches scattered over nearly every part of the earth, as will be shown in a later chapter.

CHAPTER 14
THE MEANING OF POWER

In Armenia, ten of our tractors introduced by a relief committee plowed 1,000 acres in eleven days. This work would have required 1,000 oxen, ten of our tractors introduced by a relief committee plowed 1,000 acres in eleven days. This work would have required 1,000 oxen and 500 men – and neither the oxen nor the men were available.

Ford on of one of his first tractors with a 1904 Model-B style engine in 1908.

In French Morocco, the Berbers still thresh grain by stamping with their bare feet on a small quantity placed in a bag. Three men can thus thresh about two bushels an hour. A threshing machine drawing its power from a tractor threshed ninety bushels an hour – that is, the machinery in one hour did as much as 135 men treading bags could do in the same period.

Russia has famines in spite of its immense areas of land suitable for cultivation, because its agrarian population cannot with primitive methods produce a sufficient surplus over and above their own requirements to feed the cities or, in emergency, to feed areas devastated by drought. Under present circumstances, if the surplus were produced, it could not be transported. When the Soviet Government asked our aid, we told them to buy automobiles before they bought tractors, in order to get transportation. That they did. Later they bought tractors, so that now they have from sixteen to twenty thousand tractors at work. In Russia they calculate that one tractor does the work of 100 oxen and 50 men. The saving is even greater than appears, because the upkeep of the oxen alone would ordinarily take a large portion of the crops harvested. It has not been difficult to teach the peasants to operate the machinery. The Russian peasant young man has an almost romantic regard for farm machinery.

Official tests of the tractor in England show that it costs, every factor being taken into consideration, just one half as much to plow with a tractor as to plow with horses.

The tractor is being used to revive the agriculture of Greece. There is hardly a country that has not some tractors.

Now, what does this mean? The peasants of many parts of Europe and of the Near and the Far East are poor beyond any knowledge that we have of poverty. Our poorest "poor whites" - even our tramps on the road, who are poor by profession - have more of this world's goods and certainly more comforts than most of these peasants. Even those who in this country will not or know not how to work for a living are really unable to be as poor as the peasant or the coolie.

And this is because we use so much developed power in this country that even the most ingeniously indolent cannot escape its effects. And at that we are using only a small fraction of the power we ought to use, and much of what we are using is being used wastefully. Of that, more later.

One point stands out above all others. This country uses many times more developed power per head than does any other country. We use far more in our factories - which is significant and easily comprehended. But what is much more significant and not so easily comprehended is that we use many times more power in transportation than we do in manufacturing. A very liberal estimate of all the power used in industry is 50,000,000 horsepower, while our own company alone up to December 1, 1925, had put out in cars and tractors a total available horsepower of 292,007,030. By no means all of these cars and tractors are still in service, but it is likely that more than 80 percent of them are, and to their power must be added the power contributed by all the other automobile and tractor makers, and also the power developed on the railroads.

The effect of cheap and convenient transportation is profound. It is not so long ago that a man of moderate means would live and die within a hundred miles of the place where he was born. His mode of living would differ little from that of his father, and indeed of his forefathers. That is still true throughout most of the world today but it is not true in America. One may see standing outside of almost any large building operation workingmen's cars bearing the license plates of half a dozen states. Nobody has ever disputed that the best of all education is to be gained from travel, but travel was formerly the prerogative of the well-to-do. Now, everyone can and does travel. Our state boundaries mean nothing - we could not have a war among our states because we have no cloistered states with separate identities and interests. Our Civil War could not be repeated. If Europe had cheap and easy transportation, the present artificial barriers between countries would quickly vanish because they would be an intolerable nuisance.

It is not strange, therefore, that transportation has almost wholly changed this country. The railroads built the country by making the exchange of products easy and convenient, but it remained for the automobile to break down all the barriers, because a railroad can only follow its tracks, while an automobile can go anywhere. We no longer have any really isolated districts. We have no states or sections set apart from the world, excepting here and there in the mountains, and the number of people so isolated is negligible when compared to the whole population.

And so, too, the wants of the people are increasing and the general standard of living in this country has probably increased more rapidly within the past fifteen years than in all the years previous.

Having a high standard of living may or may not be civilization - that we do not know. But we think that civilization in terms of material well-being indicates a degree of intellectual well-being, for without economic independence there can certainly be no intellectual independence. If a man spends twelve hours a day hunting his daily bread, he is not going to have much time over for clear thinking. It is natural and proper that this new era into which we are entering should be distinguished for the time being by the devotion of much of our power resource to transportation.

The automobile is not a thing of itself - it is just a way of using power. Our civilization - such as it is - rests on cheap and convenient power.

The nation started with water power but could handle only small quantities of it with the water wheel, which wasted more power than it used, and so with the invention of the steam engine, the fine natural force of flowing water was disregarded for coal power made workable through the steam engine. Now, with the ability cheaply and conveniently to transport power in the form of electricity, we are able through the water turbine to handle any amount of water power and to transport it as electricity with all the advantages of quantity production. Coal, we have learned, is not merely to be burned for its heat, but is a valuable chemical, of which heat is only one of the by-products. This heat energy is used to create steam, and through a steam turbine finally turned into electrical energy. Then we have the internal combustion engine, such as is used in the automobile with volatile oils, and in the Diesel engine with heavier oils.

We have more sources of power than ever before, and we are looking around for additional sources. There is somewhere ahead of us the utilization of atomic energy. We are everywhere searching for more and more power.

The wasteful little public utility power station is giving way to the big, centrally located power station. We are beginning to realize that the political and financial conception of developed power as something to regulate and jockey with is antisocial. Our public service commissions, with their regulation of rates, should not be allies of the financial forces which think of a generating plant as something on which to pile quantities of stocks and bonds, the returns on which are to be secured, not by serving the public but by a franchise, a monopoly, granted by some public service commission. We, the people, actually pay tax money to support commissions whose sole duty it is to see that public utility corporations shall not be allowed to ruin themselves through bad management. It is just another case of how ill-informed reformers play into the hands of shrewd financiers. These commissions were erected at the behest of the reformers to save the people from excessive charges by public service corporations - as though the people would have paid excessive rates. The public quickly reforms an ill-managed corporation by not buying its product, but the commissions which stepped in ostensibly to save the people really only save the corporations from their own folly.

Thus we have a situation in which the public service corporation is guaranteed some kind of an existence, regardless of its management. This is against the interests of the public because the corporation is not put into the position of either serving or going out of business. The public interest demands that corporations be thrown in to sink or swim. No one need worry about corporate oppression, for giving bad service destroys more quickly than can law. But the hopeful sign is that men are every day learning that the real profits of power generation are to be earned through giving it cheaply and conveniently to the public, and that, as compared with these profits, the profits of financial juggling are petty.

The source of material civilization is developed power. If one has this developed power at hand, then a use for it will easily be found. One way to use the power is through a machine, and just as we often think of the automobile as a thing of itself instead of as a way of using power, so also do we think of the machine as something of itself instead of as a method of making power effective. We speak of a "machine age." What we are entering is a power age, and the importance of the power age lies in its ability, rightly used with the wage motive behind it, to increase and cheapen production so that all of us may have more of this world's goods. The way to liberty, the way to equality of opportunity, the way from empty phrases to actualities, lies through power; the machine is only an incident.

The function of the machine is to liberate man from brute burdens, and release his energies to the building of his intellectual and spiritual powers for conquests in the fields of thought and higher action. The machine is the symbol of man's mastery of his environment.

One has only to go to other lands to see that the only slave left on earth is man minus the machine. We see men and women hauling wood and stone and water on their backs. We see artisans clumsily spending long hours and incredible toil for a paltry result. We see the tragic disproportion between laborious hand culture of the soil and the meager fruits thereof. We meet with unbelievably narrow horizons, low standards of life, poverty always on the edge of disaster - these are the conditions where men have not learned the secrets of power and method - the secrets of the machine.

To release himself to more human duties, man has trained beasts to carry burdens. The ox team and camel represent man's mind plus brute strength. The sail is man's release from the slavery of the oar. The use of the swift horse was man's dim sensing that time had value for himself and his concerns.

Did man thus increase his slavery, or did he increase his liberty?

It is true that the machine has sometimes been used by those who owned it, not to liberate men, but to exploit them. This was never accepted by society as right. It has always been challenged, and as the use of the machine became more widespread, it effectually checked the misuse that had been made of it. The right and serviceable use of the machine always makes unprofitable and at last impossible the abuse of it.

That is our idea of the import of the machine. But behind the machine is power and especially hydroelectric power. We already have nine hydroelectric plants, and two of them we developed from government dams - that is, we took over the dams and added hydropower plants to conserve the power which was going to waste. We are increasing our Fordson power plant so that it will soon have an output of approximately half a million horsepower. We have bought our own coalfields so that our supplies of coal might not be interrupted, for in 1922 we had to shut down for several days and throw hundreds of thousands of men out of work just because the controllers of the miners and the controllers of the mines could not agree upon wages and terms of work.

Of the two dams leased from the government, one is at St. Paul and the other at Green Island - both of which plants have been described in an earlier chapter. On another very large plant, we made a bid which was never acted on by Congress. That is Muscle Shoals, which is a large water-power unit capable of developing several hundred thousand horsepower and erected by the government for the fixation of atmospheric nitrogen during the war. It has not been completed, and it represents a large amount of money and - what is more important - a large amount of potential power going to waste in a section of the country that is in need of power. Our intentions concerning Muscle Shoals were set out in "My Life and Work," but later we withdrew and the reasons for our withdrawal were given in an interview with the collaborator of this book which was published in Collier's Weekly. In that interview I said in part:

More than two years ago, we made the best bid we knew how to make. No definite action has been taken on it. A simple affair of business which should have been decided by anyone within a week has become a complicated political affair. We are not in politics and we are in business. We do not intend to be drawn into politics.

We have been and still are deeply interested in Muscle Shoals as a national asset. That concerns every one of us as citizens. I have two main principles with regard to Muscle Shoals; first, it should be operated as a combined industrial unit; second, it should make nitrates which will serve as fertilizer in times of peace and as the basis of munitions in time of war. The manufacture of nitrates, of course, would not exhaust the power. The larger part would be available for general manufacturing. But first of all Muscle Shoals should be jealously watched by the nation as a most important defensive source. It is shameful that it has become the football of politics. The best way to maintain it as a ready defense source in war is to operate it as an industrial unit in peace. Its proper utilization will give the South that industrial impulse and facility which it needs. To permit it to be exploited would be a grave error.

We have in all sixteen mines in Kentucky and West Virginia, and when we took over the first mine some years ago it was with the full realization that we were entering an industry about which we knew little or nothing, which was strongly unionized in most sections, and in which the highest business practices had never found a foothold. Coal mining is one of our most backward industries. Our problem was to pay our standard wages, to provide a full year's work for the miners, and to put all industrial affairs on a man-to-man basis - the only basis on which we operate.

First of all, we cleaned up the mines and their surroundings - a mine can be clean. Such of the houses as were not worth painting, we replaced with good houses that had bathrooms, we put down sidewalks and hard surface roads, we put in street lights and a recreation building, and tried in every manner that we knew to make the little towns into first-class places in which to live. We put in our regular wage scale, and the men are now earning about twice as much as other miners in the field. The miners have proved themselves to be fine fellows - they only needed the chance. And their outlook has been broadened - in one camp alone some two hundred men now own automobiles.

During the summer months we ship coal to the head of the lakes to store an industrial supply for the Northwest. This helps to keep our mines in operation all the year round. Any reductions which may be necessary in our working force on account of seasonal conditions are always very slight and we never take any men off the payroll or reduce their wages. For some of the men we find work in cleaning up around the mines and the towns; other men we send to the Fordson and give them jobs until full mine production is needed. Part of our surplus coal we ship on our own lake boats out to the Northwest, where it is handled in carload lots by our sales agents. But there is not a great deal of surplus - our own plants will shortly take all that we can produce.

One of the curses of coal mining - one of the curses of all trades - is that often a man will remain idle unless work in his particular line shows up. No man in our employment considers himself as fixed in any particular line of work; he is ready, whenever the necessity arises, to take on some sort of work he may never have heard of before. It is not good for the country to have men regard themselves exclusively as miners, engineers, or machinists. Every man is the better for having several strings to his bow. We are planning to locate industries near the mines to have interchangeable employment, and probably we shall eventually generate a large portion of our power at mines.

Our coal costs us less than the market price over a period, although we have done little in the way of devising new methods of mining; we merely use machinery wherever possible and cut out the red tape of fixed jobs.

We could often buy distress coal for less, but we do not want coal which represents a loss to the producers - we cannot afford to be a party to a speculative product.

In the use of the coal at the Fordson power house we have the advantage of big business in being able to treat coal as a chemical, use the derivatives in our business, and burn what remains. We use both the high temperature and the low temperature distillation of coal, although, on the low temperature, we are just making a beginning. The processes are well known - most of our processes are well known. It is the combination of processes that counts. And the result is that out of coal which costs us about five dollars a ton delivered at the plant, we get a good return per ton out of by-products which gives us fuel for the boilers at a very low cost. We decided after a long research that the most economical way of using steam was through the turbine, and we shall soon have eight turbines of 62,500 horsepower each at the Fordson. Some of these are already in operation, and all of them we are building ourselves because they are of our own design and also because we found that we could turn them out ourselves faster than any manufacturer could guarantee delivery. These turbines are identical. One of the outstanding features is the generator. It is one third less in size than any other of the same capacity, and it is the first on which all-mica insulation has been used. It also uses a radically different system of ventilation from that used on other generators. It delivers current at 13,200 volts.

Each of these units produces as much power as the whole Highland Park power house.

The boiler equipment consists of eight boilers, with double-ended furnaces using powdered coal and blast furnace gas as fuels. The gas entering near the bottom of the furnace and the powdered coal 25 feet above are so proportioned in amounts, and the interior of the boiler is so arranged, that they will reach a maximum temperature before striking the boiler tubes. After these gases have passed over the boiler tubes, they circulate through super heaters to the tops of the boilers, the interior height of which is 70 feet, and thence up the eight 333-foot brick stacks, which furnish a natural draft.

Very little smoke, however, comes from the stacks, for combustion is practically complete, owing to the nature of the fuels. Not only is there a maximum production of heat by this process, but the proportion of heat that may be transferred to the water averages as high as 90 percent.

Another economy of such a fueling process is the lack of ashes and slag, there being only a small residue left in the furnace, as against a much larger amount when coal is burned in strikers.

When boilers are subjected to the high temperature caused by such efficient fueling, the furnace walls are apt to settle and crack, increasing maintenance costs. This is partially overcome by supporting the boilers from an overhead steel framework, rather than by employing foundations directly beneath.

The use of fuels which combine so thoroughly in burning, together with the practice of feeding the boiler with condensed steam (with distilled water for the make-up), to eliminate trouble from boiler scale, makes possible the continuous operation of the boilers night and day for six months or a year instead of the usual shutdown every two months or so. In line with this is the equipment which makes possible a shift of fuels from coal and gas to tar and oil in cases of emergency. Such a change may be made without shutting down the furnace and without lowering the temperature or in any way the operating efficiency of the apparatus.

The only tools in this boiler house are a slice bar, a poker, and a shovel. These are nickel plated and in a glass case! The entire interior of the boiler house is painted dark gray and enameled, and the attendants dress in white uniforms and caps. One attendant watches four furnaces, and it is his duty, after the flow of gas has been set at the proper amount, so to regulate the speed at which the coal is fed as to maintain a constant steam pressure in the boilers.

The steam generated enters the turbines at a pressure of 230 pounds per square inch and a temperature of more than 600 degrees Fahrenheit. Here it is directed against a number of steel blades or buckets, arranged fan-wise along the rim of a large wheel. Just as a current of air directed against a fan will make the fan-wheel revolve, so the steam turns the first wheel of the turbine rotor. When it leaves the wheel at the opposite side, its own direction has been changed, and it is following a circular path, opposite in direction to that of the turbine wheel. If allowed to strike the blades on the next wheel at once, the steam would tend to turn this second wheel backward, and, therefore, a set of directional blades or nozzles, fastened to the stationary housing, are so placed that the steam is turned in the proper direction once more and then thrown against the second set of blades. In this manner, the steam follows a zigzag path through nineteen wheels, comprising fifteen stages of progressive expansion and consequent decrease of pressure of the steam. In order to take care of the expanded steam, the blades in each stage are larger than those of the preceding one, the last set being twenty-six inches long, whereas those of the first stage are only three and one-half inches in length.

The steam causes the rotor of the turbine to make 1,200 revolutions a minute in the process of losing its pressure against the turbine blades. The whole construction of the turbines and boilers is in some respects unusual, but the differences are highly technical and have no place here.

But because this method of utilizing coal is so much more efficient than any we have used before, we are scrapping our power house at Highland Park - which used to be our pride - and also greatly improving our power plant at Fordson which, when we built it, we thought could not be bettered. And perhaps in another decade our new power plant will be obsolete. And then we shall scrap it!

We do not presently need half a million horsepower for our operations at the Fordson and Highland Park but we shall shortly need it in both these plants, on our railroad which we are electrifying, and in electric furnaces. For this is very cheap power.

And the cheapness of this power practically generated as a by-product indicates something of the relation which - an industry might have with the surrounding country. It is possible in any great manufacturing center that the coal used for power in the factories could also be used for heating the homes of the people. That is, it is possible to use every piece of coal twice – once for its industrial uses and once for its domestic uses. A car of coal delivered at a factory could be used to do all that is required by the factory; the chemicals, gases, tars, and other ingredients could be extracted, and the remaining coke, a pure fuel, could be sent on to the homes.

This has been done with great success and economy. It is no longer an experiment. For several winters we have demonstrated on a large scale that not only can the coal be used twice, but that the coke can profitably be sold to our employees at a considerably lower price than that made by the trade. With all the great factories coking their coal, thus providing a double use for it, other economies will come. A great waste will be prevented. When one thinks of the precious elements which have been consumed for decades on the furnace grates, all going up in smoke and being lost to human use, it becomes clear that the new method has not come too soon. Not only are the elements of coal being saved in modernized factories, and numerous other fields of endeavor enriched by the materials thus saved, but we are coming to see that our factories may become public service institutions. In the modern use of coal, gas is produced, and gas is a public utility. That part of the gas which is not used in direct processes of manufacture can be turned over to the community. The fertilizing elements extracted from coal can be utilized on the farms.

And then there is the possible effect of all this on the transportation problem. As our great factories go into these economies which really consist in getting greater usage out of their basic materials, they will come more and more to the use of power in its electrical form. Now, in our great cities electricity is used in lighting and transportation – these are its greatest services outside the factories. The multitudes of our cities are transported on electric cars to and from work. When the men are in the shops, the peak load is on the lines that furnish the factories with power. When the men are going to and from work, the peak load is on the lines which operate the transportation systems. And nothing is simpler than that the factories, before and after working hours, should turn their power over to the work of transportation.

These are only passing hints, all of them practicable and most of them already in practice, by which the industries of the nation can be of greater service to the community. Our great factories have it in their power to become public utilities in a larger sense than ever before.

And using power in chain fashion means that power will be cheaper than ever – and cheap power, rightly used, means high service and high prosperity. And it may all be had from what is now waste!

CHAPTER 15
EDUCATION FOR LIFE

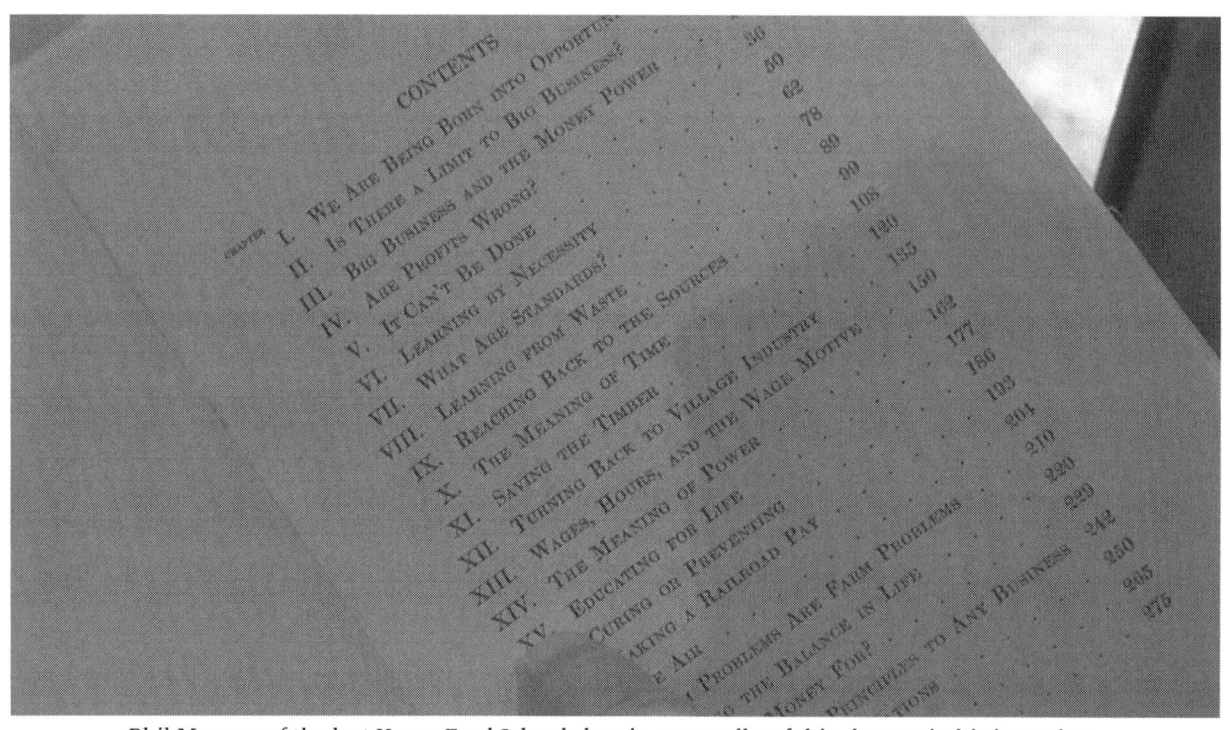

Phil Morgan of the last Henry Ford School class in 1947 talks of this chapter in his interview. See on YouTube. You can simply scan the QR code below that will take you directly to it at
https://youtu.be/mFM_Hp-vt5Q

A Persian came to the director of our trade school. As education goes he was highly educated. He had taken several degrees, both in Europe and in the United States. He was the master of many languages and had just finished four years of special work in one of our leading universities. He had not been seeking education for its own sake. He wanted to help his fellow Persians, and he was visiting our plant before he left for home because we have in our employ a large number of Persians. It was at the end of his visit that he talked with our director, and he said sadly:

"My education began in words and ended in words and when I go back to my country I have nothing to offer my people."

And he was right. He had nothing. He had been educated away from life. He had been taught the contents of a certain number of books, but he had not been taught how to better the living conditions of his people. He did not even know how to earn his own living, except by teaching to others the words which had been taught to him. He could do very little that a phonograph could not do - and it cost more to keep him than to keep a phonograph. Yet he had been inspected and stamped as educated. Educated for what? That is the question he was asking himself.

We are in favor of what might be called utilitarian education, although not at all in favor of what passes for utilitarian education. We believe that first of all a man should be able to earn his own living, and that any education which does not so fit him is useless. Second, we believe that true education will turn a man's mind toward work and not away from it and will enable him to think, and thus to earn a better living not only for himself but also for those about him. What often passes for a utilitarian education is only a scrappy training in a great number of wholly useless odds and ends.

If you train a child to expect that things will drop easily into his lap upon his slightest whine; if you train the mind to regard life as a benevolent system of Providence; if you train a boy to look for favors from others instead of looking to his own powers to create or command what he needs, then already the seeds of dependence are sown, the mind and will are warped, and life is crippled.

Emphasis is laid on this particular phase of weakness because it is so common. Unintentionally a rather soft teaching concerning the Providence of the world has fostered it. Doubtless, there is a Providence which, from an invisible plane, fulfills what is lacking in men's most sincere efforts. Human experience seems to indicate that. Men's efforts seem at times to start up corresponding currents of power which manifest themselves at critical moments, to complete a process or to give a favorable turn to seemingly unfavorable circumstances. The experience of men in all generations seems too clear on this point to leave much doubt about it.

But this Providence is not the servant of the weak - it is for those who have put forth their utmost strength. They may be weak at the moment, but they are not weak by reason of being naturally weak, but by reason of being strong and of having given all their strength to a cause or a task. This catching up, then, of the last threads, or supplying the last touch, this Providence, as men call it, comes to the help of the strong, who, being unsparing of their strength, have drained it for the moment. This is simply to say, in another way, what is already held in the old saying: "God helps those who help themselves."

We hold that it is part of our industrial duty - that is, part of our service that supports the wage motive - to help people to help themselves. We believe that what is called being charitable is a particularly mean form of self-glorification - mean because, while it pretends to aid, it really hurts. The giver to charity gets a certain cheap satisfaction out of being regarded as a kind and generous man. This would be harmless enough in itself were it not that the recipients of charity are usually destroyed - for once you give a man something for nothing, you set him trying to get someone else to give him something for nothing.

Charity creates non-producers, and there is no difference at all between a rich drone and a poor drone. Both are burdens on production. It will take easily a generation to wipe out the effects of the dole upon the peoples of Europe.

We have, therefore, not attempted to found a university or otherwise to depart from those things we intimately know. Instead, we have kept ourselves to training boys and men in the practices and ideas of our own industry, believing that here we could do the most good. We have further plans, but they have not matured. It is rather a serious problem to know quite what to do with boys between sixteen and twenty, for they have just about as much responsibility as healthy young animals. That is something ahead of us.

Our first effort was in the direction of helping boys who did not have the chance to help themselves. Our thoughts in this direction have been more fully told in "My Life and Work." We started this school - the Henry Ford Trade School - in October, 1916, and we admit to it orphans and widows' sons or others who would have no chance even to learn a trade, let alone to get an education, because whatever they might earn was needed for the support of the home. We planned to make a school which would not only be self-supporting, but in which the students could earn at least as much as, if not more than, they could in some outside employment which had no future.

We now have 720 boys in the school, of whom 50 are orphans, 300 the sons of widows, 170 the sons of Ford employees, and 200 from scattered sources. We have to date graduated 400 boys, most of whom have found places in our company. A boy in the beginning is given a scholarship which carries $7.20 a week, which rises to $18 a week, and in addition each boy gets $2.00 a month as thrift money to put into the bank, and a hot luncheon at noon. The average scholarship allowance is $12 a week, including a vacation of four weeks. We make this allowance to the boys that they may contribute to the support of themselves and their mothers while they attend our school. The waiting list for the school is now 5,000. From the start, the school has been governed by three principles: first, that the boy is to be kept a boy and not turned into a premature working man; second, that the academic training is to go hand in hand with the industrial education; and third, that the boy is to be given a sense of responsibility by being trained on articles which are to be used. Nothing is done merely for practice.

The instruction is divided into sections: A week in the classroom and two weeks in the shop. So closely does the classroom dovetail with the practical work that the students are able to master a subject in much shorter time than is common in most educational institutions. The whole Ford Plant at Highland Park is their textbook and laboratory. Lessons in mathematics become concrete shop problems. Geography is closely allied to export activities, and the metallurgical classes have everything, from blast furnaces to heat treat departments, to observe and study in connection with the classroom work. The academic course includes English in its usual branches, mechanical drawing, mathematics, including trigonometry, physics, chemistry, metallurgy, and metallography. The industrial course includes the practical application of the principles learned in the classroom as well as a thorough training on every type of machine used in tool making.

The boys produce a few Ford parts, a wide variety of Ford tools, as well as such delicate precision instruments as gauges, which require accuracy to the ten thousandth of an inch. Most of the cut-away motors seen in Ford sales rooms are made by the boys out of rejected parts. All work done in the shops is bought by the Ford Motor Company if it passes inspection. This makes the school practically self-supporting, besides making the boys realize that they have a responsibility that extends outside of the classroom.

It is recognized that the average boy would far rather play than study or work, so the usual sports and athletics associated with school days are encouraged. During academic periods, an hour a day is spent on the athletic field under competent instruction. The school has its football, baseball, and basketball teams and is a force to be reckoned with in local scholastic athletics. The large auditorium is at the disposal of the boys every Friday for entertainments.

When a boy graduates at eighteen, he is master of a highly paid trade by which he may earn money enough to continue his education if he so desires. If not, he is skilled enough to command a good job anywhere, though he is first offered a position with the Ford Motor Company.

Inasmuch as every boy has earned his way, he need feel under no obligation to the company after he has graduated, though, as a matter of fact, most of the boys prefer to work for the company.

It must be remembered that the boys in this school are not selected because they are bright and promising. They are selected because they need the money and opportunity. Without our interest, some of them would go on the human scrap-heap. The oldest of the graduates is only twenty-five, but already some of these graduates are showing their heads above the crowd. One is now a foreman. Several others are assistants to executives and in line for promotion, while those who are at machines in the shops are mostly doing so well that it will be a matter of only a short while before they have higher places. But the most significant fact is that the foremen of departments are glad to get the boys on graduation.

We do not in general take boys who are physically unfit, but there have been exceptions. I recall two who were lamed by infantile paralysis, and once we take a boy we look after him. For instance, one boy was hurt by an automobile on the street and developed a tubercular knee. He had a number of operations and was in the Ford hospital for perhaps a year - but not as a charity patient. The hospital account was merely charged to the boy, and some day he will probably pay it. We had a Chinese-Filipino boy who started his savings because of a hospital bill. He had run away from home, worked his way across the Pacific, and somehow managed to reach Detroit, where he was picked up by the police. He had heard of our industries and wanted to work in them. He was an exceptional case, and we took him into the trade school. He was not a good student. Soon he fell ill. We sent him to the hospital where he ran up a bill of seventy-five dollars. These bills are not deducted from the pay of the students, unless they so request, but this youngster really wanted to pay his bill. Each week he paid something on account, and when he had liquidated the bill he had so formed the habit of saving that he each week put a sum in bank, and when, finally, he quit the school - he was a rover - he had $540 in bank. He had landed in Detroit with seventy-five cents.

The average earnings of the graduates who have been out four years are between eight and nine dollars a day, or approximately twenty-five hundred dollars a year - which is, I believe, rather higher than the average earnings of college graduates. If we were out for a record, we should pick our boys differently, but we are out to help those who are most in need of help.

Many of the graduates of the trade school go forward into another school, which is every day increasing in importance, and that is our apprentice school. The vital need of the company is for expert toolmakers. Our productive machinery is so arranged that most of the jobs can be learned in less than a day, but in order that the machinery may be kept in condition to operate and also for building machinery we need a large force of skilled machinists. Therefore, we opened an apprentice school for training men between the ages of eighteen and thirty to be what are technically known as toolmakers. The course is three years, and it is open to anyone in the factory under the age of thirty. It is a self-supporting school. The apprentices put in eight hours a day in the tool rooms, being guided by the foreman and a special instructor, and each week they receive lessons in mathematics and mechanical drawing. At the time of writing, 1,700 are enrolled in the school and their wages average from $6 to $7.60 per day. They fully earn their money.

All of this education may be classed as utilitarian, and it has to be, but it does not seem to draw the boys or the men away from going farther with education. A certain number naturally stop learning when the teaching stops - that is the way of human nature. But a surprisingly large number continue in night schools to get more general and special education. Indeed, we have had so many applications for the day shifts in order that the men might go to night school that we have been forced to make a rule against placing a man in a day shift for any educational reason because it seemed unfair to make some men work at night simply because others wanted to work during the day.

The third section of our educational work is what we call the Service School, the purpose of which is partly to prepare foreign-born students for work in our branches abroad, but more largely to spread the idea of our methods of production. For we have no trade secrets. If we are doing anything which another manufacturer may find use for, then we want that manufacturer to have the benefit of what knowledge we possess. That we take as our duty.

We should like to create in every country a nucleus of workers having a thorough knowledge of modern transportational, power, and haulage units, and an understanding of the principles and technique of modern industrial production.

To ground the student thoroughly in this knowledge, he works in department after department. Instructors call on each student while he is at work, observe his progress, and ask him questions about his job. The cooperation of department foremen is, of course, absolutely necessary to the efficient functioning of the system, and such cooperation has been given in an extremely satisfying degree. Faithful, conscientious effort on the part of the student is also necessary. And the men as a whole have acquitted themselves well.

No student is allowed to go from one department to another until he has mastered his present work. Owing, no doubt, to the widely different environments from which many of the students have come, mastery of the phases of manufacture presents varied degrees of difficulty. In nearly every instance, however, the tenacity of the student has overcome the problems at last.

The course is two years, and the students are paid six dollars a day – which they earn. We have at present 450 students, many of whom are college graduates. They include 100 Chinese, 84 Hindus, 20 Mexicans, 20 Italians, 50 Filipinos, 12 Czechoslovakians, 25 Persians, and 25 Puerto Ricans. We have also on the way a large number of Russians, 25 Turks, and a group from Afghanistan. The Chinese are among our best students – they are slow but extremely thorough. We have had students from nearly every country in the world. The least adaptive of all our students, whatever the nationality, are those who come with preconceived notions. Their progress is naturally difficult and slow. But we do our best to fit them to carry the best industrial practices to their own people. We believe that in doing this we are helping to solve international problems in a practical way.

CHAPTER 16
CURING OR PREVENTING

Many men take poverty as a natural condition. It is an unnatural condition. In the United States, there is no reason for it. Every man has not the ability to be the director of serving enterprises, just as every man has not the ability to jump five-foot fences, but with the subdivision of labor and the provision of so many jobs which require no skill, every man has the opportunity to earn a living. Some men will always be failures if left to their own direction. Thousands of farmers ought to be working in shops. They are wasting their time trying to farm - they have not the sense of management. Thousands of men in small business who are trying hard to make ends meet but never succeeding would do very well in a large corporation where they might have direction. Then, also, we have the effects of a bad industrial system which operates on the short-sighted profit motive, and which makes employment intermittent by, from time to time, through high prices, reducing the number of buyers.

Charity is no help in any of these cases. It is only a drug. There are emergencies when men and women, and especially children, need help, but these cases are not actually as numerous as they seem to be. The very fact that charity may be had increases them, for charity holds out the promise of something for nothing. The cases of real need can be looked after on a personal basis without destroying the self-respect as is done by the machinery of organized charity. We may not be able to teach people to help themselves, but we can direct them how to help themselves, and in time this direction will have its effects.

It is these thoughts which cause us to avoid anything and everything which have in them a suggestion of charity. Some years ago, we refitted a home for orphans, and once a week I went out there to see how it was getting on. We employed managers who were supposed to know how to run such homes. Probably they were qualified, as such qualifications go, but they had no conception of what a home for children ought to be - they seemed to think of the place as an institution in which to confine children. Finally, we had to give it all up for the sake of the children, and we found homes for them in families. The sickliest boy we had was adopted by a German woman who already had six children!

We rarely make subscriptions, but sometimes we have to consider making subscriptions, and the last moderately large one that we made was to an institution in Detroit. My son thought we ought to give something, and I suggested:

"We can do one of two things: We can either give a little and forget about it, or we can give a lot, get right into the management, and see to it that the place is self-supporting."

We chose the latter course as being more useful. Our hospital is an experiment in seeing if a hospital can be made both self-respecting and self-supporting. Part of the story of this hospital was told in "My Life and Work." The hospital has nothing to do with the Ford Industries. We own and control the hospital absolutely because we want to carry out in it certain theories which we believe will benefit the public.

Hospitals are undoubtedly public necessities. A vast amount of dissatisfaction exists concerning both the medical profession and hospital management. There is a feeling that the treatment of disease, the care of the sick, and the instruction of the well, should be put on a sounder basis. Surgeons of national reputation are working toward the grading of hospitals according to merit. Many people are still afraid to go to hospitals - especially to municipal ones.

We could see no reason why a properly administered hospital could not give the highest medical and surgical service under the best possible conditions at an established schedule of going rates and be made to pay for itself.

The unit of a hospital is the room. We gave the men who had been selected to head the staffs a carpenter and some wall board and asked them to work out an ideal hospital room and bath - a room which would have all the space needed and none over. They devised a room - a unit. The building of the hospital was then only a matter of designing a building to fit the rooms, with whatever accessories were necessary. The result is the present brick and stone structure. The opening of the hospital was interrupted by the war. The government took it over in August, 1918, as General Hospital Number 36 and turned it back again in October, 1919. Then the original plan went on.

This is the plan. The hospital staff, which consists of about one hundred surgeons and physicians, are all on salary from the hospital and do not engage in private practice. There are six services - Medicine, Surgery, Obstetrics, Pediatrics, Laboratory, and X-Ray. Each of these services is headed by men of recognized attainments. In the beginning, there was a preponderance of Johns Hopkins men, but as the hospital has grown the staff has ceased to be representative of any single school. Now the men are so drawn that some fifteen or twenty of the leading medical schools in this country and Canada are represented. A majority of the men have been in graduate work both here and abroad. Several are members of the Royal College of Surgeons.

The nurses were at first graduate nurses and employed by the hospital on full time. They receive the Ford rate, a minimum of six dollars for a day of eight hours. They are assigned from four to six rooms, according to the condition of the patients. All the meals are served by special maids, so that detail is taken away from the nurses. A bathroom with ice water in addition to hot and cold water being attached to each room, supplies of linen being always at hand, and most of the unnecessary steps of the nurse being eliminated, she finds no trouble in properly caring for her quota of patients. She works eight hours instead of the usual twelve hours and has no reason to be tired and cross.

Last year, we made provision for pupil nurses by opening the Clara Ford Nurses' Home and the Henry Ford Hospital School of Nursing and Hygiene. The underlying thought is to train nurses to a real profession in which the care of the ill will be the sole objective. To this end, the new home has considerably better appointments than most first-class hotels. The home and the educational building are on the hospital grounds but at some distance from the hospital. The home has 309 individual rooms, all finished and furnished alike. Each room has a private bath. The rooms are grouped about central entrances or elevators with a sitting room and kitchenette for each group, to carry out the home idea. Connecting with a reception hall on the first floor are eight small parlors where the young women may entertain friends. Dining rooms, kitchens, laundry, sewing room, and trunk room are in the basement. At the rear of the building is a sunken garden extending out from between the two wings. The whole environment of the dormitory is planned with the aim of providing a complete change of atmosphere for the nurses after leaving the hospital wards or classrooms.

The School of Nursing and Hygiene conforms to the architecture of the Hospital and Nurses' Home. This building is two stories high and 120 feet by 50 feet. Besides the classrooms and laboratories, there are two squash courts, a swimming pool, and an auditorium-gymnasium.

The nurses, while in the hospital, are held to a high standard of duty. Exactly the same policy is followed with the nurses as with the workers and executives in the factories - good pay, short hours, the best facilities for work, and plenty of work.

The hospital has both in-patient and out-patient departments, and although it tries to cooperate with outside physicians and surgeons, attendance and operating within the hospital are exclusively the function of the hospital staff. The fees are fixed in advance according to the diagnosis and according to a scale.

The standard rooms - those in the new hospital - are $8 a day, which includes board and nursing.

The hospital reopened with a waiting list of nearly five hundred in the latter part of 1919. Every patient on entering, either the in or the out department, goes through a thorough physical examination with blood tests, and so on, and a diagnosis is made on the basis of full information. The examination is continued through X-rays and the other well-known forms of medical inquiry, whenever the regular examination discloses any condition which ought to be further gone into. An examination takes about two hours and the charge for it is $15. It is thoroughly inclusive, and the hospital authorities regard it as a prerequisite to intelligent work.

Every patient is a private patient. It is a rule of the hospital that the privacy of a patient must be kept inviolate. A room may be entered only by the doctors or nurses in charge in their professional capacities or by such guests as the patient wishes to receive and his condition permits. A patient is a patient, not an exhibit.

The hospital neither encourages nor discourages its use by the wealthy. All patients pay according to the prearranged agreement, and in the eye of the hospital, all the patients are of equal standing. The fees are payable in advance, but no one needing medical or surgical treatment has ever been turned away. Some method is always found by which the patient can meet the financial requirements in a wholly self-respecting way. We take it that self-respect forms a part of a patient's health.

The hospital is not self-sustaining, but it will become nearly so in course of time. It is doubtful if a hospital which does all it ought to do in the way of research can become entirely self-sustaining. Some things must be paid for out of humanity's general treasure. Our first object is not to make the hospital pay, but to equip it to do its work. Any profits which accrue will be plowed back into the hospital.

We think we are finding out something about hospital management, but having the hospital has also brought us flatly up to the question: "Why should there be need for a hospital? Cannot most of these diseases be prevented?"

And that has taken us into broader questions. Take the matter of food, for example.

There must be a right food if there is to be good health. Bees create their queens by selective feeding, and the effect of food on health, disposition, morals, and mental power is just now a great and challenging problem.

The doctors are beginning to find out that illnesses spring from food. They have not yet gone a great distance in this direction, but I understand some very important work is being done. Men who are careful of their diet do not often fall ill, while those who are not careful always have something or other the matter with them.

The best doctors seem to agree that the cure for most indispositions is to be found in diet and not in medicine. Why not prevent that illness in the first place? It all leads up to this - if bad food causes illness, then the perfect food will cause health. And that being the case, we ought to search for that perfect food - and find it. When we have found it, the world will have taken its greatest single step forward.

It is going to take some time to get this food. It may not exist in the world today in any form. It may be produced from some existing food or from some combination of existing foods. It may be that a new plant will have to be evolved. The one thing certain is that this food will be found. It would have been found long ago if only the attempt to find it had been earnestly made, but it is only lately that we have begun to realize that food is all-important.

This whole affair of food must be put on a business basis. Science working alone does not move as quickly or as surely as when it is working as part of a business enterprise. Scientific men are just like other men in needing management. A scientific discovery is a fine thing of itself, but it does not begin to help the world until it is put on a business basis. Direct any set of men to a definite end, and in the course of time they will reach it; do not ask for an opinion in advance as to whether or not what you want can be done, for then you will only get all the reasons why it cannot be done. But if you say what you want and keep behind the men with whatever resources are necessary, the men will stay with their problem day and night until they solve it. That is what we are going to do with food.

Someday, someone will bring about a condition which will make hospitals unnecessary.

CHAPTER 17
MAKING A RAILROAD PAY

We have owned the Detroit, Toledo & Ironton Railroad for about five years. A great deal has been written and said about this road, because, until we took it over, it had been through more than a dozen receiverships and reorganizations. We have no record that it ever earned any money before we bought it – that is, earned money for the stockholders. It has earned fairly well for the bankers who from time to time have reorganized it.

The road has earned money for us and would earn more were it not that an Act of Congress limits the return on our investment to 6 percent. We are limited in our service by laws conceived in part by ill-informed theorists who cannot understand the real function of profits, and in part by those who see in regulated business the inevitable necessity for banker finance.

These are the advantages under which we took the road:

(1) A complete freedom from banker control.
(2) A large traffic originating in our own industries.
(3) Direct connections with all of the big trunk lines of the country. The old road had these connections also, but it took small advantage of them.

These were our disadvantages at the beginning:
(1) A thoroughly demoralized working force.
(2) The bad will of the public and the shippers.
(3) A ramshackle road that started nowhere and ended nowhere.
(4) A roadbed hardly fit for use and rolling stock and motive power which were all but junk.

Out of the chaos which existed when we took it over, we have now a railroad which, while not first class in other than men and management, earned in 1925 more than two and a half millions of dollars, or about half of what we paid for it.

This result has not been brought about by magic. We have not yet put the new electrical short line between Flat Rock and Detroit into operation. This short line represents the highest type we know of concrete construction with the wires carried on concrete arches. This cut-off road is owned by the Detroit and Ironton Railroad Company, the stock of which is owned by us. We have not made the short cuts which we intend to make on the road and for which we have bought the right of way. We have not laid all the heavy rail we intend to put down, and we have not touched many of the worst grades. We shall make over the road, but we have not yet done it. The earnings have been made with only a small addition to the equipment which was already in use when we bought the road. We have simply brought in management. That is to say, we have:

(1) Cleaned up the road and everything about it.
(2) Put all the equipment in good condition.
(3) Put in what we think are proper wage scales, and have demanded work for pay.
(4) Abolished all red tape and division of duties.
(5) Played square with the public and the people who work for us.

(6) Made all our improvements with our own money.

The point in the management of this railway is not the money it has earned or where or how it gets its traffic. The point is that this railway has utterly discarded many of the precedents of railroad operation and is doing its job with the utmost directness at much lower than the former average operating ratio and at the same time paying the highest railway wages in the country. The railroad is really more remarkable for the time-honored formulas it neglects to observe than it is for the profits it earns.

We did not buy the railroad because we wanted to own a railroad. We did not want to go into the railroad business. It was simply that the right of way interfered with some of our River Rouge extensions. The railroad wanted so much money for a small portion of its land that we thought it would be cheaper to buy the whole railroad. Once we bought the railroad, we had to run it according to our own principles of management. Of course, we did not know whether our principles would apply to the management of a railway, but we thought they would. We found that they did. We have not been able to do much yet. When we get the road into the shape we want, perhaps it will amount to something.

Our factories were in Detroit long before we bought this railroad, and the railroad was there, too. It would seem that the railroad should have had as much business from us then as it has now. We have spent more money than the old railroad could have spent, for it had no credit, but it could easily enough have used what facilities it already had in such a way as to get more business and build itself up. We really have spent very little money except out of earnings.

For the fiscal year ending in June, 1914, the old D. T. & I. reached an operating ratio of 154 percent - that is, it spent three cents to earn two cents. It was capitalized in 1913 at $105,000 a mile! Nobody knows how many millions have been raised on the strength of this railroad. In the reorganization of 1914, the bond-holders paid around five million dollars in assessments. That is what we paid for the road and we could have paid less. We paid what we thought to be a fair price, which is the only price we ever pay. Our price happened to be above the market price. We paid sixty cents on the dollar for the bonds, although they were being offered between thirty and forty cents without takers. The bonds were in default. In fact, no security ever issued by this railroad had, up to the time of our purchase, made a return to any investor. We paid a dollar a share for the common stock and five dollars a share for the preferred stock. These stocks did not have a market price because there were no buyers. We made our bid for the securities on the basis of giving fair value as nearly as we could estimate it. We did not get a bargain. We did not want a bargain. We think our management experience has been sufficiently large to permit us to turn a profit on any investment we may make. Every transaction must have at least two sides, and so we are just as much opposed to paying too little as we are to paying too much.

The road taken over, the first step was to put in the Ford principles of management. The principles are extremely simple. They may be compressed into three statements:

(1) Do the job in the most direct fashion without bothering with red tape or any of the ordinary divisions of authority.

(2) Pay every man well - not less than six dollars a day - and see that he is employed all the time through forty-eight hours a week and no longer.

(3) Put all machinery in the best possible condition, keep it that way, and insist upon absolute cleanliness everywhere in order that a man may learn to respect his tools, his surroundings, and himself.

Railroad management, because of long usage, the demands of legislation, and for a dozen other reasons, has become exceedingly complex. A big railroad divides up into numerous circles of authority; so do many manufacturing corporations. The Ford Motor Company has only two divisions - office and shop. It has no rigid lines of authority. The people are supposed to get through the work. This same system went into force on the railway.

The divisions of work among the men were abolished; an engineer may now be found cleaning an engine or a car or even working in the repair shop. The crossing tenders act as track walkers for their districts, the station agents sometimes paint and repair their own stations. The idea is that a group of men have been assigned to run a railroad, and among them they can, if they are willing, do all the work. If a specialist has some of his special work on hand he does it; if he has no such work he does laborer's work or whatever may be to do.

We abolished the legal department and all the divisions in the clerical department. We wiped out the Detroit office and all the freight solicitors and a considerable line of executive officers. The legal department was costing the old road $18,000 a year - it now costs $1,200 a year. The new principle is to settle all claims for damages at once on a fair basis according to the facts. The whole clerical force - which includes the administrative officers - consists of ninety persons. The executive officers are in two rooms; the whole accounting force is in one small building. The travelling auditor makes reports on any conditions he finds. It is no one's business to spy on any one else because no one has any exclusive business to spy on. The job, not convention, rules. The old railway had 2,700 employees for a freight business running to 5,010,000 tons. The force was at once reduced to around 1,500. Now, handling twice the old tonnage, the road has 2,390 employees and these include the mechanics in a large repair shop where the old engines are being made over.

The railway unions have made no objection of any kind, for all the men are being paid well above the highest union scale. The management of the road does not know whether a man is union or non-union; the unions do not seem to care, either, for the road has been exempted from all wage negotiations and also from all strike orders.

Cleanliness is an integral part of our plan. The first thing we did was to clean the railway from end to end and to paint every building. New ties are being laid at the rate of about 300,000 a year, and the sixty-pound rails are being replaced by eighty- and ninety-pound rails. The new stone ballast has to be as exact and to be kept as exact as a straight edge can make it. No employee may smoke on the premises. The engines are being made over at an average cost of around $40,000 each; they are being practically rebuilt, and when they come out of the shop they are show engines. They have to be kept that way. No hammer of a size to damage an engine is allowed in a cab. An engine must be cleaned after every trip.

Give a man a good tool - a fancy polished tool - and he will learn to take care of it. Good work is difficult excepting with good tools used in clean surroundings.

These are not unimportant points; they are fundamental. They make for the working spirit. They are as important as the wages. The work would not be returned for the wages were not the conditions so arranged that the work is possible. Section sheds are all standard and have cement floors, every tool and piece of material is in a standard rack, and a supply car goes over the stock once a month. These houses, as well as the stations, have to be kept painted and absolutely clean - stations and platforms have to be swept at least three times a day. Locomotives are now cleaned by a machine which was designed at Fordson and which saves three men and does the work in two and a half hours less than before. The locomotives and all the machinery in the repair shops are enameled to an automobile finish. Cabooses are kept clean and they are comfortable - often the brakemen come in before time to scrub the floors.

It is said that a D. T. & I. man always carries in his hand a bunch of cotton waste. It is the insignia of the road. But that cotton waste is not thrown away once it is used. It goes back to a cleaning plant and comes out as new. No scrap is thrown away. It all goes back to our reclamation plants.

One hears a great deal about railroad wages. No dispute on wages ever takes place in the Ford Industries; the wages are always somewhat ahead of what the workman reasonably expects. When an ordinary laborer goes on the railway, he is paid, according to our rule, five dollars a day for sixty days; then he goes on to the six dollars a day minimum.

Excepting in a few instances, the men running the road today are the men who were with the old company. We do not like to discharge men. Whenever, we take over a property, we keep all of the old employees who are willing to work and to fall in with our ideas of management. Very few fail to fall in step with our policies. Those few we let go, because invariably they are the men who want jobs and not work.

The train master of one of the most important divisions of the road began as a section hand when he was sixteen years old. He got ten cents an hour and often was not paid for three months. His father was a road supervisor of the same section, along with three other supervisors and numerous foremen. Now this train master has charge of the whole division and there are no road supervisors. Instead, we have a few maintenance foremen who work on their own initiative instead of being directed from above. As this train master put it to the foremen when the new plan went into effect:

"Wouldn't you fellows rather put in a bolt or a tie when you see it is needed than wait around for me to come along and tell you to do it?"

The foremen have their pay raised on their work. Everyone on the road has his pay raised according to his work. All the foremen are workers - not one of them stands around just bossing. If you come upon a gang you cannot tell who is the boss. We judge the men solely by results. For instance, a section in charge of one young man was always in first-class shape - the rails were always right, the ties good, the ballast straight lined, and the buildings fresh with paint. We raised the young man without telling him. When his first check under the new scale came to him, he took it to the superintendent.

"There is a mistake in my check," he said.

Then he was told that he had been raised, and why. The section next to him was in bad condition, but the moment its foreman heard of the pay raise that section began to get better. We find it good business to pay solely on ability, and where two men are doing the same job and one is getting more than the other, to let it be known why; thus, we rarely have a request for an increase in pay, the men know they will get more when they are worth more and that asking will not help. Also we have no Grievance Committee or committees of any kind other than Safety Committees. Any man may go directly to headquarters and he knows it. The cause of derailments is a sore spot with every railroad and under the old methods the track men always got the blame. Now they have a chance and we can place the real blame, and we find that it is seldom with the track men.

We had some trouble with the track gangs in the beginning. They were nearly all foreigners, and we found that being related to the foremen was the best credential for a job. Now relatives are not allowed in the same gang. We are having an increasing number of young high school graduates coming into the section gangs. They are no longer taking the white collar. They see that manual labor can be performed under decent and self-respecting conditions.

This is particularly noticeable in the bridge gangs. Formerly these gangs were made up without regard to the residence of the members, and the men slept in dirty camp cars reaching home only on Sundays and sometimes not then. Now we have the road divided into fifty-mile stretches, the gangs are chosen from men who live along the stretch, and with fast motor cars we see that each man reaches home every night. The morale of these gangs used to be low; now it is high. Incidentally, we save the pay of seven cooks and the keep of the men. This saving has been transferred to their pay and they can have real homes.

We have no seniority rules. Such rules are not fair to the community. If a man has been in service a long time, he ought to be better than a newcomer; if his experience has only taught him to dodge work, then the new man, in the public interest, ought to go ahead of him. The engineers on most of the railroads are, because of the rules, usually old men. We have quite a number of young men. We care nothing about age anywhere in our industries. We are after the best man, regardless of age. The absence of rules helps in many ways. As a yard master who has been on the railroad for thirty years - he is sixty-eight years old - said:

"Say a car comes in marked 'Rush' and no yard engine is around. In the old days, if I asked a regular engine and crew to shift that car, they would just tell me to chase myself - that moving cars around the yard was not in their working agreement. Now any engine available will shift the car. The men are paid to work, not to debate rules."

The wages are paid for a strictly forty-eight-hour week, with no overtime, and also there is no piece work at all. The lowest paid man on the D. T. & I. receives $1,872 for a year of 2,496 hours. According to the statistics of the Interstate Commerce Commission for Class I railroads, the average compensation for railroad employees, excluding general division officers in 1923, was $1,588 for a year of 2,584 hours - that is, the D. T. & I. men receiving the lowest pay get $25 a month more than the general average of railroad pay for the highest-class roads. Take some specific wages. The D. T. & I. freight conductors get from $3,600 to $4,500 a year as against from $3,089 to $3,247 on other lines; the brakemen get from $2,100 to $2,820 a year as against from $2,368 to $2,523; and the engineers from $3,600 to $4,500 as against the general average of from $3,248 to $3,758. The average pay of office employees on the D.T. & I. is $8.11, and of operating men $7.26.

In addition to the wages, the road has an investment plan. The impulse to invest is right, and it is a thousand criticisms upon our civilization that a man cannot invest where he works, so that not only may he have an additional income, but that his work may take on added interest. If there were more opportunities for solid industrial investment in business with which men are acquainted, there would be far less of appeal in the false bonanza schemes that are exploited.

The plan has been in operation only since October, 1923, but up to date, employees have subscribed for certificates to the amount of $600,000 and more than one half the men are investors. They pay for the certificates out of wages and are permitted to buy up to an amount the installment payment on which will not exceed one third of the wage. No interest is guaranteed, but the men are paid 6 percent if they find it necessary to withdraw. It is essentially a profit-sharing plan drawn in accordance with the railroad laws and rulings.

The earnings of the D. T. & I. are in part due to the business of the Ford Motor Company and in part to the better division of rates with connecting roads. The old road did not have enough traffic to make a fight on the division it received for its part of a through haul, and it received divisions which were often below the actual cost of transportation. It took what it could get; under our management all these rate divisions have been revised, upon a fair and just basis. The operating ratios tell the really important story. In 1920, under the old management, it had an operating ratio of 125.4 percent; in the first year of the new management and with practically the same equipment, it had a ratio of 83.8 percent. In 1922, it spent a great deal of money on repairs and the ratio was 83.3 percent as compared with the operating average of 79.31. The present operating ratio is around 60 - which is less than the average of the country for far better equipped roads.

Another point we make and carry through all our industries - no man may work on Sunday.

The experiment is not unimportant. For a long time the country's railways have been at war with their employees or with the public - and sometimes with both. The war has been so long drawn out that the purpose of the railways seems sometimes to be forgotten. I believe in private ownership. I think time does not hallow the practices of business. Under private ownership it is possible to conduct any business so that it will pay high wages and yet give cheap service.

CHAPTER 18
THE AIR

We have added the making of airplanes to our industries because we are manufacturers of motors and therefore every phase of motor transportation interests us. We are not as yet really manufacturing airplanes, according to our interpretation of manufacturing. We are largely experimenting to see whether it is possible to produce an airplane which will require no more skill in its management than does a motor car, which can be manufactured and sold so cheaply as to be within the means of a large number of people, and which will be as safe from accident and as fool-proof as is the motor car.

We are proceeding slowly, as is our wont. We are working on a number of models, and we are running two air lines from Dearborn - one to Cleveland and the other to Chicago. These air lines, excepting for a mail contract, carry only our own goods, for we are in the business of making motors and do not intend to go into the business of aerial transportation. But unless we have regular air lines running under our own supervision, we cannot obtain the data on performance necessary to proper production. We cannot go into production until we are absolutely sure of what we are doing. When we shall have that surety, only the future can tell. But the development is going on far more rapidly than did the development of the motor car, for we introduced the motor car into a world unfamiliar with machinery, while now nearly every man understands at least something of motor-driven machinery. The step from the motor car to the airplane is not nearly as great as the step we have already taken from the horse carriage to the motor car. We do not have to convince the public that transportation through the air is desirable. The public wants quick transportation. It is now only necessary to provide safe transportation at a low cost, and then to convince the people that the stunt airplane is no nearer to the commercial airplane than the racing motor car is to the truck.

The military airplane - and because of the war nearly all of the attention in recent years had to be given to the war planes - requires great skill in its piloting, just as the driving of a racing motor car requires great skill. The military airplane has to be very fast and flexible. The pilot has to know how to go into nose dives and tail spins - and how to get out of them. Ninety per cent of the efficacy of a military airplane is in its pilot.

We have not been working along war lines, although we know that the airplane must perform a high part in all future military operations, but we believe that we can be of the greatest service for both war and peace in developing the commercial airplane. For, once we know enough about commercial aeronautics, it will not be difficult to turn out military airplanes as needed and to find the proper pilots for them.

This work in the air, however, is not primarily my work. It was my son Edsel, President of the Ford Motor Company, who first became interested in aviation, and it took a long time to convince me that it had a commercial feature. The direction of the work depends on my son. My generation brought out the automobile. It remains for the next generation to bring out the airplane, although already the progress with the airplane has been much more rapid than was the progress with the motor car.

We now own as a subsidiary the Stout Metal Airplane Company, which produces an all-metal monoplane. We have an airport at Dearborn and also a mooring mast for dirigibles. We have a factory for building the metal airplanes. This factory was recently destroyed by fire, but a new and better factory is being built.

We are giving more attention at present to the airplane than to the dirigible but we believe that each type has its place in air navigation. The airplane seems to be well fitted for fast express work and the dirigible for the carrying of heavy loads. It is our general thought - although nothing is as yet conclusive - that the dirigibles will take the long main routes of air travel, with the planes acting as feeders. But we are not committed to either type - we want to learn all that we can about both types.

Ford Stout 2-AT Pullman "Maiden Dearborn" circa 1925.

The principle is fundamental with us that an airplane, before it can be considered commercially, must be developed to a point where it can support itself in the air financially as well as physically.

The all-metal monoplane appealed to us particularly, because of the simplicity of its construction and the fact that it might be put into production. The biplane, with its fabric planes and wire and wooden bracings, has to be made by hand, and we are not interested in hand production. Also the metal airplane may be left outdoors in any weather without the danger of harm.

Our interest in the dirigible is indicated by the fact that we erected a mooring tower 210 feet high. We have as yet done very little with the lighter-than-air machines and have not as yet used the big mast. Our principal experimenting has been with the heavier-than-air machines.

We started with these two fundamentals: A commercial airplane must have, (1) the ability to accomplish the most ton miles per horsepower, and (2) the ability to stay in the air the most hours per day. That is, the best commercial plane is the one that will make the most ton miles per dollar per day. This is what we expect from an airplane and what we shall achieve:

(1) Absolute reliability of structure under all conditions of weather or fire hazard.
(2) Absolute dependability of power plant, accomplished, possibly, by multiple engines.
(3) A speed of 100 miles per hour, with full load, in horizontal flight at sea level, on not more than three fifths of

the maximum horsepower.

(4) Pilot located forward to assure unobstructed vision when planes become common over air routes, particularly in bad weather.

(5) A pay load of at least four pounds per horsepower, with fuel for six hours of flight.

(6) Ability to operate twenty hours per day in the air with load.

Two major requirements must be met before we can have real commercial aviation or commercial air lines. The first is a real airplane engine, air-cooled and without electric ignition, if possible. The second is an absolutely dependable navigation apparatus, probably a specially developed radio system. These points we are working on, and it is only a matter of time before we shall get what we need.

We began our first air lines in April, 1925 - that is, we have had more than a year of experience with all-metal planes fitted with Liberty engines. We have during this period been flying daily, except Sunday, over a 260-mile course to Chicago and return, and 127 miles to Cleveland and return, a total of 774 miles per day. We have not had a single accident, we have not had a day's interruption of service, and it is the exception for a plane not to arrive exactly on time.

Our loads vary from 1,000 to 1,500 pounds per trip, with an average of about 1,200 pounds, in addition to 150 gallons of fuel, 14 gallons of oil, and often an extra pilot in training. On one occasion a plane was flown to Cleveland with a complete Ford car, body and all.

Our experience thus far indicates that the cost of transportation can be brought well within commercial limits and the service made speedy and reliable.

For the first three months of operation our actual average speed between Detroit and Chicago, with loads, was ninety-six miles per hour, but during the next two months, after bad weather had set in, this average dropped to ninety-three miles per hour, because most of the winds encountered were crosswise of the course. Another speed handicap was that the ships flying to Chicago, leaving at 12, travelled against a wind that the plane did not have in its favor coming back, since the summer wind dies down about 5pm and the ship is not due at Ford Airport until 6:30pm As this work is being done with an ordinary Liberty engine turning at normal engine speed, we believe the record is rather remarkable, particularly the fact that we have had but one dead-stick landing during the whole period of operation. Trips were made with as much as 2,700 pounds of useful load.

We are experimenting with a large plane with three motors, so that it may keep the air with one motor dead, but for an ordinary commercial freight aviation, or for the personal aviation that is so near at hand, a single engine will be sufficient except when used over mountains or where landing fields are not available. Commercial passenger lines will probably all use three-motored ships.

Flying equipment standing on the ground is a liability, like a motor truck standing still or an ocean steamship at the dock. It earns its pay by ton-mile service and must be in the air the greatest possible number of hours per day. It should not be necessary, in commercial airline work, to have more than one plane on the ground for two in the air, and even this ratio can be bettered. This will be possible, however, only when power plants and other devices are interchangeable, so that operators can change any defective equipment almost immediately and get the machines back into the air promptly. The parts in all the planes we are making are interchangeable to a degree. Essentially, when we have closed on our design, they will be interchangeable just as are our motor-car parts.

The future of aviation does not lie in selling thrills to the public but in carrying people and loads from place to place in the service of industry.

So much for air lines.

The airplane will soon be a part of our life. What it will mean, no one knows; we have not yet found out what the automobile means.

CHAPTER 19
FARM PROBLEMS ARE FARM PROBLEMS

Is farming the industry of food production, or is it a way of living - or is it just something to talk about? And what is a farmer? We speak of farmers as though they were all alike. That we know is not true. There are wheat farmers, cotton planters, cattle, sheep, and hog raisers, fruit farmers, dairy farmers, not to speak of the diversified farmers who try a little of everything.

But they do have this in common: They are all sections of an industry which only to a small degree has as yet realized that it is an industry.

The old farm and the old plantation were nearly self-contained. In the days when opportunities were scarce, the question of getting enough to eat and having a place to sleep stood out above everything else. A farmer did not expect to make money. Indeed, he did not often see any money. What few things he needed over and above what he could raise or make on the farm he traded for in kind. The tradition of the farm is not a money tradition. It is a living tradition.

The spinning wheel and the hand loom are no longer on the farm. Farm people buy their clothing. The farm is no longer isolated - the automobile, the telephone, and the radio have attended to that. The farmer has moved out of his little, individual, self-contained world into the great world which is a world of industry and which has money enough to regard as common necessities what the farmer formerly regarded as extreme luxuries. The farmer wants as much money for his work as the industrialist gets for his work. The farmer claims that he works harder than the industrialist, and probably he does, but the world does not pay for sweat. It pays for results. Industry, through the application of management and power, has been able to obtain results.

We cultivate several thousand acres at Dearborn; we also have a dairy herd of around three hundred cows; and near our coal mines in Kentucky, on mountain soil that was not supposed to be good for much of anything, we are growing garden vegetables and fruit. Most of my own life has been spent on a farm. We are in touch with farming nearly everywhere through the sales of automobiles and tractors. And so we are not without knowledge of farm needs and farm wants.

There is a farm problem. No one quite knows what that problem is; it has to do with finding a way for the farmer to make a living. Some say that the solution will be found in raising farm prices and lowering general prices. It is always in the public interest to lower prices; it is never in the public interest to raise prices, and especially food prices. The exact nature of the problem is confused. Of course it is. It has to be. For the moment we begin talking about an established institution as a problem, then it is actually not a problem at all - the thing is over with and done. A post mortem will tell what the man died of, but it will not bring him back to life. The old kind of farm is dead. We might as well recognize that fact and take it as a starting point for the devising of something better.

It is not a kindness to help the farmer to dodge the facts and to keep him going on stimulants. The real trouble is that the world has passed on and the farm has stood still. It is now little business in a world of big business. More than that, it is a part-time job in a world that asks for a living on the basis of a full-time job. If a man's time is worth any more than that of a setting hen, then the farm is no place for him to work through the whole year. There is not enough for him to do that is worthwhile doing. He spends from half a month to a month a year in getting ready to start nature into production and in harvesting what nature has produced. During the remainder of the year, he is taken up with fruitless tasks which keep him occupied but do not gain him a living.

Take the balanced farm which rotates its crops and has a certain amount of livestock. The truck farm, the dairy farm, the pig farm, the cotton plantations, the fruit orchards, and other specialized activities are on a different basis. Consider the average balanced farm - the farm managed in the average way. It will have a certain number of fields on which the crops will rotate in the usual manner. Also, it will have a small herd of cattle, some pigs and poultry, and perhaps some sheep. If the farmer has modern ideas, he will have only a few horses or none at all, and he will have an investment in automobiles, tractors, and harvesting machinery.

With machinery, the work of plowing, planting, and harvesting will not extend over more than ten or fifteen days during the year. At the extreme outside, his outdoor work on crops, exclusive of garden crops, cannot extend beyond a month. The rest of the year he spends in tending the livestock and marketing it either as meat or as milk. He will not have enough live cattle to make a first-class, well-arranged barn pay, and he will have to do most of the work of feeding and milking by hand in the hardest and most wasteful manner. He sells part of his crop directly, and the rest of it he sells through the animals. A good deal of his work has to be done by hand, especially in and about the barn, for neither his production nor his arrangements are such as to justify the use of much machinery. He cannot take advantage of any of the economies of volume production, and hence he is up early and late drudging along through his daily tasks. I know what that drudgery is; I have worked on a farm.

The single-crop farmer is through for the year with a month or half a month's work. During the remainder of the time he watches nature work for him. The present complaint is that as a result of all his work, even the balanced crop farmer has little or nothing to show for his labor. Is this a temporary condition due to the World War or some other unusual circumstance, or have we reached a point where the whole of farming must be revamped?

Industry has to be revamped every little while; the man in industry who does not keep up with the times simply passes out - we do not notice his going. The war and the boom and the upset condition of the world and all the land and other speculation which went with inflated prices served to bring on the crisis in farming affairs more rapidly than it might otherwise have come, but the crisis had to develop some time, and it might as well be now as any other. The war did not do so much to change the condition of the farm as it did to change the thoughts of the farmer; since the war he has expected to earn a living and something more. That is why we have a problem.

The farmer is trying to live as well as the man employed in industry - and the farm as at present managed does not give such a living. It never has given such a living. Few have ever made any money out of farming. This may seem to contradict what are supposed to be the accepted facts. The one-crop farmers most certainly have never made much money out of farming. They started with virgin land and in their crops sold the fertility of the soil - that is, they sold off their capital investment. They have made their largest sums in selling their farms on the basis of crop yields. Each successive purchaser has bought less than the man before him - although he has paid a higher price. With each year of farming, the land is less fertile. Now the price of land is so high and the taxes are so high that the land cannot be mined to pay the fixed charges. For the process is mining rather than farming - it is an exploiting of natural resources. This kind of farming is not good for the country; the older farm states already have great numbers of abandoned farms, just as the oil states have abandoned oil wells. The farmer with a moderate-sized farm who rotates crops and keeps a little livestock seems to have made some money in the past, although now he says that, with the wages of farm labor what they are, he cannot come out even. And farm workers are paid much below the average of factory workers and have to work harder.

But has any farmer ever made money? His land has increased in value and that has brought him money when he sold; sometimes he has realized this added value in the form of a mortgage. But he has lived rigorously and those farmers who think they have made money have done so by spending little and banking the equivalent of low wages for themselves and their families. And even with the farms which are thought to pay, it is hard to say whether the profit has been gained out of the sale of farm products or out of the sale of livestock. We cannot count the controlled war prices in any summing up of farmers' profits; they did not amount to much anyway, for those war dollars had small buying power. Before the war some money was made out of exploiting virgin land, but, barring these operations and barring increased land values, it is to be doubted whether the money said to have been made out of straight farming would prove to equal the wages of common labor during the same period.

Is there any help for this situation? The farmers say that they have to pay too much for the things they buy - that their prices are out of line with the prices of the products of industry. They also say that, while they get but little for their products, the consumers pay high for them. But suppose the prices of manufactured commodities do come down, and the costs of distribution are cut, will a condition result in which the farmer can make a profit? No changes merely in distribution will bring the earnings of farming in line with the earnings of industry - the same energy will yield more money in industry than it will in farming as it is now carried on.

Obviously, giving more credit to the farmer is not going to help him. The farmer is paying out too much now in mortgage interest, discount on short-term loans, and taxes. Adding further interest charges to the total will only increase his costs of production and put still farther away the possibility of earning money. Far too many farmers have been taught to think that money can take the place of management. Very few business ills are ever cured by money. A business may be short of money through some extraordinary circumstance that has nothing to do with earnings, but when the earnings are insufficient to provide capital improvements and a living profit over, then there is something wrong with the business as a business, and borrowing money will serve only to postpone the investigation of what is really the trouble until it is too late to do anything about it. Generally speaking, borrowing is a vice, and although it may be pleasant enough for the farmer to be able to borrow money when he likes, in the end he is only going to be worse off for that borrowing.

Intelligent work, not money, is the main requisite for production. There is no magic in loans. That ought to be apparent to everyone now, for the farm situation did not become critical until after a period when the farmer could borrow as much as he wanted. The record of farm bankruptcies and mortgage foreclosures may be taken as an indication of the bad state of farming, or again, it may be taken as an indication that money has been unwisely borrowed. A farmer does not plow with money; he does not sow with money; he does not cultivate with money; he does not harvest with money. His problems are of production, not of finance.

And, following the same line, his problem is not one of marketing. Marketing remedies are being urged upon the farmer just as the financial remedies are being urged. One must produce before one can market, and no matter how skillful a merchant the farmer may become, he will not, by reason of that skill, be a better farmer. The central problems of farming have to do with the working of the land for grain, fruit, vegetable, or dairy products. If land is yielding ten bushels of wheat an acre, then no manner of marketing will enable the owner of that land to compete with a farmer who is getting thirty bushels an acre.

There is room for very great improvement in the manner of marketing all farm products, and these improvements can be brought about, but not until production is in better shape. Real business always starts with production and, once we have proper production, improvements in marketing are bound to follow, for the very pressure of production forces better distribution. Marketing is only getting the fruits of production to the people for consumption, and when distribution is in very bad shape, the place to start an investigation will be found in production.

Look at farm production. The first point which must strike anybody is the amount of useless labor expended. During half a month, or at the most a month, the farmer is employed in the production of crops. During all the rest of the time, he is tending livestock or doing odd jobs.

It is supposed that a good farm should keep a herd of cattle, but the unspecialized farmer cannot afford to keep more than twenty-five cows, and as a rule he will have no more than half a dozen. He cannot keep these cows clean - which is bad for both the farmer and for the public. They have to be milked by hand. That is wasteful and dirty. The milk has to be carried in every day to the sales point. This also is wasteful, for the farmer does not have a full load. Having a community wagon to pick up the milk from a number of farms is a slight improvement, but not a very great one, because there is no reason for doing so much transporting of milk. If ten or twenty farmers in a region were to combine their herds, then it would be possible to put up a modern, sanitary building in which the business of dairying could be carried on as an industry and follow industrial principles. It could be arranged to feed, milk, and clean the cows by machinery, with a minimum of human labor. People have been keeping cows for so long that they think there is only one way of looking after them, when, as a matter of fact, if only we should get a big enough dairy farm and discard the traditions, we could make use of electric power and do nearly everything by machinery.

Our dairy farm at Dearborn is managed exactly as though it were a factory. We have a concrete building which is absolutely clean, and the cows in it are clean, for they are washed every day. The washing, the milking, the feeding, in fact, everything connected with the care of the cattle, is done by machinery. We employ only about the same number of men as would ordinarily be required for a herd of twenty-five cows, and we pay these men factory wages and they work only eight hours. Management makes their work so effective that we can afford to pay them well.

It is an utter waste of time and effort to keep livestock in small units, and the farmers can earn far more out of shares in community livestock poolings than they could ever hope to earn out of tending small herds of their own. This applies to all of the livestock on a farm. The result will be cheaper products for the consumers and higher profits, although not higher prices, for the producers.

Prices are now high and profits low because of the wastes of production.

Taking away a farmer's livestock leaves him only his land to look after - that is, he is left with no more than a month of work. Farming then shows up as the part-time job it really is, and straight farming will eventually have to be considered only as a side issue. Farming is no exception to what might be called the rule of nature that one month's work will not support twelve months of living. The real problem of farming is to find something in addition to farming for the farmer to earn a living at. That is the plain, rough truth.

And as has been set out in a previous chapter, the decentralization of industry will provide these jobs to supplement the farm work. Industry and agriculture have been considered as separate and distinct branches of activity. Actually they fit into each other very neatly. But first we have to rid ourselves of many traditions. For instance, a horse is now a pleasure animal and is far too expensive to keep on a farm excepting as a luxury. It takes from three to five years to develop a work horse. It takes but a few hours to make a tractor. A horse eats every day in the year - an "eight-horse" farm withdraws forty acres a year from the farm's return to feed itself. A tractor eats only while it works.

At Dearborn, in plowing time, we string fifty or sixty tractors in a line. They are run by men taken out of the factories and paid the usual factory wage. All the essential operations of the farm are done in this fashion, and altogether we do about fifteen days' work a year -and keep the land in a high state of productivity.

And then the farmers can go into some other kind of work. The farm has its slack seasons, and so has industry; the two can be made to fit in together, and the result will be more and cheaper goods and food for everyone.

Is there enough work to employ the farmers? There is plenty of work to be done. No one has any conception of the amount of work that can be done in this country - if prices are kept down and wages and profits up.

All this cannot come about in a day. Industry did not change overnight. But the start toward industrial farming will be made when the farmers realize that they cannot farm with laws or with dollars - that the problems of the farm are farm problems and nothing else.

CHAPTER 20
FINDING THE BALANCE IN LIFE

In the first chapter the question was asked: Are we going too fast?

The impression seems to be that the only place to which one may go quickly is destruction. And since we are said to be going fast, then we must be going to the devil. Are we? But is not most of this talked of speed used to get the day's work over and done with?

What is really bothering most people is how to put in their spare time. That used to bother only what was called the "leisure class." The workman in the old days, it is true, had plenty of spare time, for he was employed only a small part of the year. But his spare time could hardly be called leisure - he spent it trying to keep body and soul together. Now, we find in our own industries that eight hours a day through five days a week gives all the production that is necessary to ask for on the man basis. Our workmen have leisure. Contrast this with the good old times - before management and power came into industry. Take the testimony of one Samuel Coulson, given before a Parliamentary committee in England in 1832. Coulson had children in the mills.

Q. "At what time in the morning, in the brisk time, did those girls go to the mills?"

A. "In the brisk time, for about six weeks, they have gone at three o'clock in the morning, and ended at ten, or nearly half-past, at night."

Q. "Had you not great difficulty in awakening your children to this excessive labor?"

A. "Yes, in the early time we had to take them up asleep and shake them, when we got them on the floor, to dress them, before we could get them off to their work; but not so in the common hours."

Q. "What was the length of time they could be in bed during those hours?"

A. "It was near eleven o'clock before we could get them into bed after getting a little victuals, and then at morning my missus used to stop up all night, for fear that we could not get them ready for the time."

Q. "Were the children excessively fatigued by this labor?"

A. "Many times; we have cried often when we have given them the little victualling we had to give them; we had to shake them, and they have fallen to sleep with the victuals in their mouths many a time."

It was no problem for those children to employ their leisure time! Nor had the adults a problem, for the twelve-hour day was usual and the sixteen-hour day not at all exceptional. Those people were going fast. Today only the machines are going fast. But our machines have to be tended with a clear brain, and management has to have a clear brain - else industry will drift back into the old man-killing stage.

Working all the while muddles the brain. Playing all the time muddles the brain. We have to find some kind of a balance. This is something new in the world.

In the not very distant past, people were divided into those who worked and those who played. It is easy enough to work all the time - although, after a while, not much brain goes into the work. It is not quite so easy to play all the time, but I understand that it can be done.

The day's work is the center of everything. If the day's work be not done, then leisure must vanish. The world cannot be supported by play alone. The force of all this came up to me in my own life a long while ago, and ever since I have been searching for a balance. In the early days, of course, there was no balance. It was work, work - all the while. That must be. But always have I found fun in a great many directions, the greatest fun of all being in the day's work. But it does not do to have only one interest, for then one cannot really get a perspective on that interest. There is recreation in the trees and in the birds, in walking across country, in motoring, in hunting up the objects which our fathers and our forefathers used, and reconstructing life as they lived it. They knew how to order some parts of their lives better than we do. They had much better taste; they knew more about beauty in the design of commonplace, everyday things. Nothing that is good ever dies. That is why we are taking over and reconstructing in their periods a couple of old inns - one in Massachusetts and another not far from Detroit.

These old inns with their fine ballrooms reminded us more pointedly that one thing had passed out of life, and that was real dancing. Dancing had become commercialized; it had gone from the home and the ballroom to badly ventilated restaurants where, with only a few square feet of floor amid the tables, there could be no real dancing.

The old American dancing was clean and healthful. In the square dances and the circle two-step, one finds rhythm and grace of motion, and people are thrown together and have to know one another. The old dances were social. The modern dances are not. The same two people may dance together all evening but the old dances gave one a dozen partners in an evening.

As a young man I liked to dance, but the only dances we knew were what are now called the "old-fashioned dances"- the schottische, the polka, the chorus jig, quadrilles, gavottes, and the like. The younger people nowadays, so we found, did not know these dances, and the older people - those who really needed dancing - had grown rusty. They thought they were too old. One never gets too old to dance. A number of men and women past seventy now come to our dances, and one fiddler who is eighty-five cannot only fiddle, but can dance as he plays - which is getting ahead of the story.

In our new laboratory building at Dearborn we partitioned off a corner which gives a ballroom big enough for seventy couples. We gathered together an orchestra. Out of Budapest we brought a cymbalum - without knowing whether we could find anyone to play it. A young Hungarian in the shops heard we had it and asked a chance to try his hand. He has proved to be a real musician and is no longer in the shops. Then we have a dulcimer -the mother of the piano - and which, like the cymbalum, is played with little hammers, and of course we have a violin and a sousaphone. This is the orchestra we have finally fixed upon. We searched out and reprinted all the old music we could find, but a deal of that music existed only in the minds of the old-time fiddlers who played and called at the country dances.

That started us hunting for fiddlers, and we have already had forty or fifty of them from all over the country playing for us, not so much for their playing, but to record the old country tunes. We are getting quite a library of old dance music, and Mr. Edison and the Victor people have recorded some of it for the phonograph.

It is fine to see how these old fiddlers come to life through their music. More than thirty years ago, out at the Botsford Tavern, when they had dances nearly every week, was a group of players who were rated as first class. We began to hunt them up. They had all prospered and had more or less retired. Through one we found another until finally we got all the members of the old orchestra together and gave a party, and it was a great party. The old men played for two hours, and they forgot that they were old. They had something in their music which the younger men - who are probably better players - do not seem to have, and they were keen, too. The oldest of them was dancing and playing and he was eighty-five!

We are all getting a great deal of fun out of dancing. We have our dancing classes two nights a week, and everyone has to learn to dance in absolutely the correct way, for a fine part of the old dancing was its deportment. The rules are followed. There is no holding up of two fingers for a dance and no "cutting in." The ladies do not enter the room unescorted and must slightly precede the gentlemen. No one is expected to cross the center of the ballroom. Everything is formal. The instructions are all in the manual we have had written.

No one objects to the formality. They like it as a change from the casualness which is so often rudeness. The experiment as an experiment is a success. It has been demonstrated that, given a choice, people would rather have the tuneful music and the dances that go with it than the tuneless music with its ugly dances.

Our complete repertoire is fourteen dances - The Two-Step, The Circle Two-Step, The Waltz, The Schottische, The Polka, The Ripple, The Minuet, The Lanciers, The Quadrille, The Varsovienne, and so on through the infinite variety of combinations. These dances have to be danced! There is no improvisation of steps.

We are not, as has been imagined, conducting any kind of a crusade against modern dancing. We are merely dancing in the way that gives us the most pleasure. It seems to be rather a popular way, for a number of outside classes have asked to be taught, and we are looking after as many of them as we can.

Primarily, we are having a good time out of the things of yesterday, and that is the reason for the Wayside Inn and the Botsford Inn.

The Wayside Inn, at South Sudbury, Massachusetts, is one of the oldest in the country - we are a new country and nothing is very old, but the Wayside Inn has housed George Washington and the Marquis de Lafayette and, through Longfellow's "Tales of a Wayside Inn," has become a part of the nation. When it came up for sale we bought it, not at all as a personal matter, but to preserve for the public. The Inn expressed the pioneer spirit - and the pioneer spirit is what America has, over and above any other country. If ever we lose that spirit, if ever we get to the point where a majority of the people are afraid to do things because no one before them has done them or because they are hard to do, then we shall stop going forward and start to go back.

I deeply admire the men who founded this country, and I think we ought to know more about them and how they lived and the force and courage they had. Of course, we can read about them, but even if the account we are reading happens to be true, and often it is not, it cannot call up the full picture. The only way to show how our fore-fathers lived, and to bring to mind what kind of people they were, is to reconstruct, as nearly as possible, the exact conditions under which they lived.

Those of us who are older can still think in terms of the life of the pioneers, but the generation growing up is in a different world from the one we grew up in. The younger generation knows a good deal about automobiles and airplanes and the radio and the movies, but it has little to go on when it comes to comprehending the pioneers and what they stood for.

At first we had no intention of doing more than buying the Inn and restoring it. But, since it is on a public road, there was nothing at all to prevent its surroundings from being exploited. We had to preserve the setting, and so we bought enough additional land for that.

We went about getting the Inn back into its original condition - all except one bedroom. This we have named the "Edison Room" and have furnished it as of the time of Mr. Edison's birth.

Henry Ford, John Burroughs, and Thomas Alva Edison in Florida – circa 1914.

There was a good deal to be done. We tore out the brick work which had closed up many of the old fireplaces, and now we have sixteen big fireplaces – some of them big enough to hold logs that take three men to lift. We have restored the floors.

The old Inn was lighted by candles in wall sconces and in candlesticks. These had been replaced by ordinary electric-light fixtures. We could not, as a practical matter, go back to candlelight, for the fire risk would have been too great. We finally managed to get sconces such as were used in the Inn, and to get candle-shaped electric lights which very well imitate the old candles.

Then we went out to find some of the relics of the Inn which had disappeared. Most of them we have found. One trunk, for instance, we located and brought back from Kansas. The old Bible we managed to repair, and we put it in its old Bible case so that it will last for a long time. The old clock had not been running for many years. It was made in England in 1710, and many of the parts were badly worn, although other parts, in spite of all the years of service, were as good as new. We made new parts to replace the worn ones, but we saved all of the old parts and have them in a case.

Thus, bit by bit, we have the Inn about as it was when Washington passed there during the Revolution. The furniture did not give us much trouble. We had rather a large collection of New England furniture of the period, and the Inn itself had a great many fine pieces which only needed expert repairing.

Having finished the Inn and bought all the surrounding land, we then began to put the whole neighborhood into somewhat of its former condition. We picked up two old sawmills of the time - one of them in Rhode Island. These we are reassembling. On the property was already a grist mill with a breast water wheel which was grinding only feed. This we are putting back into the exact condition it was in during the Revolution - with an overshot wheel - so that it will grind wheat, rye, and corn. We are working on an old blacksmith shop and shall have it ready, with the forge, tools, and benches of the time. Perhaps we shall get more of these shops together, for there is a lesson in the old village industries.

In the barn of the Inn we are gathering the coaches and rigs of the time. The coach house is not large enough to hold more than a couple of specimens of the collection. One of the most interesting of the old coaches is the "Governor Eustis," in which it is said Daniel Webster and Lafayette rode in 1825 to the dedication of the Bunker Hill Monument. We have a collection of old plows and other farming tools, and we have oxen to draw them, just as the pioneers had.

By the time we get through, we expect to have this section, not a museum of Revolutionary days, but a natural, working demonstration of how the people of those days lived. We have both lost and gained in the movement of modern industry. Our gains are many times greater than our losses; we can keep all of the gains and repair some of the losses.

The Wayside Inn represents a period of about two hundred and fifty years ago. On the Grand River Road, sixteen miles from Detroit, stands another inn, formerly known as the "Sixteen Mile House," but now as the "Botsford Inn," after Frank Botsford, who was its proprietor for a long time, although the inn has not been operating as such for many years. It dates back about one hundred years and is a fine specimen of the last century's type of roadhouse in a comparatively new country - for Michigan was a wilderness when Massachusetts was a fairly settled country.

We bought this inn, moved it back from the road, and we have made it over to simulate the original inn. It is now open to the public. We have the old kitchen with the big fireplace which had been closed, and the Dutch oven, but also, we have, concealed, a new kitchen, just as we have at the Wayside Inn, with electrical cooking apparatus and every known modern aid. You may pass from a kitchen of a hundred years ago into a kitchen of today.

For a long time we have been active in collecting for preservation all kinds of Americana. That collection has grown until now it covers several acres in one of our buildings at Dearborn. It is not as yet an ordered collection.

We want to have something of everything - we have types of every sort of wagon and carriage ever used in this country, from the covered wagon of the pioneer to the last style of buggy. We have nearly every type of agricultural instrument, every type of musical instrument, we have all kinds and sorts of furniture and household effects. One of these days the collection will have its own museum at Dearborn, and there we shall reproduce the life of the country in its every age.

CHAPTER 21
WHAT IS MONEY FOR?

A foreign manufacturer, visiting our plants, said: "We have to fix our profits in advance, or we should not be able to pay our charges. Unless we can calculate on the basis of a certain output and certain profit, we should have to go out of business. How do you manage that?"

The question was perfectly sincere, and the man meant well. But he was trying to drive with the cart before the horse. He had been setting out to gain a certain profit instead of starting out to render a certain amount of service – and let the profit take care of itself.

We regard a profit as the inevitable conclusion of work well done. Money is simply a commodity which we need just as we need coal and iron. If money be otherwise regarded, great difficulties are inevitable, for then money gets itself ahead of service. And a business that does not serve has no place in our commonwealth.

The most common error of confusing money and business comes about through the operations of the stock market. And especially through regarding the prices on the exchange as the "barometer of business." People are led to conclude that business is good if there is lively gambling upward in stocks, and bad if the gamblers happen to be forcing stock prices down.

The stock market as such has nothing to do with business. It has nothing to do with the quality of the article which is manufactured, nothing to do with the output, nothing to do with the marketing, it does not even increase or decrease the amount of capital used in the business. It is just a little show on the side.

It has very little to do with dividends. A large part of trading in stocks is without reference to dividends. Except with the sober investing class, the dividend is of little consequence; at least, it is not the main objective. Some of the most "active" stocks do not pay dividends. The profits sought from stock trading have no relation to the earnings of industry by the production of goods. The price of a stock often depends wholly on how many people want to buy the shares that are for sale.

The state of the stock market may make a deal of difference to the officers and directors of a company if they are dabbling in the stocks and trying to make money out of the securities of the company instead of out of its service. These stock market companies are of little consequence: they flicker and die out. But they do serve to convince people that the stock market has something to do with business, whereas, if not a single share of stock were to change hands, it would make no difference to American business. And if every share of stock changed hands tomorrow, industry would not have a cent more or a cent less capital to work with.

This whole stock activity, therefore, is on a par with organized baseball, so far as the fundamental interests of business are concerned: it is a side show, unrelated to the basic principles of business and supplying none of the necessities of business. It has only a spasmodic and accidental relation to values. If the extreme speculative element were removed, the natural buying and selling of stocks would be but a mere side line of banking.

We further hold, however, that strings on a business held by those not engaged in it are hindrances, because often it compels the business to become a money-maker instead of a commodity-maker. When the chief function of any industry is to produce dividends rather than goods for use, the emphasis is fundamentally wrong. The face of the business is bowed toward the stockholder and not toward the consumer, and this means the denial of the primary purpose of industry.

The absentee stockholder is one of the principal, though concealed, items in the unnecessary and preventable costs of living.

All this is defended, of course, by the statement that stock represents a contribution to enable industry to function. The story, however, is not so simply told. When preferred stock, for example, becomes a burden on production, the benefits of industry become private instead of public, and this cannot be defended on any terms. There comes to mind an instance where a charge of fifty dollars was added to the cost of an article to meet the demands of stockholders. In another case one hundred and twenty-five dollars per article was added for the same reason.

Industry is not money - it is made up of ideas, labor, and management, and the natural expression of these is not dividends, but utility, quality, and availability. Money is not the source of any of these qualities, though these qualities are the most frequent sources of money.

Any business is better off when its money comes from the buyers of its product. Such money is not a charge on the business or on the public. Money that enters in any other way becomes a charge upon the business. Its main interest is its own increase, and the public never gets through paying on the original investment.

But stock speculation is not without value - some really good men lose at it and in consequence are compelled to go to work. The stock habit takes too many men's minds off their legitimate business. Anything that drives them back to their proper sphere is a benefit. Wealth is not increased by stock activity; at best, it only changes hands. Wealth is not created; it is but a score in a game. I was once quoted as saying that the stock market was a good thing for business. The reporter omitted my reason - "because it drives so many men back to legitimate business by breaking them."

Business used to be conceived as existing solely for the benefit of its owners. Now the pendulum has swung the other way, and there is a notion that business exists solely for those who work in it and more especially for the wage earners. That is as great a misconception as that business exists to produce shares which may be traded on the stock market. We had a very curious instance of this in the essays of a number of college men who worked in our shops during a vacation period.

What they wrote was interesting. They were keen, inquisitive, and intelligent; they were not partisan, except with that perfectly human partisanship which instinctively takes the side of the working man as against the corporation. With the exception of one or two men, all pronounced the employer-employee relation as good, that the working conditions were good, and so on. But not one said a word about the product. If a hospital had been examined after this manner, the report would have said how comfortable the doctor's offices were, what nice accommodations were provided for the nurses, and how easy and delightful was the arrangement of the interns' hours. Not a word about the service of that hospital to the health of the world. That is, those college men assumed that industry is to be judged by its benefits to those who are in it! As if the worth of schools is to be judged by the personal gain of teachers, or the worth of hospitals by the financial benefits derived by the doctors. Schools are to be judged by pupils - their work. Hospitals are to be judged by healed patients - their work.

It is not long since the emphasis in industry was on the profit for the owner. The emphasis now is on the profit to the wage earner. That is as far as we have got in the popular judgment of industry. It is right, of course, that wages should receive their just emphasis. But no judgment of industry will ever be sound until industry is first given the test of public service. The question of profits and wages will never find sound solution until the service motive in industry is completely established. The first responsibility of industry is to the public.

The factory justifies itself by its usefulness to society at large. If it neglects so vital an element as wages, it simply disqualifies itself from rendering any service at all. For these things all go together.

Business does not exist to earn money for the capitalist or for the wage earner. The narrow capitalist and the narrow trades unionist have exactly the same view of business - they differ only on who is to have the loot.

Review the actions of each. First, we can assume that any product or process worth developing has come into being through men who worked at the thing itself, for the sake of its perfection and not exclusively nor even primarily for profit.

Then, the development having reached a certain stage, it is capitalized. Men of money see the opportunity to make more money. They set up plants, install machinery, and go to work. But the real product they aim to make is dividends, not commodities. Commodities are thought of only as a means to the dividends. If, in a pinch, anything must suffer, it will be the commodity, not the dividends. Every exertion will be made - wage reduction, quality reduction, quantity reduction, price increase - anything to save dividends.

Engineers have another interest altogether. Today's standard represents for them the level of today's achievement; they hope to excel it tomorrow. It is just here that engineering science is the enemy of shortsighted finance. A group of money brokers have installed a battery of expensive furnaces to produce dividends! Furnaces are not designed for that. Their purpose is to produce metal. The engineers produce a better furnace. It is then up to the financial controllers to say whether they will scrap the old furnaces and put in the new, giving the public the benefit of lower costs, or cling to the old and prevent the new.

Of course, this costs money. The money, however, has been previously provided by the public. Every concern which deals well with the public has money to keep up with progress. The surplus of any industrial firm is far more a fund to insure future progress than it is a payment for past performance. The financial controller of business, having no vision on this side of the matter, protests the unnecessary expenditure. But the engineer, having regard to the service results, makes the expenditure out of self-respect.

Take the wage side. Wages furnish purchasing power, and the whole process of business depends on people who are able to buy and pay. On the other hand, when special pleaders begin to declare that wages should absorb all the economies, all the increased profits made possible by industrial improvements, it becomes necessary to call attention to the essential class nature and limited benefits of such a view.

It has been seriously proposed that all the advantages accruing from better management, such as increased production, lower costs, higher values, should be made over to wages.

Our own industries form an example. Most of our improvements are internal, that is, they occur within the management of the business, the laying out of the work, the simplifying of the method, the saving of useless labor and wasted material, all of which permit the service to be rendered at less cost than formerly.

There are three ways whither this decreased cost, which is really increased profit, might go. We could say: "We will keep it all, because it was our ability that made this saving possible." Or we could say: "We will take this difference between what the article used to cost and what it costs now and put it into the wage envelopes of the men." Or we could say: "It costs less to produce this service, therefore the selling price ought to be reduced an equal amount and the buyer given the benefit."

In the first instance, the argument could be: the extra profit belongs to those whose brains made it possible. In the second instance, the argument could be: the extra profits belong to the workers, the producers. In the third instance, the argument could be: the buying public has the right to necessities and service at the lowest possible cost.

Stating the arguments gives the answer. The benefit belongs to the public. The owners are not the public; the specific group of employers are not the public. The owners and the workers will get their reward by the increased amount of business the lower prices bring. As has been pointed out previously, industry cannot exist for a class. When it is conceived of solely as making money for a class instead of providing goods for all, then it becomes a complicated affair which frequently breaks down - breaks down so frequently that pseudo-scientists have created what they call "business cycles." It appears from their writings that the order of business is wholly established and that it can run only so long without smashing. That is the superficial money idea of business.

We need have no slumps in business. We need never have unemployment. The old pioneers driving west made twelve miles a day. Then was achieved the unheard-of speed of sixteen miles an hour. Today we can cover six or seven hundred miles in twenty-four hours of automobile driving. The point is, we have attained such a speed that slowing down for economic crossings or curves does not mean anything. When the limited, while passing a crowded section, cuts down from sixty to thirty miles an hour, it does not mean that the train has stopped or even slumped. But those who are fearful are always looking out for signs of a slump. Often it would seem that the neurasthenics manage business!

The best time to study our economic machinery is lost because, when affairs are "prospering," the majority are so interested in getting the utmost out of the machine that they will give no time to improving it as it runs. The only time that we stop and seriously look at our economic machinery is when it breaks down. A bad machine broken down is not much worse than a good machine broken down. The best way to get a line on the machines is to watch them when they are working at supposedly highest precision.

And that is what we refuse to do. Even our economic observers watch the progress of business mainly to foretell symptoms of breakdown. It is now an established business to keep a lookout for signs of hesitation or collapse, so that those who pay for the lookout may run for cover first. But no one pays for, indeed most resent, service that looks toward prevention of breakdown by attention to the system while it is working full speed.

We are losing a great opportunity if we regard business depressions as unpreventable epidemics. Medical science chooses to follow a line that makes public health continuous; only the scientific habit of mind can lead us into the desire to make public prosperity continuous. Our recipe for "hard times" is to lower prices and increase wages. And it would take the efforts of only a few large companies thus to check the panic of any depression brought about by other than some great destruction such as war or a calamity of nature.

But serious social losses befall us because of our refusal to consider economic questions when the sun is shining and when everything is going fairly well. The seeds of bad times are in the mistakes which we make in good times. Yet in good times no one wants to hear of the mistakes we may be making. The policy then is to "get while the getting is good." When the machinery runs down because of our ignorance of all the natural laws which regulate economic health, there is plenty of discussion. But the accident has happened, and the longer or shorter period of recovery and repair must be lived through.

These seasons of prosperity and adversity grow two types of thinking, the conservative type appearing with prosperity and the radical type with adversity. Both these types probably are essential, but, undeniably, neither of them, acting alone, achieves much for progress. The radicals are right in saying that the conservatives make no progress, and the conservatives are probably right in saying that the professional radicals could not manage any of the things whose management they criticize.

But this cannot be denied: the responsibility always rests upon those in charge, and they happen to be labeled "conservatives"- their responsibilities forbid them the irresponsibility of the radicals. Just now, and probably for a long period ahead, until such distinctions as "conservative" and "radical" cease, the conservatives will be in charge of the economic machinery through sheer right of being able to make it work as well as it does.

With that point of fact agreed upon, what follows? Simply this: it devolves upon the "conservatives" to regard themselves as trustees of power in behalf of all the people. In the past they have been pretty good trustees with regard to themselves. They have introduced certain improvements in the system for the benefit of banks and business men. They have shown their ability to make our crazy-quilt economics yield more square meals and more independence and more homes for more people than has been done anywhere else in the world.

It is clearly up to them now, as trustees, to show what they can do further in the way of making our system fool-proof, malice-proof, and greed-proof for the benefit of every person in the land. It is a mere matter of social engineering. It may have the effect of reducing "personal fortunes," but it will not have the effect of reducing working capital. What right has a "personal fortune" to be anything but working capital? The time is here when the commanding law is, "to whom much is given, of him shall be much required."

But most harmful of all is the thought that the economic machine can ever be repaired by the government. Interference by the government usually boils down to having the government levy taxes and give the proceeds to those who clamor loudest for them. What are called "progressive programs" simmer down to: "We can force the country to do things for us." The whole list of programs which assume that the "Government" is an inexhaustible source of privilege and favor, the whole list of proposals that the country does this for this class and that for that class, is the expression of the mendicant type of mind. Mass weakness looks like strength, but it is not. It does not propose itself to do the thing it suggests, it proposes that the "doers" do for it. This type of mind never proposes to serve the country, but to make the country serve it.

It is true that the strong ought to serve the weak, but not to confirm them in their weakness. Service to the weak is disservice, unless it has the effect of bringing the weak to strength and independence. Fostering the handout attitude of mind is extreme unkindness. That is why our customary charity is such a contemptible thing. It weakens those who are willing to give, and it weakens those who are willing to receive. Charity is an evasion of effort.

Not only is the whole movement toward dependence on government basically wrong as to fact, but it also destroys every possibility of the very good it seeks. First, this idea is wrong in fact, because when government is explored, it is found to have nothing to give except what is given to it. Second, this idea is destructive of the very good it seeks, because it shuts off the source of whatever wealth or power the government might have for collective use. When, for example, the Government of Russia was seized, what was found? Nothing. The millennium did not come. Instead, disorder entered, and what measure of benefit there was in the old order was lost. With the supposed source of blessing in their hands, the inaugurators of the new system found there were no blessings to dispense – not even the common blessing of bread.

Our legislative channels are choked with proposals to give gratuities in every direction, to organize a paternalism that leaves no corner of life free from the patronage of government agencies, to benefit class as against class, and interest as against interest, without end. Legislators have in large measure begun to think that their function, as members of government, is to serve as nursemaids to the people, instead of clearing the field of action that the people may do things for themselves. Lawmaking bodies have an impression that this is the activity which makes them most popular with the masses. They think that in this they truly represent the people's desires.

Much of this legislative action takes the line of attempting to curb the imperfect economic machine by statute. Is not the public in its political capacity just as unscientific as in its commercial capacity? Our governmental economics are grotesque. Most of the laws in restraint of economic progress have been enacted with a view to curbing the element of human selfishness which is mixed in all gainful activity, but as no law can do this, the net result has been the binding of business in chains.

Look at taxes – for the largest governmental activity everywhere seems to be in the line of taxes. Few seem to have studied the relation between high taxes and poverty – that high taxes breed poverty by making production less efficient. Neither do we examine into the true functions of government.

It is rather significant that the only forms of taxation submitted directly to the people are those forms which can be made to appear as payable by a succeeding generation. The big appeal is to class consciousness. It is right that the tax burden should be distributed according to the ability to pay, but it is wrong that the tax function should be used as a means of class propaganda. There are no class divisions in the actual workings of any tax – the people all pay it. When the man of large means makes honest returns and pays large taxes, it is the public that has supplied the money. When the dishonest man evades the tax, it is still the public that pays the difference.

One way to get a correct angle is to penetrate behind the dollar sign to the thing itself. That will throw a lot of tax injustice into relief. When a business is on the point of expanding, suppose the income tax man should come along and say, "Give me your new machinery fund." Is the money which the government would get under such conditions half as useful to the country as the factory expansion would be, with its increase of employment and national resource? As a matter of fact, is it really dollars that are collected under such circumstances, or is it commodities that are confiscated?

Think of the inheritance tax as collectable in actual possessions rather than in money. Suppose the collector says:

"We must take one of the furnaces, four of the ovens, two of the elevators, ten of the machines, 25 percent of your coal pile, as an inheritance tax."

That would be comprehensible on the theory that some wrong perpetrated against society was represented by the goods seized. It would be comprehensible on the theory that it is wrong to seize a living man's possessions, but right to take them from his children when he is dead. It would be comprehensible on the theory that government deliberately permits criminal increase of machinery and jobs while an industrial manager lives, but quickly abolishes machinery and jobs when the manager is no more.

And yet, such action would be far more just than the present one. Inheritance is always expressed in dollars, yet the dollars are seldom there. What most heirs inherit in these days is a job, a business to be maintained, a responsibility to be shouldered. To inherit the managing control of a factory or other business is to be saddled with a task, upon the wise performance of which depends the employment of men and the livelihood of families.

This is all part of the fallacy which has steered our country and other countries wrong on so many matters touching industry – the fallacy that business is money, and that big business is big money.

CHAPTER 22
APPLYING THE PRINCIPLES TO ANY BUSINESS

The principles that have been given are universal - or, at least, we think so. And we have applied them through all our industries without finding it necessary to make any changes. However, there is always the feeling that since our industries are today comparatively large, they were always large, and that what we do is peculiar to large industry. In a way, that is true, but it is largely a question of scale. Our principles remain the same. To be specific:

I have been asked: "How would you apply your theories of business if, instead of having a large plant making automobiles and tractors, you had but a small shop, employing twenty-five men, which manufactured nothing that had to do with automotives? Or what would you do if you were in the retail business with a store doing, say, one hundred thousand dollars a year?"

These questions cannot be answered right out of hand, or in a sentence. For the answer hinges on whether you regard yourself as committed to a certain size of business or to a certain policy of business.

Size is only a stage; at one stage your finances will let you do only this. In the next stage you can do a little more. And so on. One can never reach the point where one may manufacture or sell in exactly the fashion that one would like - that is, with the greatest possible economy in every direction. As resources go, the Ford Industries have large resources, but we shall never reach the point where whatever we happen to be doing cannot be improved upon.

Size is purely an incident to a policy of manufacturing. It is nothing in itself.

At first we could do but little; then, gradually, we could do more and more, and today we are able to do a great deal - although we have more ahead to do than we have behind us done. We are going forward all the time. A few weeks ago, a visitor who knew our plants rather well three years ago was talking with one of the executives. He mentioned some process familiarly. The executive did not know what he was talking about.

"Don't you remember the way you make that part? I think you showed it to me yourself. It was a new way that had just been devised."

"How long ago was that?"

"Just three years - you surely remember."

"Three years is a long time. A lot of things have happened in three years. There are many things that we are not doing today in the way we did them three years ago."

These methods are changing so constantly, not because we like changes for themselves, but because the firm policy of always striving to lower the price and raise the quality just naturally forces improvements. And size comes just as naturally, because the market is always broadening and requiring more goods. The question to ask one's self is not: "What are the best methods for a man with a business like mine to adopt?" But: "What am I in business for? Whither am I going? What do I want to do?" If a man has twenty-five employees and intends never to hire more and never to do beyond a certain amount of business, then I should say that he is in a most dangerous condition unless he is making a luxury - whatever a luxury may be. The small manufacturer is always in danger if he is not making as well as anyone in the trade can make, for he always runs the chance of a large manufacturer coming along with methods that permit him to turn a profit at a sales price less than the cost to the smaller man. That is not a misfortune even for the man who is put out of business. It is the inevitable march of progress. The man who cannot or will not do business well has to drop out – or learn to do business well. And it is only a waste of time and money for him to combine with others in an attempt to stop progress. An association to keep the incompetent in business will have just as great a chance for success as an association to alter the course of the sun.

It is inevitable that the business of the country shall be done by very large companies which reach back to the source, and, taking the raw material, carry it through the necessary processes to the finished state. Just as soon as a business gets beyond a certain size the control of materials has to be absolute, for, regardless of costs, it is not otherwise possible to avoid the stoppages of strikes or the advent of unskilled management. For what is the use of building a great plant and planning work with the utmost care, if the plant may be made idle or the plans thrown out by some force, the control of which is in other and perhaps unfriendly hands?

Each extension, however, depends on the need of the period; if you use a thousand tons of steel a month, it is not worthwhile to run a steel plant – unless the steel you require is a special kind which is not made in large quantities. If you can make that thousand tons of steel cheaper than you can buy it, then you should make it. Or again, you may have to manufacture because you cannot depend on the quality of what you buy in the market. That has happened to us many a time. We have never manufactured a part or gone to the source of a raw material unless we rendered a service in so doing. We never make for the sake of making.

This, I think, answers the question of how our methods might be put to use by the smaller manufacturer. It is not the method but the objective that controls. Your methods are formed by what you are trying to do; they do not determine your purpose. To my mind it is starting wrong to put methods ahead of purpose.

The whole subject of manufacturing and retailing divides into two classes, not according to size, but according to purpose. If the purpose be to perform the greatest possible service, which in a business way means doing all that is in one's power to manufacture or distribute the largest possible amount of goods at the least possible cost, then the methods will form themselves quite naturally and according to circumstances. If, on the other hand, one wants to get the largest possible profit regardless of service, then one is not in business and there are no business rules which apply. It is just a matter of taking what one can take when one can take it.

There is, however, another kind of business between the two extremes which ought to be mentioned – for it is perfectly honorable. This is the business which has to do with the filling of special orders of one kind or another where the buyer is under no necessity of paying the price asked by the producer. Jewelry is in this class, and so is what is called merchant tailoring. Some men would rather have their clothing made than buy it readymade – although with the present-day ability to fit any one in ready-mades, there seems to be no absolute necessity for going to a tailor. Why should not the manufacturer who makes thousands of overcoats be in a better position to give you just the right coat than the man who makes only a comparatively few to order, and then mostly in the way that the customer directs, instead of in the way that the tailor's experience has taught to be best?

But perhaps rather than classify business as luxury and necessity – for these words are almost meaningless or even misleading – it would be better to classify business according to its appeal. The appeal to the mass of the people is one kind of business, and the appeal to the class is another. The second kind of business cannot be very large, for its appeal is limited to not more than 10 percent of the population.

First, take the second kind of business – the appeal to the 10 percent. It is just as good as any other sort of business, excepting that the area of service is sharply limited. There is not the slightest objection to high prices for quality – provided that the quality be given. And also, provided that there be no effort to force only the high-priced goods upon the 90 percent of the people who can afford only the lower prices.

Any business which directs itself to the 10 percent of the people may be large or small according to the degree in which it makes something that the whole 10 percent want, but at the best it cannot be very large, for the consumers are not there. As the price increases, the whims or special desires of the customers more and more rule, and the field of appeal narrows so that the best way of making may have to give way to the customer's way – which probably will not be the best way. This sort of business is really more in the nature of personal service than business in the sense of serving the whole people. Inevitably, it is a now-and-again sort of business, for its appeal is not to a large enough class to permit continuous quantity methods of manufacture.

Take a familiar article - a watch. As a young man, my first plans for going into quantity production were centered about watches. Under the right manufacturing conditions and the proper design, a first-class watch which would keep accurate time could be made to retail at fifty cents. Probably ten million a year of them could be sold - year in and year out. If the watch were made to sell at fifty dollars, quantity methods of manufacture might still be employed, but the business could hardly expect to grow very quickly after the first few years. For the market for fifty-dollar watches is very much smaller than that for fifty-cent. watches. If the watch were made to sell at one thousand dollars, then the customers would control the manner of production. A manufacturer could not afford to make a large line of thousand-dollar watches, and he would have to be prepared to make many of his watches to order - for a man paying that much for a watch would undoubtedly have special features in mind. He most certainly would not want all thousand-dollar watches to be exactly alike. He would be paying out some of his money, not for the watch, but to have something different from what other people had.

Take another instance; a builder of small homes for the masses of the people according to a fixed standard might expect to grow to any size; a builder of office buildings could not - for each job would have to be separately considered.

The point is that it is not size but intention that governs the methods to be adopted.

Take the matter of clothing - that is a universal necessity. No one knows how much clothing the country requires. It all depends on the price. If the price be high, a man will wear his suit as long as he can. Buying a new suit will be on a par with buying a home or a farm. As the price drops, the purchase will be easier and easier to make, and when the price gets very low, even the poorest will buy clothing freely.

In the end it is the way that an article is made, and not the way that it is sold, that governs, and if a product requires an unusual degree of salesmanship it is always a question whether the product is right. The question behind manufacturing is not: "How can I best serve the salesmen?" It is: "How can I best serve the consumer?"

If you find the answer to the second question, then it is quite inevitable that you will also find the answer to the first question, for there is a conflict between the two ideas only when the approach is through the salesman instead of through the consumer.

One product is enough for any factory, if it is going to grow large through service. And it is natural that the selling should be subordinate to the manufacturing. For if true business is serving the greatest number at the lowest price, then it is not logical to put mere persuasion above service.

Salesmanship can, however, be as truly service as can manufacturing. Personal salesmanship and retail merchandising are, considered from the service end, much alike.

Their problem is to get the goods from the manufacturer to the consumer in the cheapest possible manner.

But the same principles hold; they merely have to be applied differently. The retailer who would perform the largest service must, like the manufacturer, study his market to see what it is that the largest possible number of customers will need.

And just as the methods of the manufacturer are determined by the kind of service he wants to render, so also are the methods of the retailer determined. If the service be to the masses, then the selection of articles to be sold will be limited to the low-priced, high-quality articles that appeal to the 90 percent, and the business will become large. The largest retailer can hardly be as large as the largest manufacturer because of the geographical limits imposed upon him. But at that there seems to be no reason why retailers should not be many times larger than they now are. We have no really large retail establishments. But then there is a question whether size always makes for economy of handling in the retail establishment.

It is doing anything in less than the best way, not competition, that matters. If we do that which is before us to do in the best way that we know, that is, if we faithfully try to serve, we do not have to worry much about anything else. The future has a way of taking care of itself.

And to return to the opening question. The way for the little man to use the best methods is to get big.

CHAPTER 23
THE WEALTH OF NATIONS

The preservation of peace among nations is held as an ideal toward which it is our high duty to strive. No one can question the undesirability of war. War is destruction. It diverts production from serving the needs of mankind. It puts nothing into the world and takes much from it.

But war is not a cause. It is a result. It is a result of poverty – especially of poverty of thought. Just so long as great masses of people live in poverty, just so long will there be war. The urge to war, springing as it does from the desire to take the fruits of another's production, will ever be present, until the peoples of the world have learned to produce in abundance for themselves – until it has been proven that it is easier to make than to take.

Agreements not to make war, agreements to arbitrate differences between nations, and all the paraphernalia of diplomacy are of only temporary use in preventing war, because they treat war as a disease – whereas it is only the symptom of a disease. It is, indeed, more than possible that such agreements as expressed in the League of Nations or its adjunct, the World Court, may really be promoters of war by stifling investigation into its real causes. Agreements to limit armament are on a different basis, for they recognize war in a very frank way. They agree to limit for the time being the expense of getting ready for the next war, and thus they set free energy which may be used for production and the eventual alleviation of that poverty which causes war.

Every war has an economic cause. The wars which seem to spring from mere lawlessness may always be traced back to poverty. Poverty has never been eliminated by the repetition of any form of words. No man will today confess to an implicit belief in Aladdin and his Wonderful Lamp, but when we get into politics, our childhood belief returns, and we take it as true that some arrangement of words in a treaty, or a resolution, or a law will create as the Lamp created. All the treaties that have been duly engrossed and signed to date have served to prevent only such wars as no one wanted. Therefore, denouncing war is not very important. Agreeing not to go to war is not very important. That which is really important is the turning away from the treatment of war as a cause, which at the best is a negative treatment, and the turning toward, not the prevention of war or the preservation of peace, but the making of prosperity universal. And prosperity can be made the natural state of being. That has been demonstrated, and the United States has made the demonstration.

The United States most certainly has a mission, but that mission is not to put more words into a situation that already has far more words than it needs. Neither is it our mission to lend money. Every dollar that we lend to Europe only serves to postpone the day of reckoning, only serves to continue the poverty and misery which were acute before the war and are now even more acute. One of the chief functions of the League of Nations to date has been to arrange for the making of loans that postpone the facing of realities. What has heretofore been said about borrowing money in business applies with equal force to the borrowing of money by nations. The nations of Europe do not need money, although they think they do. There is not a single condition in Europe which money alone will remedy. The mission of the United States is not to cultivate a false spirit of internationalism which would merge Europe's troubles with our own, but to demonstrate by example at home and abroad that the present state of Europe is wholly unnecessary and is due solely to a misconception of the economic system.

It is well enough to talk about internationalism and the damage which narrow nationalism has done to the world. It is utter folly for people, because they are organized under separate governments, to imagine themselves as inevitable enemies. In that sense, nationality has been a hoax. A nation is only a homogeneous economic unit. If it is not homogeneous and cannot be efficiently governed, then it is not a proper unit. Sometimes what ought to be an economic unit is split into two or more parts. We have long since learned that our state lines are not economic boundaries, and we pay no attention to them, but Europe sets up political boundaries and then tries to make economic boundaries out of them with disastrous results – as, for instance, Germany and France.

But to insist on Americanism is not to insist on a narrow nationalism. The essential principles of Americanism are the goal toward which all civilization is striving. This is not said in any bombastic way, for the principles were born before the United States. The United States was created as a nursery in which these principles could be brought to full growth, that all the nations of the earth might see, and seeing know, the practical nature of liberty in all things. The mission of the United States is to give a demonstration to the world of the reality and endurance of certain principles.

War will never be stopped by the pacifists, and peace will never be won by the war makers. As long as there exists on earth the warring type of mind, and it has instruments to execute its purpose, war is possible. But, as was shown in the last war, the military strength of the peace-able, the non-war-making nations, is greater than that of the war-making nations. War, as a method of accomplishing anything, is now resisted, and in the future will be more and more resisted, until even the war-making mind will learn its futility.

Can you imagine the United States starting a war? Can you imagine the United States refusing to crush a war started against it? It is not our well-known inclination to peace that guards us, it is our well-known disinclination to stand for any one disturbing our peace.

Pacifism is an excellent doctrine if preached to those parts of the world where the war-making mind is rampant. To arm the bandits of the world and disarm its law-abiding citizens is not the way to stop international hold-ups. Counseling the decent citizen to disarm himself as an example to the thug indicates unfounded confidence in the thug's susceptibility to Christian example. It is just a pious fiction.

Militarists are helpless to bring peace. They are specialists in force, just as pacifists are specialists in sentimentality.

The people are not going to become as soft as pacifists would like to see them, nor as hard as extreme militarists desire; but they are going to excel in the strategy of common sense. The fact that our people are not war-starters is not going to prevent them from being war-stoppers, and such effective war-stoppers that war-starters will hesitate.

What we have most to fear in the lessening of our effectiveness is the taking of political promises as substitutes for thought and work. The largest single cause of poverty in Europe since the war has been the abject dependence upon government to do what government cannot do. The irony of this system is that the government which adopts it must continue to do more and more; and as the demand for more increases, the ability to do anything decreases. For there is nothing in government that does not come from the people; and a people in whom the spirit of self-help is killed contribute less and less to that which they desire – until in the end both people and government fall into a common helplessness. When Russia performed that amazing right-about-face and abandoned official communism for a partial return to private enterprise, it simply testified to the indispensability of self-help to any people.

Government can create a monopoly, but it cannot create a supply. It can arbitrarily fix prices, but it cannot create buying power. It can apply promise poultices; it cannot enable any business to stand on its own feet.

Legislative action simply gives protection to defects and keeps them in existence.

The strength of the United States lies in the fact that government aid to business and agriculture has never gone far enough seriously to affect the independence of either industry or agriculture. It is fortunate in some respects that so much governmental energy has been given to fighting business – business never had a chance to get soft. We have had, it is true, the tariff, which perhaps was an aid before we had any real business, but it is a noteworthy fact that none of the really great businesses of this country - those which strive to their utmost to render service - have arisen because of the tariff or stand in the slightest need of its protection. Those businesses which claim that they need tariff protection will usually be found to be backward in method, producing poor stuff with ill-paid men; and this is inevitable, because they have not had on them the pressure to do better, and instead of creating markets for their products among their own employees, they have been satisfied to sell to limited markets or to take advantage of the artificial tariff-created, high-priced market at home to sell at lower prices in foreign countries.

One of the great steps which the United States might take would be to wipe out all tariffs on imports. That would be a real contribution to the world, and also it would be a real contribution to American industry. The whole world outside the United States has not the productive capacity to supply our wants. In only a few industries could foreign manufacturers sell below home manufacturers, except where our prices for home consumption are stupidly high. In the cases where it would be necessary for us to make lower prices, we should be benefited, for these are our low-wage industries, and competition would force the reorganization and re-planning of these industries, and then, as has been previously explained, they would have to pay higher wages, and this would mean increased purchasing power and consumption. We have now the capacity to absorb almost limitless quantities of well made, rightly priced goods. The world would be benefited by having to sell to us on a straight competitive basis, for then they, too, would be forced into the volume which makes for high wages.

Industry abroad grew up differently from ours. Great Britain, being the first of industrial nations, could export practically all of its products to the non-industrial nations, and also it built up a great sea transport system, because it had the men to make the ships and sail them. A tariff would only have clogged its operations, and it had no need to create a home market because, being first in the field, it had no competition. When Germany turned into an industrial state, it evolved an elaborate program of state aid to industry, both by tariff and subsidy, and now, since the war, all the nations of Europe have tried to further their industries somewhat on the German plan. It has been taken for granted everywhere that industry must look for its well-being, not to the people at home, but to markets a broad, and hence the maze of tariff walls, of export and import licenses, of government help and regulation - in fact, one finds abroad everything but production.

The facilities to produce are present, but these facilities are greater than the ability to consume, and there can be no peace on this earth until the ability to consume is brought up and kept up to an equality with the ability to produce. This equality cannot be brought about until what we have called the wage motive replaces the profit motive.

Outside the United States, the wage motive has never gained a foothold. Business is mostly in the hands of financiers and is run for profit and not as a serviceable element in the common social life. No really big business exists outside the United States, and what pass for big business are only unsteady financial pyramids, quite un-equipped to give service. It is taken for granted that capital and labor are not engaged in a joint enterprise. The wage motive is not allowed to take hold, for between government regulation and taxes and trades union regulation on output, the opportunity to reorganize does not get a chance. We see labor governments go into power on the pretense of doing something for the workingman, we see capitalistic governments go into power on the pretense of helping capital. But so great is the claptrap of the politicians that we never see governments going into power without quack remedies - going into power under the promise of helping the people to help themselves. No one will face the facts.

Political nostrums cannot help Europe or any part of the world. No division of property can be of the slightest help, because there is not enough property to divide. Salvation has to come through the production of more property, but that production also will be ineffective and merely make for turmoil unless with it is raised the power of consumption.

Our company is not without experience in the feasibility of raising the power of consumption, for we have branches, or affiliated companies or associated companies, operating in most parts of the world, and in all of them we use exactly the same methods as we use in our plants in the United States, and in all of them we pay approximately the same minimum wage as we pay in the United States, and the results have in every case been exceedingly interesting. Our wages abroad run from two to three times the usual wages paid, but because we are organized to pay high wages we get cheap production. These foreign plants are not little American settlements. Usually they are set up and started by men who have been trained at Detroit, often by nationals of the country where the plant is located. But once under way, all the employees are drawn from the locality. Our Irish plant is all Irish, our English plant is all English, our plant in Brazil is all Brazilian, and so on over the world. We feel that we could not be of service following any other course.

Take our plant at Cork. My ancestors came from near Cork, and that city, with its wonderful harbor, has an abundance of fine industrial sites. We chose Ireland for a plant because we wanted to start Ireland along the road to industry. There was, it is true, some personal sentiment in it. We began the plant in 1917, but because of the war it was not completed until 1919. Originally, it was designed to manufacture tractors for distribution through Europe, but free production was so hampered by politics that we changed the whole plant into a foundry, which now supplies our plant in England and which will eventually supply other European plants.

Cork has for many years been a city of casual labor and extreme poverty. There are breweries and distilleries, but no real industry. The best that a man could hope for was two or three days a week on the docks, for which he would receive sixty shillings, or fifteen dollars, for the hardest kind of "Stevedoring" (*loading or unloading of a vessel*). If he went out as an agricultural laborer, he could not expect to get more than thirty or thirty-two shillings a week. None of this work was steady.

The men and their families did not really live. They had no homes - only hovels. No clothing but what they had on. We started our plant with three men from Detroit to direct operations. Now we have under regular employment about eighteen hundred men. They work eight hours a day, five days week steadily. The minimum wage is two shillings three pence per hour, or eighteen shillings a day. The average wage is two shillings and sixpence an hour, or a sovereign a day - five pounds a week. This is steady money, week in and week out - something that few, if any, of the men had ever before known. We have no labor turnover whatsoever, and always have a long waiting list. The Irish are supposed to be temperamental. We have never had a complaint about the repetitive work. The only complaints we ever had were during the first few months, when some of the men found it hard to do without smoking while at work.

The payment of these higher wages had an immediate effect in the homes of the men. You can see it in the wife of a new man. The wives usually bring down lunch for their husbands. For the first few weeks, the wife will be wearing a shawl over her head. Then she will have a hat, and a few weeks later she will be in a frock or a suit. The men no longer spend their evenings hanging around grog shops in old clothes and a kerchief. They have clothes in addition to their working clothes, and you will see them in the evening strolling out to see the pictures with their wives, and they are wearing collars and swinging canes. While once it was the custom for a man to get drunk as soon as he got paid, we have no trouble whatsoever with drinking. Where once the men were apt to turn up on Monday morning somewhat the worse for wear, they are now fresh and bright. In spite of the fact that none of the men ever had any previous experience with money, they have quickly learned to buy wisely and to save.

Not the least interesting of the developments at Cork has been the attitude of the workmen toward destructive revolution. Our superintendent was several times ordered to turn the plant over to the making of munitions for the Irregulars. He always refused. Then, one day, a motor lorry with fifteen soldiers swung into the plant, and the young lieutenant in charge handed the superintendent a list of the machinery that he proposed to take away with him. The superintendent tried to tell him that the machinery would be useless and that one needed more than machinery to manufacture munitions. But the lieutenant had his orders and was going to carry them out - he demanded immediate action. The superintendent said something to this effect:

"We have eighteen hundred good, strong Irish boys working in these shops. I don't know what they will do if I tell them that you propose to take out some of this machinery, but I think we can both guess what they will do. My advice to you is to get out before there is any real trouble."

The lieutenant took the advice. Well paid workers do not go in for merely destructive revolution. Some of our employees already own automobiles. It is only a question of time and the reduction of taxes before most of them will own motor cars, and then the whole standard of living will rise as it has risen in this country.

Much of the labor of England is unionized, and men are held strictly to their crafts. We have no crafts in our industries, and although we are not opposed to unions, we have no dealings with them, because there is nothing that they can furnish to aid us in our management. We pay higher wages than any union could demand for its members generally, we have steady employment, and we are not interfered with.

The standard of living among our employees in England is high, the men do good work, and our costs are low – not as low as in the United States, because we have not the volume of production, but we have volume enough to demonstrate that with management attuned to high wages and no individual limits on production, England can be made a high wage and therefore a high consumption country. Every man in the plant is an investor in our certificates.

We first introduced our cars into France in 1907, and we had plans for the erection of an assembly plant when the war broke out in 1914. Shortly, we were called upon to supply cars, first for ambulance uses and then for general uses, so that, in 1916, we opened an assembly plant at Bordeaux, sixty miles from the coast. For three years, this plant served only for war, turning over more than eleven thousand cars to the French Government, most of which are still running, although now for peace purposes. That, however, is not the point. The point is that at the Bordeaux plant we employed 300 men in our usual way, and they fell into our methods of production without difficulty. Now we have a building in Paris, erected on our standard lines with a capacity for assembling 150 cars and trucks a day. As might be imagined, the thrift record of the French workers is exceptional. The industrial workers of France are supposed to be socialists. We have heard nothing of this in our plant. In Copenhagen, where we established a plant in 1919, we met for the first time a labor government which regulated hours, wages, and conditions of work, and practically made union regulations a part of the law of the land. We hired barbers, preachers, blacksmiths, plumbers, unskilled laborers, and whoever applied, and put them to work, side by side, on the machines – as has been our custom everywhere. We paid a minimum wage of what corresponded to $5.25 in the United States, with some of the men getting as much as a dollar more.

Our superintendent was asked to classify the plant according to law. Each shop had to have a classification and go under a certain scale – we were paying far above the ordinary scale. We could not classify – we could not qualify as a blacksmith shop, which was the nearest classification! And then, too, the men who were not blacksmiths objected to being forced out of good jobs.

Our plant was put there to serve and does serve, but it could not have served had it been forced into an academic classification.

Our experiences at Antwerp, at Rotterdam, at Barcelona, and at Trieste have been quite the same as in other parts of Europe. We have found everywhere men willing to work consistently for the wages we pay – to work so well that we get cheaper and better results than do those in the same territory who pay lower wages. And everywhere a higher standard of living has come with the higher wages. But everywhere the governments step in to put many of the products of the worker above his purchasing power. For instance, our touring car sells in one country, solely owing to government charges, for about two and one-half times the price in the United States. Such taxes not only stifle consumption, but they create an army of non-producers.

Our branches in South America tell the same story, of wages and progress, except that most of these branches have gone into territory that never before had other than the crudest of industry, and hence we had to draw our workers from unskilled peons, with the exception of the branch at Buenos Aires. Our other South American branches are at Santiago, Chile; Sao Paulo, Brazil; Pernambuco, Brazil; and Montevideo, Uruguay. We cannot pay our full standard Ford wage in any of these countries, because the high purchasing power of the dollar would make wages as paid in the United States grotesque. We shall raise wages as the countries build up.

Paying regular wages to people in countries which are entirely new to industry was an interesting experiment, and more interesting still has been the watching of what the automobile is doing to such countries. For while Brazil takes up one fifteenth of the earth's surface and has extraordinarily rich natural resources, it has not had the transport facilities for development. A country develops only according to the ease of transport, and most of Brazil has only six months of transport by motor because, during the other six months, the roads are too heavy for any car to force through.

Our branch is hardly more than a year old, but already the high wages, (higher and more steady than would seem), are beginning to have an effect. The workers have not yet made much change in their housing conditions but they are buying more clothing, they are buying a few furnishings, and they are saving money. They do not yet quite know what to do with their incomes, but they do not quit work because they have more money than they need – which was what we were afraid of – nor have they developed spendthrift habits. Soon they will begin to develop more needs, and the process of material civilization will start. The automobile will make a great nation out of Brazil. The natives, though totally unused to machinery of any kind or to discipline of any kind, fell very quickly into the work of assembly and repair. They seem to learn quickly – probably because they can see good reasons for learning.

The Orient too, is awakening in many directions and, as has been said in a former chapter, we have no more ardent students at Detroit than those who come from India and China. These men see that the only salvation of their countries lies in the introduction of power so that a home consuming market can he built up. They resent, and rightly, attempts to exploit their starvation labor by foreign capital, but they are anxious indeed to learn how to do for themselves. We can help the Orient only by establishing industrial institutions on modern lines, which means that these institutions will create their own markets through the payment of high wages. Road building goes on everywhere. The automobile is the greatest modern source of roads. The formula for getting good roads is, first get your automobiles. It is not good roads that have brought automobiles, but automobiles that have forced good roads. It has always been said that the caste system in India is an absolute bar to development, but in our schools we have Indians of all castes, and they work side by side, apparently forgetting that they ever heard of caste. What they may do when they return to India is another matter, but if they can forget caste while working for us, then caste is not as powerful as it is represented.

But of what concern are these comparatively trivial incidents of work? They have about them no pomp or circumstance. What difference does it make to suffering humanity if a man in Cork who used to wear a kerchief about his neck is now wearing a collar? Changing from a kerchief to a collar is only a symbol. But it is an important symbol. It denotes that one man has been assisting in production – that he has helped to bring something into the world – that he has made the world a mite richer. Political action cannot construct – it can start destruction or it can try to hold things as they are – which is only destruction by slow process, for life cannot be made to stand still.

What the world chiefly needs today is fewer fervent diplomats and politicians and more men advancing from kerchiefs to collars.

CHAPTER 24
WHY NOT

This book has concerned itself with things material - with the supply of the material wants of humanity. Man, through the ages, has sought health, wealth, and happiness. Health does not of itself bring wealth, and happiness does not necessarily follow the obtaining of either health or wealth, or both of them. Happiness is something for the individual, but, whatever happiness may or may not be, surely it is more apt to grow out of health and wealth than out of illness and poverty.

There is a fairly general agreement that if civilization means anything at all it should mean the opportunity to every man, woman, and child on earth to have at least decent shelter, food, and clothing, with as much over as individual merit may warrant. Unless that much be accomplished, we may say that civilization is a failure. It matters not what books may be written, what buildings put up, what works of art created - nothing matters, if the opportunity be not given for anyone who wills to live as befits a human being.

The world has been baffled by poverty. Sometimes it has been so baffled that it has made a virtue of poverty, and men have set up that they were proud to be poor. The only escape for poverty was held out by religion promising Heaven as a surcease from sorrow, or by various ill thought out or, half thought out communistic theories, which, while not promising wealth, could promise an equality of misery. Trained thought has avoided the one big question of the world. Indeed, anything that had to do with the actual provision of goods - with the making easier of the lot of what was called the "common man" - had been charged with having the taint of commercialism. It was noble enough to talk about the alleviation of poverty, but quite ignoble to do anything about it in a concrete way.

Only now are we beginning to realize that any study which has not as its end the welfare of the common man is not worthwhile. Take science, philosophy, and religion. It is idle to say that one deals with reality more than the other. They all deal with realities. Facts are not all on one plane. Science is not limitedly material. Religion is not limitedly spiritual. Matter and spirit are terms we use to make distinctions which perhaps do not exist. Yet science and philosophy entirely, and religion to a degree, have largely kept aloof from any materialism which had to do with anything so commonplace as bread and butter.

The coming of the industrial era, although it rapidly increased actual wealth, made a new problem in its distribution, and while it made the rich richer, at first it made the poor still poorer. The production by power and machinery was far greater than by hand, but the industrialists had no conception that power and machinery were destined to make a new world. They thought in the old terms of hand production, and many of them still think in those terms. Even reformers thought in the same terms. We had the golden age of oratory - smothering with words the cruelties of exploitation. Most of our economic and social conceptions date from this age. There was much talk of "good employers" and "bad employers," and the disposition of the employer had a deal to do with the welfare of his employees. No one thought of the employer as other than a man who "gave" jobs. For a long time, it did not occur to any one that the employee was quite as necessary to the employer as was the employer to the employee - that the relation was not sentimental. A manufacturer who ventured to correct the worst evils incident to production was set down as a "philanthropist" - that word having come to designate a slightly senile and eccentric old gentleman who went about distributing unmerited aid to people lacking the self-respect to refuse it.

Men talked of democracy and associated it with liberty, but whenever they obtained self-government - which was supposed somehow to be the same as democracy and liberty - immediately they sought autocracy under some other name. They wanted the state to regulate under the conception that it could take the place of individual leadership and that industry, being a new thing, needed regulation, when the truth was that industry had not found its function and needed freedom to find itself. The multitude of laws which we have today - a wilderness of statutes and ordinances - does not indicate an increase in men's rights and liberties. Doubtless, mankind's liberties will be greatly expanded by growth of character and by recognition of the need for economic liberty (not freedom from economic law, but liberty within economic life). But we are being daily made aware that while anybody can make a statute, it takes a wise man to make one that roots in basic rights. Very often a statute hinders progress because progress itself will cause some readjustment, and people are naturally averse to readjustment even for progress.

And then, curiously, legislation seems capable, in whatever form it may be cast, of working oppositely from the intention which commanded the best support for it. The tariff began in an effort to protect jobs of workingman and render the country self-dependent; it ended in the disgraceful spectacle of non-competitive trusts. From a fence to keep out harm, the tariff became a stockade which kept out the benefits of fair competition. The principle had elements which commended it to honest intelligence, but the administration of it became an oppression.

One could fill a volume with the legislation which has passed because of its good promise, but which once passed has been manipulated for private advantage against the public rights.

But all this time, while we were floundering and it was being truly said that government had failed, the men who put work before talk were working, and they were working with such large results that they have discovered the real meaning of power and machinery - that it was brought into this world to free man, not to enslave him, and that there is a new morality which is active and not merely passive.

A man can make a soap, or a phonograph, or a car, or a gas, or a magazine, and he can say, "I want to make the best article I can, of equal quality all the time, easily procurable always, and always so satisfactory that people will never want anything but my product."

Would you say that he was showing morality? No, you would say that he was just showing sound business sense. But that is morality.

If the man had said, "I want to make a soap that will cheat and injure every purchaser," we should not stop to consider his morality. We should know that he was insane.

Morality is doing the sound thing in the best way; it is the larger view and the longer view applied to life. For what we are doing is not making this or that: we are making life, and the opportunity of life, and the conditions of life; and the measure of our morality is the measure of our wisdom - how well are we doing it?

Let us say of life at least what we say of soap: "We want to create for everybody the best life conditions possible, a high level of opportunity - a life that people will be glad to live." Then we are applying sound sense to life.

The advantage of what we call moral is that it is natural; it represents the way that life must go if it is to go at all. The good is natural. Morality is a part of good management. The good manager may resent the word as applied to his work, he may retort that it is only common sense. But that is morality - the plain, practical development of life according to its nature.

The social effect of this morality finds expression in devoting business to the service of the whole people instead of to the service of the few. The expression, "spirit of service," sounds idealistic. The spirit of service is just a knowledge that no man can survive, no industry can survive, no government can survive, no system of civilization can survive which does not continually give service to the greatest possible number. The only interest one can have in anything is the service one gets from it or gives to it. As normal, creative individuals, we are satisfied only with the service we render in our work; as members of civilization or government, we are satisfied only with the measure of service they render us.

And this service does not demand altruism. It only demands that enlightenment replace un-enlightenment.

Altruism clogs progress; it blocks the way of the presently possible by insisting on the presently impossible. For instance, unemployment insurance and old-age pensions make unemployment and destitution in old age more probable by charging the daily product with an extra load which limits consumption and therefore limits production to a scale which prevents the advantages to be had from large uninterrupted production.

But let this be made clear. There is no way out from poverty except through work. The world has tried everything but work. And the hardest of all work must come in the management. Most of the so-called "economic" problems would be completely solved if industries were managed by men who know industry. The experts, research men, and easy chair philosophers are making economic mysteries out of nothing. There would be no economic mystery in a ditch-digger failing as a surgeon. The same kind of nonsense exists when mere money-brokers endeavor to manage productive business.

The majority of "labor troubles" are caused by managers who have no first-hand knowledge of labor. They are "boss troubles," usually, and can be permanently settled by a new kind of manager - one who knows the job so well that no walking delegate, or anyone else, can tell him how it should be done. A man who must be told his own business by someone outside of it will render his best service by quickly getting out of business.

Not only labor troubles, but the difficulty of industry in keeping pace with possible improvements and increase of service, come from this cause. Industry exists to make things that people use. But when managed by men who know nothing of the factory, whose interest is confined to the balance sheet, its principal product becomes dividends. That leads to those economic situations about which whole libraries are written. They are not economic at all. There is nothing in business itself that necessitates failure; but men who enter business unprepared by training in its special points take failure with them. Business never fails; only men do that. The way into business is through the door of work.

I am sometimes asked whether it is better to go into business for oneself or take employment. Employment as a career competes with private business in a way which few realize. Employment now offers a career such as men sought in their own business and often failed to attain.

The very growth of business has tended to give employment a status which even business ownership did not have fifty years ago. A great deal of nonsense has been written about the freedom of the workman under the old system. The old-time guild system held nothing of the ideal. The union rules and repressive traditions of that system weighed heavily alike upon master and man, and led to little satisfaction for the individual and to no prosperity for society.

The urge to create has never been so heartily encouraged nor its field so widely extended, as in modern industrial employment. Take the world of design, as only one example: the best the past has left us in industry is its designs, but the world of design has expanded illimitably since the arrival of industry with its extension of service and its encouragement of individual effort. Where there was one designer set free to do his natural work, there are now hundreds. And even if some modern designs are not good, it does not follow that all the old designs were good. Some of them were very bad. And even if all our modern designs were bad, it would still be better to have our own designs than slavishly and un-creatively to follow designs of a previous generation.

What we are achieving today is a greater freedom than was ever before possible - we know that we can make the possession of the mere necessities of life an incident. In our own factories we find that five days a week are enough to give our production - that we can get more production in five days of eight hours each than we could get in a six- or seven-day week of ten hours a day. That extra day of leisure is going to bring large results, for the people will learn more about living, will have time to expand their sense of need, and therefore will increase their consumption.

The world can have what it wants of goods if the spirit of service - the wage motive prevails. But we shall have to have a change in spirit. The day of dead conservatism or wild radicalism has passed. We need a new conservatism in government which will not promise that anyone can live without work, or that all shall have castles, and which will not hold the man who does better than his fellows as a menace. Its menaces will be the groups that encourage waste, inefficiency, limitation of production, limitation of wages, limitation of opportunity, limitation of development in industrial processes, limitation of competition, or any other system founded on class selfishness. It will apply itself equally to the man who withholds a day's work and the man who evades competition under tariff protection.

The new conservatism will understand that legislation of itself can bring no good economic conditions into existence – it can only clear the way. The people are no longer fooled by the promise that laws can bring prosperity. All that the law can do is to give legal standing and recognition to the people's conviction that fair play ought to rule everywhere.

We are not living in an age of industrial expansion; the very expression shows a lack of grasp of what is going on. We are living in an age when for the first time it is possible to supply a fair part of the needs of all peoples if they really want their needs supplied.

We are not living in a machine age. We are living in an age when it is possible to use power and machinery in the public service – and at a private profit.

But what of the future? Shall we not have over-production? Shall we not someday reach a point where the machine becomes all powerful and the man of no consequence?

No man can say anything of the future. We need not bother about it. The future has always cared for itself in spite of our well-meant efforts to hamper it. If today we do the task we can best do, then we are doing all that we can do.

Perhaps we may overproduce, but that is impossible until the whole world has all it desires. And if that should happen, then surely we ought to be content.

TODAY AND TOMORROW

Portrait of Henry Ford circa 1919.

Henry Ford on the cover of Time Magazine, January 14, 1935.
Photo credit: Jeffrey White Studios, Inc. - Time Magazine

Phil Morgan of the last Henry Ford School class interviewed by Paul Akers of Generosity Press.

This particular interview is also on YouTube. You can simply scan the QR code below that will take you directly to it at https://youtu.be/mFM_Hp-vt5Q

TODAY AND TOMORROW

By Henry Ford

*The vintage 1926 Henry Ford book
now adapted for today's digital devices*

TODAY AND TOMORROW

Timeless Wisdom for a Modern Digital Age

(Newly Annotated and Illustrated)

Contributors
Paul Akers (Introduction)
Samuel Crowther (Original Collaborator)
Greg Otterholt (Modern English - Annotations & Illustrations)

Now available in print / eBook / and audio-book

Go to **generositypress.com**
for more details, resources, and a video introduction.

Copyright © 2018 by Generosity Press
All rights reserved,
including the right of reproduction
in whole or in part in any form.
ISBN 978-0-9906010-9-8

Edited and digitized for print, eBook and audio-book by Greg Otterholt
Assistant Editor - Shannon Waterman
Book Cover - Jayme Newby

Manufactured & Produced in the United States of America.

Check out **paulakers.net** for additional books and business resources.

Manufactured by Amazon.ca
Bolton, ON